REVISED EDITION

THE METAPHYSICAL FOUNDATIONS

OF MODERN PHYSICAL SCIENCE

by Edwin Arthur Burtt

HUMANITIES PRESS

ATLANTIC HIGHLANDS, N.J.

First published 1952 in the United States of America by
Humanities Press International, Inc., Atlantic Highlands, N.J. 07716.
First paperback published 1980. This is a reprint of the second (latest)
edition.

©Edwin Arthur Burtt, 1924; 1932

Library of Congress Cataloging–in–Publication Data

Burtt, Edwin A. (Edwin Arthur), 1892–
  The metaphysical foundations of modern physical
science.

  Previously published;   Rev. ed. 1952.
  Revision of thesis (Ph. D.)—Columbia University,
1925 under title: The metaphysics of Sir Isaac
Newton.
  Bibliography: p.
  Includes index.
  1. Science—Philosophy—History. 2. Metaphysics—
History. 3. Mathematics—Philosophy—History.
I. Burtt, Edwin A. (Edwin Arthur), 1892–
Metaphysics of Sir Isaac Newton. II. Title.
B67.B8   1989   500.2'01   89-15426
ISBN 0-391-01742-X

All rights reserved. No part of this publication may be reproduced or
transmitted, in any form or by any means, without permission.

Printed in the United States of America

Preface

The general scope of the problem attacked in this book is sufficiently indicated in the introductory chapter. Suffice it to add here merely that my attention was directed to its profound importance in consequence of assuming responsibility for an advanced course in the history of British philosophy at Columbia University. An intensive study of the classic English thinkers early taught me that no one could hope to appreciate the motives underlying their work till he had mastered the philosophy of the one Englishman whose authority and influence in modern times has rivalled that of Aristotle over the late medieval epoch—Sir Isaac Newton.

I wish to express my special indebtedness to Dean F. J. E. Woodbridge, of the Department of Philosophy, Columbia University, for the stimulus of his teaching and for his own critical interest in Newton's philosophy; to Prof. Morris R. Cohen, of the College of the City of New York, an authority in this field; to Dr. J. H. Randall, Jr., whose extensive researches in the same field have made his criticisms most helpful; and finally to my wife, without whose faithful companionship and co-operation the task would have been quite impossible of fulfilment.

A word about the quotations in the following chapters. Since I have dealt in large part with hitherto untranslated source material, I must accept responsibility for the translations of: Copernicus (except for the Letter to Pope Paul III, where I have used Miss Dorothy Stimson's translation in her *Gradual Acceptance of the Copernican Theory of the Universe); Kepler; Galileo (except his *Dialogues Concerning the Two Great Systems of the World* and *Dialogues and Mathematical Demonstrations Concerning Two New Sciences,* where

I have used the translations noted); Descartes, as regards all the quotations taken from the Cousin edition of his works; More's *Enchiridion Metaphysicum;* Barrow; and Newton, as regards the quotations from Horsley's edition of his works, Vol. IV, pp. 314–20. The remaining quotations are from translations already in the field.

I wish to express hearty thanks to my friend and colleague, Professor T. V. Smith, of the University of Chicago, who has shared with me the labour of reading the proofs.

E.A.B.

University of Chicago.

Preface to the Revised Edition

Would that I were competent to rewrite the present volume with a clear grasp of all that has happened in the world of science since the days of Newton, and especially in the light of contemporary transformations in physics! In lieu of that I am persuaded that the best plan is to leave the body of the work with none but minor changes. No historical researches during the last six years with which I have become acquainted seem to require any essential changes in the survey here embodied, so far as it reaches.

The concluding chapter, however, has been almost entirely rewritten. Its original emphasis is no longer quite consonant with my present philosophic leads, and it failed to bring out the lessons of the historical study in such a form as to yield pertinent suggestions for contemporary speculation.

E.A.B.

Stanford University, Calif.,
November 1931.

Contents

CHAPTER I: INTRODUCTION   15
  (A) The Historical Problem Suggested by the Nature of Modern Thought   15
  (B) The Metaphysical Foundations of Modern Science the Key to This Problem   25

CHAPTER II: COPERNICUS AND KEPLER   36
  (A) The Problem of the New Astronomy   36
  (B) Metaphysical Bearings of the Pre-Copernican Progress in Mathematics   41
  (C) Ultimate Implications of Copernicus' Step—Revival of Pythagoreanism   52
  (D) Kepler's Early Acceptance of the New World-Scheme   56
  (E) First Formulation of the New Metaphysics—Causality, Quantity, Primary and Secondary Qualities   63

CHAPTER III: GALILEO   72
  (A) The Science of "Local Motion"   72
  (B) Nature as Mathematical Order—Galileo's Method   74
  (C) The Subjectivity of Secondary Qualities   83
  (D) Motion, Space, and Time   91
  (E) The Nature of Causality—God and the Physical World—Positivism   98

CHAPTER IV: DESCARTES   105
  (A) Mathematics as the Key to Knowledge   106
  (B) Geometrical Conception of the Physical Universe   111

(c) "Res extensa" and "Res cogitans"   115

(D) The Problem of Mind and Body   121

CHAPTER V: SEVENTEENTH-CENTURY ENGLISH
PHILOSOPHY   125

(A) Hobbes' Attack on the Cartesian Dualism   126

(B) Treatment of Secondary Qualities and Causality   130

(c) More's Notion of Extension as a Category of Spirit   135

(D) The "Spirit of Nature"   140

(E) Space as the Divine Presence   143

(F) Barrow's Philosophy of Method, Space, and Time   150

CHAPTER VI: GILBERT AND BOYLE   162

(A) The Non-Mathematical Scientific Current   163

(B) Boyle's Importance as Scientist and Philosopher   167

(c) Acceptance and Defence of the Mechanical World-
View   172

(D) Value of Qualitative and Teleological Explanations   177

(E) Insistence on Reality of Secondary Qualities—Conception of Man   180

(F) Pessimistic View of Human Knowledge—Positivism   185

(G) Boyle's Philosophy of the Ether   189

(H) God's Relation to the Mechanical World   194

(I) Summary of the Pre-Newtonian Development   203

CHAPTER VII: THE METAPHYSICS OF NEWTON   207
Section 1:   Newton's Method   207

(A) The Mathematical Aspect   209

(B) The Empirical Aspect   212

(c) Attack on "Hypotheses"   215

(D) Newton's Union of Mathematics and Experiment   220

Section 2: The Doctrine of Positivism   227

Section 3: Newton's General Conception of the World, and
of Man's Relation to It   231

Section 4: Space, Time, and Mass   239

(A) Mass   240

(B) Space and Time   244

    (c) Criticism of Newton's Philosophy of Space and
        Time   256

Section 5: Newton's Conception of the Ether   264

    (A) The Function of the Ether   265

    (B) Newton's Early Speculations   269

    (c) Development of a More Settled Theory   279

*Section 6: God—Creator and Preserver of the Order of the
        World*   283

    (A) Newton as Theologian   284

    (B) God's Present Duties in the Cosmic Economy   291

    (c) The Historical Relations of Newton's Theism   297

CHAPTER VIII: CONCLUSION   303

BIBLIOGRAPHY   329

INDEX   345

The Metaphysical Foundations
of Modern Physical Science

CHAPTER I.   INTRODUCTION

A. Historical Problem Suggested by the Nature of Modern Thought

How curious, after all, is the way in which we moderns think about our world! And it is all so novel, too. The cosmology underlying our mental processes is but three centuries old—a mere infant in the history of thought—and yet we cling to it with the same embarrassed zeal with which a young father fondles his new-born baby. Like him, we are ignorant enough of its precise nature; like him, we nevertheless take it piously to be ours and allow it a subtly pervasive and unhindered control over our thinking.

The world-view of any age can be discovered in various ways, but one of the best is to note the recurrent problems of its philosophers. Philosophers never succeed in getting quite outside the ideas of their time so as to look at them objectively—this would, indeed, be too much to expect. Neither do maidens who bob their hair and make more obvious their nether bifurcation see themselves through the eyes of an elderly Puritan matron. But philosophers do succeed in glimpsing some of the problems involved in the metaphysical notions of their day and take harmless pleasure in speculating at them in more or less futile fashion. Let us test the modern world-view in this manner. What are the problems whose correct treatment, it has generally been taken for granted, constitute the main business of metaphysical thinkers? Well, most conspicuous of these is the so-called· problem of knowledge; the main current of speculative inquiry from Descartes onward has been permeated by the conviction that investigation into the nature and possibility of knowledge forms a necessary preliminary to the successful attack upon other ultimate issues. Now, how did all this come about? What assumptions were people accepting when they plunged themselves into these profound epistemological ponderings? How did these assumptions get into men's thinking? To raise such questions at a time when everybody vigorously believes that philosophy must do this sort of thing, is, of course, inopportune and futile, but now that some contemporary philosophers have made bold to discard epistemology as the study of unreal puzzles, the occasion is ripe to suggest them. Does the problem of knowledge lead thinking into false directions, and nullify its conclusions by unsound premises? What are the premises anyway, how are they related to the other essential features of modern thought, and what was it at bottom that induced people in modern times to think in this fashion? The central place of epistemology in modern philosophy is no accident; it is a most natural corollary of something still more pervasive and significant, a conception of man himself, and especially of his relation to the world around him. Knowledge was not a problem for the ruling philosophy of the Middle Ages; that the whole world which man's mind seeks to understand is intelligible to it was explicitly taken for granted. That people subsequently came to consider knowledge a problem implies that they had been led to accept certain different beliefs about the nature of man and about the things which he tries to understand. What are those beliefs and how did they appear and develop in modern times? In just what way did they urge thinkers into the particular metaphysical attempts which fill the books of modern philosophy? Have these contemporary thinkers who decry espistemology really made this whole process thoroughly objective to themselves? Why, in a word, is the main current of modern thought what it is?

When "the main current of modern thought" is spoken of in this wholesale fashion, a brief word might be injected to show that a certain obvious danger is not blindly fallen into. It may very well be that the truly constructive ideas of modern philosophy are not cosmological ideas at all, but such ethico-social concepts as "progress," "control," and the like. These form a fascinating key to the interpretation of modern thought and give it a quite different contour from that which it assumes when we follow up its metaphysical notions. But with that aspect of modern thinking we are not concerned in the present treatment. In the last analysis it is the ultimate picture which an age forms of the nature of its world that is its most fundamental possession. It is the final controlling factor in all thinking whatever. And that the modern mind clearly has such a picture, as clearly as any previous age that one might wish to select, it will not take us long to see. What are the essential elements in that picture, and how did they come there?

Doubtless it is no mystery why, amid all the genetic studies entered upon with such confidence to-day, the precise nature and assumptions of modern scientific thinking itself have not as yet been made the object of really disinterested, critical research. That this is true is not due merely to the fact, itself important enough, that all of us tend easily to be caught in the point of view of our age and to accept unquestioningly its main presuppositions: it is due also to the associations in our minds between the authoritarian principle and that dominant medieval philosophy from which modern thought broke in successful rebellion. Modern thinkers have been so unanimous and so vigorous in their condemnation of the manner in which large propositions were imposed on innocent minds by external authority that it has been rather easily taken for granted that the propositions themselves were quite untenable, and that the essential assumptions underlying the new principle of freedom, the manner in which knowledge was successfully sought with its support, and the most general implications about the world which seemed to be involved in the process, are thoroughly well grounded. But what business have we to take all this for sound doctrine? Can we justify it? Do we know clearly what it means? Surely here is need for a critical, historical study of the rise of the fundamental assumptions characteristic of modern thinking. At least it will compel us to replace this easy optimism with a more objective insight into our own intellectual postulates and methods.

Let us try to fix in preliminary fashion, although as precisely as we may, the central metaphysical contrast between medieval and modern thought, in respect to their conception of man's relation to his natural environment. For the dominant trend in medieval thought, man occupied a more significant and determinative place in the universe than the realm of physical nature, while for the main current of modern thought, nature holds a more independent, more determinative, and more permanent place than man. It will be helpful to analyse this contrast more specifically. For the Middle Ages man was in every sense the centre of the universe. The whole world of nature was believed to be teleologically subordinate to him and his eternal destiny. Toward this conviction the two great movements which had become united in the medieval synthesis, Greek philosophy and Judeo-Christian theology, had irresistibly led. The prevailing world-view of the period was marked by a deep and persistent assurance that man, with his hopes and ideals, was the all-important, even controlling fact in the universe.

This view underlay medieval physics. The entire world of nature was held not only to exist for man's sake, but to be likewise immediately present and fully intelligible to his mind. Hence the categories in terms of which it was interpreted were not those of time, space, mass, energy, and the like; but substance, essence, matter, form, quality, quantity—categories developed in the attempt to throw into scientific form the facts and relations observed in man's unaided sense-experience of the world and the main uses which he made it serve. Man was believed to be active in his acquisition of knowledge—nature passive. When he observed a distant object, something proceeded from his eye to that object rather than from the object to his eye. And, of course, that which was real about objects was that which could be immediately perceived about them by human senses. Things that appeared different *were* different substances, such as ice, water, and steam. The famous puzzle of the water hot to one hand and cold to the other was a genuine difficulty to medieval physics, because for it heat and cold were distinct substances. How then could the same water possess both heat and cold? Light and heavy, being distinguished by the senses, were held to be distinct qualities, each as real as the other. Similarly on the teleological side: an explanation in terms of the relation of things to human purpose was accounted just as real as and often more important than an explanation in terms of efficient causality, which expressed their relations to each other. Rain fell because it nourished man's crops as truly as because it was expelled from the clouds. Analogies drawn from purposive activity were freely used. Light bodies, such as fire, tended upward to their proper place; heavy bodies, such as water or earth, tended downward to theirs. Quantitative differences were derived from these teleological distinctions. Inasmuch as a heavier body tends downward more strongly than a lighter, it will reach the earth more quickly when allowed to fall freely. Water in water was believed to have no weight, inasmuch as it was already in its proper place. But we need not multiply instances; these will sufficiently illustrate the many respects in which medieval science testified to its presupposition that man, with his means of knowledge and his needs, was the determinative fact in the world.

Furthermore, it was taken for granted that this terrestrial habitat of man was in the centre of the astronomical realm. With the exception of a few hardy but scattered thinkers, the legitimacy of selecting some other point of reference in astronomy than the earth had never suggested itself to any one. The earth appeared a thing vast, solid, and quiet; the starry heavens seemed like a light, airy, and not too distant sphere moving easily about it; even the keenest scientific investigators of ancient times dared not suggest that the sun was a twentieth of its actual distance from the earth. What more natural than to hold that these regular, shining lights were made to circle round man's dwelling-place, existed in short for his enjoyment, instruction, and use? The whole universe was a small, finite place, and it was man's place. He occupied the centre; his good was the controlling end of the natural creation.

Finally, the visible universe itself was infinitely smaller than the realm of man. The medieval thinker never forgot that his philosophy was a religious philosophy, with a firm persuasion of man's immortal destiny. The Unmoved Mover of Aristotle and the personal Father of the Christian had become one. There was an eternal Reason and Love, at once Creator and End of the whole cosmic scheme, with whom man as a reasoning and loving being was essentially akin. In the religious experience was that kinship revealed, and the religious experience to the medieval philosopher was the crowning

scientific fact. Reason had become married to mystic inward-
ness and entrancement; the crowning moment of the one, that
transitory but inexpressibly ravishing vision of God, was likewise the moment in which the whole realm of man's knowledge gained final significance. The world of nature existed that
it might be known and enjoyed by man. Man in turn existed
that he might "know God and enjoy him forever." In this gra-
ciously vouchsafed kinship of man with an eternal Reason and
Love, lay, for medieval philosophy, a guarantee that the whole
natural world in its present form was but a moment in a
great divine drama which reached over countless æons past
and present and in which man's place was quite indestructible.

Let us make all this vivid to ourselves by the aid of a few
verses from that marvellous poetic product of the philosophy
of the Middle Ages, the *Divine Comedy* of Dante. It but puts in
sublime form the prevailing conviction of the essentially *human* character of the universe.

> The All-Mover's glory penetrates through the universe, and
> regloweth in one region more, and less in another.
>
> In that heaven which most receiveth of his light, have I
> been; and have seen things which whoso descendeth from
> up there hath nor knowledge nor power to re-tell;
>
> Because, as it draweth nigh to its desire, our intellect sink-
> eth so deep, that memory cannot go back upon the track.
>
> Nathless, whatever of the holy realm I had the power to
> treasure in my memory, shall now be matter of my
> song . . .
>
> Much is granted there which is not granted here to our
> powers, in virtue of the place made as proper to the
> human race. . . .
>
> All things whatsoever observe a mutual order; and this the
> form that maketh the universe like unto God.
>
> Herein the exalted creatures trace the impress of the Eternal
> Worth, which is the goal whereto was made the norm
> now spoken of.
>
> In the order of which I speak all things incline, by diverse
> lots, more near and less unto their principle;
>
> Wherefore they move to diverse ports o'er the great sea of

being, and each one with instinct given it to bear it on.
This beareth the fire toward the moon; this is the mover in
the hearts of things that die; this doth draw the earth
together and unite it.
Nor only the creatures that lack intelligence doth this bow
shoot, but those that have both intellect and love . . .
Gazing upon his son with the love which the one and the
other eternally breathes forth, the primal and ineffable
Worth,
Made whatsoever circleth through mind or space with so
great order that whoso looketh on it may not be without
some taste of him.
Then, reader, raise with me thy sight to the exalted wheels,
directed to that part where the one movement smiteth
on the other;
And amorously there begin to gaze upon that Master's art,
who within himself so loveth it, that never doth he part
his eye from it.
See how thence off brancheth the oblique circle that beareth
the planets, to satisfy the world that calleth on them;
And were their pathway not inclined, much virtue in the
heaven were in vain, and dead were almost every potency
on earth;
And if, from the straight course, or more or less remote
were the departure, much were lacking to the cosmic
order below and eke above.

From the description of Dante's final mystic union with
God:

O light supreme, who so far dost uplift thee o'er mortal
thought, re-lend unto my mind a little of what thou then
didst seem,
And give my tongue such power that it may leave only a
single spark of thy glory unto the folk to come;
I hold that by the keenness of the living ray which I endured I had been lost, had mine eyes turned aside from it.
And so I was the bolder, as I mind me, so long to sustain it
as to unite my glance with the Worth infinite.
O grace abounding, wherein I presumed to fix my look on

the eternal light so long that I consumed my sight thereon!

Within its depths I saw ingathered, bound by love in one volume, the scattered leaves of all the universe;

Substance and accidents and their relations, as though together fused, after such fashion that what I tell of is one simple flame. . . .

Thus all suspended did my mind gaze fixed, immoveable, intent, ever enkindled by its gazing.

Such at that light doth man become that to turn thence to any other sight could not by possibility be ever yielded.

For the good, which is the object of the will, is therein wholly gathered, and outside it that same thing is defective which therein is perfect. . . .

O Light eternal, who only in thyself abidest, only thyself dost understand, and to thyself, self-understood, self-understanding, turnest love and smiling:

That circling which appeared in thee to be conceived as a reflected light, by mine eyes scanned some little,

In itself, of its own color, seemed to be painted with our effigy and thereat my sight was all committed to it,

As the geometer who all sets himself to measure the circle and who findeth not, think as he may, the principle he lacketh;

Such was I at this new seen spectacle; I would perceive how the image consorteth with the circle, and how it settleth there;

But not for this were my proper wings, save that my mind was smitten by a flash wherein its will came to it.

To the high fantasy here power failed; but already my desire and will were rolled—even as a wheel that moveth equally—

By the Love that moves the sun and the other stars.[1]

Compare with this an excerpt from a representative contemporary philosopher of influence, which embodies a rather extreme statement of the doctrine of man widely current in modern times. After quoting the Mephistophelian account of

[1] Selections from the *Paradiso*, Cantos I, X, and XXXIII, Temple Classics edition.

creation as the performance of a quite heartless and capricious being,[2] he proceeds:

> Such, in outline, but even more purposeless, more void of meaning, is the world which Science presents for our belief. Amid such a world, if anywhere, our ideals henceforward must find a home. That man is the product of causes which had no prevision of the end they were achieving; that his origin, his growth, his hopes and fears, his loves and his beliefs, are but the outcome of accidental collocations of atoms; that no fire, no heroism, no intensity of thought and feeling, can preserve an individual life beyond the grave; that all the labours of the ages, all the devotion, all the inspirations, all the noonday brightness of human genius, are destined to extinction in the vast death of the solar system, and that the whole temple of Man's achievement must inevitably be buried beneath the debris of a universe in ruins—all these things, if not quite beyond dispute, are yet so nearly certain, that no philosophy which rejects them can hope to stand. Only within the scaffolding of these truths, only on the firm foundation of unyielding despair, can the soul's habitation henceforth be safely built. . . .
>
> Brief and powerless is Man's life; on him and all his race the slow, sure doom falls pitiless and dark. Blind to good and evil, reckless of destruction, omnipotent matter rolls on its relentless way; for Man, condemned to-day to lose his dearest, to-morrow himself to pass through the gate of darkness, it remains only to cherish, ere yet the blow falls, the lofty thoughts that ennoble his little day; disdaining the coward terrors of the slave of Fate, to worship at the shrine that his own hands have built; undismayed by the empire of chance, to preserve a mind free from the wanton tyranny that rules his outward life; proudly defiant of the irresistible forces that tolerate, for a moment, his knowledge and his condemnation, to sustain alone, a weary but unyielding Atlas, the world that his own ideals have fashioned despite the trampling march of unconscious power.

[2] Bertrand Russell, *A Free Man's Worship* (*Mysticism and Logic*) New York, 1918, p. 46, ff.

What a contrast between the audacious philosophy of Dante —reposeful, contemplative, infinitely confident—and this view! To Russell, man is but the chance and temporary product of a blind and purposeless nature, an irrelevant spectator of her doings, almost an alien intruder on her domain.[3] No high place in a cosmic teleology is his; his ideals, his hopes, his mystic raptures, are but the creations of his own errant and enthusiastic imagination, without standing or application to a real world interpreted mechanically in terms of space, time, and unconscious, though eternal, atoms. His mother earth is but a speck in the boundlessness of space, his place even on the earth but insignificant and precarious, in a word, he is at the mercy of brute forces that unknowingly happened to throw him into being, and promise ere long just as unknowingly to snuff out the candle of his little day. Himself and all that is dear to him will in course of time become "buried in a universe of ruins."

This is, of course, an extreme position; at the same time is it not true that the reflective modern man, in his cosmological moods, feels this analysis of the situation thrusting itself upon him with increasing cogency? To be sure, there are always some who try to avoid cosmology; there are likewise a few idealistic philosophers and a much larger number of religious enthusiasts who confidently hold to a different view, but would it not be safe to say that even among their ranks there is much secret fear that something like the above conviction would be found inescapable if the facts were faced with absolute candour? For there is a truth on such matters as on all others. In any case, speculation has clearly been moving in this direction: *just as it was thoroughly natural for medieval thinkers to view nature as subservient to man's knowledge, purpose, and destiny; so now it has become natural to view her as existing and operating in her own self-contained independence, and so far as man's ultimate relation to her is clear at all, to consider his knowledge and purpose somehow produced by her, and his destiny wholly dependent on her.*

[3] This author has now adopted a less extreme position on these points. (Revised Edition.)

B. The Metaphysical Foundations of Modern Science the Key to this Problem

One hardly philosophizes to-day in the true sense of the word unless one understands how it was that this veritable upheaval in the main current of intelligent thought has historically come about. And this is precisely the question we wish to ask. But, and this is now the interesting point, when the question is raised in just this form, one soon realizes that a study of modern philosophy—that is, of the writings of those men whose names fill the histories of modern philosophy—gives one little help in the attempt to answer it. For modern metaphysics, at least beginning with the work of Berkeley and Leibniz, has another and more significant connecting thread than that of its epistemological interest; it is in large part a series of unsuccessful protests against this new view of the relation of man to nature. Berkeley, Hume, Kant, Fichte, Hegel, James, Bergson—all are united in one earnest attempt, the attempt to reinstate man with his high spiritual claims in a place of importance in the cosmic scheme. The constant renewal of these attempts and their constant failure widely and thoroughly to convince men, reveals how powerful a grip the view they were attacking was winning over people's minds, and now, perhaps even more than in any previous generation, we find philosophers who are eager above all things to be intellectually honest, ready to give up the struggle as settled and surrender the field. A philosophy akin to Russell's in the relevant essentials, ventures to-day to call itself by the name "naturalism," implying the assurance that a frank facing of the facts by a normal mind, free from malicious inner distortions, will inevitably lead to acquiescence in his results.

What is the reason for the failure of these attempts? A possible answer to this question is, of course, that they were condemned to be ineffectual from the start, that the modern view of man's relation to his environment, though never acknowledged before in quite this form, is after all the truth. The pathetic characteristic of human nature which enables man easily to think more highly of himself than he ought to think— to swallow gullibly a flattering notion of his own importance in the drama of the ages—might fairly well explain the fact that in all the dominant currents of thought in almost all previous times and places, even where the theoretic interest had become strong, he was prone to fancy that there was something imbedded in the eternal structure of things more akin to that which was most precious in himself than particles of matter in their changing relations. That the scientific philosophy of the Greeks, with all its sublime passion for the very truth of things, arrived in its turn at an exalted philosophy of man, might be due to the circumstances insisted upon by some historians of thought, that the zenith of Greek metaphysics was attained quite consciously through the extension, to the physical realm, of concepts and methods already found helpful in dealing with personal and social situations. It might be the result of a misapplication, to the universe at large, of a point of view legitimate enough in a certain field, the misapplication being based in the last analysis on the unwarranted assumption that because man, while here, can know and use portions of his world, some ultimate and permanent difference is thereby made in that world.

There might be, however, another possible answer to this question. It is obvious, from a casual observation of the medieval and modern methods of attacking the difficulties of metaphysics, that a radical shift has been made in the fundamental terminology used. Instead of treating things in terms of substance, accident, and causality, essence and idea, matter and form, potentiality and actuality, we now treat them in terms of forces, motions, and laws, changes of mass in space and time, and the like. Pick up the works of any modern philosopher, and note how complete the shift has been. To be sure, works in general philosophy may show little use of such a term as mass, but the other words will abundantly dot their pages as fundamental categories of explanation. In particular it is difficult for the modern mind, accustomed to think so largely in terms of space and time, to realize how unimportant these entities were for scholastic science. Spatial and temporal relations were accidental, not essential characteristics. Instead of spatial connexions of things, men were seeking their logical connexions; instead of the onward march of time, men thought of the eternal passage of potentiality into actuality. But the big puzzles of modern philosophers are all concerned with space and time. Hume wonders how it is possible to know the future, Kant resolves by a *coup de force* the antinomies of space and time, Hegel invents a new logic in order to make the adventures of being a developing romance, James proclaims an empiricism of the "flux," Bergson bids us intuitively plunge into that stream of duration which is itself the essence of reality, and Alexander writes a metaphysical treatise on space, time, and deity. It is evident, in other words, that modern philosophers have been endeavouring to follow the ontological quest in terms of a relatively new background of language and a new undercurrent of ideas. It might be that the reason for the failure of philosophy to assure man something more of that place in the universe which he once so confidently assumed is due to an inability to rethink a correct philosophy of man in the medium of this altered terminology. It might be that under cover of this change of ideas modern philosophy had accepted uncritically certain important presuppositions, either in the form of meanings carried by these new terms or in the form of doctrines about man and his knowledge subtly insinuated with them—presuppositions which by their own nature negatived a successful attempt to reanalyse, through their means, man's true relation to his environing world.

During the last generation these ideas of science have been subjected to vigorous analysis and criticism by a group of keen thinkers, who have asked themselves what modifications in the traditional conceptions would be demanded if we sought to overhaul them in the light of a broader and more consistently interpreted experience. At present this critical investigation has culminated in a rather extensive transformation of the major concepts of scientific thinking, furthered on the one hand by radical physical hypotheses of a gifted student of nature like Einstein, and on the other by the attempted reshaping of scientific methods and points of view by philoso-

phers of science such as Whitehead, Broad, Cassirer.[4] These
are the most timely and important happenings in the world of
scientific philosophy at the present moment. They are compelling people to ask more fundamental questions than have
been asked for generations. They are prodding scientists into
an extremely healthy state of scepticism about many of the
traditional foundations of their thinking. But the kind of work
which these pioneers of thought are eager to see done is only
a part of the job that really needs to be done. And that job
in its entirety cannot be done merely by confining one's interest
to the securing of a consistent conception of method in physical
science, nor by a careful analysis of the categories of physics
as they reveal their meaning to us in the present era of scientific achievement. Cassirer sins on the first count; Whitehead
and Broad on both counts. To follow the remarkably acute
German scholar is to gain a magnificent historical perspective
but to forget, in the very laboriousness of the effort, the
pervasive influence of the movement studied on cosmological
thinking among modern intelligent folk generally. To follow
the English critics is in addition to take much out of the past
for granted which needs just as vigorous prying-into as the
contemporary problems to which our inquiring attention has
been drawn.[5] We inevitably see our limited problem in terms
of inherited notions which ought themselves to form part of a
larger problem. The continued uncritical use in the writings
of these men of traditional ideas like that of "the external
world," the dichotomy assumed between the world of the
physicist and the world of sense, the physiological and psy-

[4] See especially, A. N. Whitehead, *The Principles of Natural
Knowledge,* Cambridge, 1919; *The Concept of Nature,* Cam-
bridge, 1920; *The Principle of Relativity,* Cambridge, 1923;
C. D. Broad, *Perception, Physics, and Reality,* London, 1914;
Scientific Thought, London, 1923; E. Cassirer, *Das
Erkenntniss-problem in der Philosophie und Wissenschaft der
neueren Zeit,* 3 vols, Berlin, 1906–20; *Substance and Function
and Einstein's Theory of Relativity* (trans. by W. C. and M. C.
Swabey), Chicago, 1923; see also the earlier studies of K.
Pearson, E. Mach, H. Poincare, and for fuller familiarity with
the field the works of Minkowski, Weyl, Robb, Eddington.

[5] This no longer applies to Whitehead. (Revised Edition.)

chological postulates taken for granted, as, for example, the
distinction between sensation and act of sensing, are a few
illustrations of what is meant. Our questions must go deeper,
and bring into clear focus a more fundamental and more popularly significant problem than any of these men are glimpsing.
And the only way to come to grips with this wider problem
and reach a position from which we can decide between such
alternatives as the above is to follow critically the early use
and development of these scientific terms in modern times, and
especially to analyse them as presented in their first precise
and, so to say, determinative formulation. Just how did it come
about that men began to think about the universe in terms of
atoms of matter in space and time instead of the scholastic
categories? Just when did teleological explanations, accounts
in terms of use and the Good, become definitely abandoned
in favour of the notion that true explanations, of man and
his mind as well as of other things, must be in terms of their
simplest parts? What was happening between the years 1500
and 1700 to accomplish this revolution? And then, what ultimate metaphysical implications were carried over into general philosophy in the course of the transformation? Who
stated these implications in the form which gave them currency
and conviction? How did they lead men to undertake such
inquiries as that of modern epistemology? What effects did
they have upon the intelligent modern man's ideas about his
world?

When we begin to break up our puzzle into specific questions like these we realize that what we are proposing is a
rather neglected type of historical inquiry, that is, an analysis
of the philosophy of early modern science, and in particular
of the metaphysics of Sir Isaac Newton. Not that much of
this has not been written; indeed Professor Cassirer himself
has done work on modern epistemology which will long remain a monumental achievement in its field. But a much more
radical historical analysis needs to be made. We must grasp the
essential contrast between the whole modern world-view and
that of previous thought, and use that clearly conceived contrast as a guiding clue to pick out for criticism and evaluation,
in the light of their historical development, every one of our

significant modern presuppositions. An analysis of this scope and to this purpose has nowhere appeared. Such considerations make it plain, also, why this arduous labour cannot be avoided, as some present-day thinkers fondly hope, by making a large use in our philosophizing of the categories of evolutionary biology. These categories have indeed tended to supplant, in disquisitions about living matter at least, much of the terminology of mechanical physics. But the whole magnificent movement of modern science is essentially of a piece; the later biological and sociological branches took over their basic postulates from the earlier victorious mechanics, especially the all-important postulate that valid explanations must always be in terms of small, elementary units in regularly changing relations. To this has likewise been added, in all but the rarest cases, the postulate that ultimate causality is to be found in the motion of the physical atoms. So far as biology has its own peculiar metaphysical assumptions, they are as yet covered up in the vagueness of its major concepts, "environment," "adaptation," etc., and must be given time to reveal their specific nature. It is the creative period of modern science, then, in the seventeenth century chiefly, to which we must turn for the main answer to our problem. As for pre-Newtonian science, it is one and the same movement with pre-Newtonian philosophy, both in England and on the continent; science was simply natural philosophy, and the influential figures of the periods were both the greatest scientists. It is largely due to Newton himself that a real distinction came to be made between the two; philosophy came to take science, in the main, for granted, and another way to put our central theme is, *did not the problems to which philosophers now devoted themselves arise directly out of that uncritical acceptance?* A brief summary of Newton's work will show that this is very possible.

Since his day, a two-fold importance has generally been ascribed to Newton. Popularly, he has profoundly affected the thinking of the average intelligent man by his outstanding scientific exploits, of which the most striking was his conquest of the heavens in the name of human science by identifying terrestrial gravitation with the centripetal movements of the celestial bodies. Great as is the name of Newton to-day, it is difficult for us to picture the adoration with which he was regarded all over Europe in the eighteenth century. It seemed to men, if we are to trust the voluminous literature of the time, that such achievements as the discovery of the laws of motion and the law of universal gravitation, represented an incomparable, uniquely important victory of mind, which it could fall to the lot of only one man throughout all time to realize—and Newton had been that man. Henry Pemberton, who edited the third edition of the *Principia* for Newton, and who wrote one of the numerous commentaries on it, declared that ". . . my admiration at the surprising inventions of this great man, carries me to conceive of him as a person, who not only must raise the glory of the country which gave him birth, but that he has even done honour to human nature, by having extended the greatest and most noble of our faculties, reason, to subjects which, till he attempted them, appeared to be wholly beyond the reach of our limited capacities." [6] The admiration of other scientific minds is represented by Locke's designation of himself, beside the "incomparable Mr. Newton, an under-labourer, employed in clearing the ground and removing some of the rubbish that lies in the way to knowledge";[7] or by the famous tribute of Laplace who remarked that Newton was not only the greatest genius that ever had existed, but also the most fortunate; inasmuch as there is but one universe, and it can therefore happen to but one man in the world's history to be the interpreter of its laws. Literary men like Pope found expression for the prevailing veneration of the great scientist in such a famous couplet as:

Nature and Nature's laws lay hid in night;
God said, "Let Newton be," and all was light.[8]

[6] *A View of Isaac Newton's Philosophy*, London, 1728, Dedication to Sir Robert Walpole.

[7] *Essay Concerning Human Understanding*, Epistle to the Reader.

[8] Epitaph, intended for Newton's tomb in Westminster Abbey, *Poetical Works*, Glasgow, 1785, vol. II, p. 342.

Emmanuel College Library

while the new authoritarianism that developed under Newton's name, attacked so violently by Berkeley in his *Defence of Free Thinking in Mathematics,* was still deplored twenty years later by eager inquirers such as George Horne:

> The prejudice for Sir Isaac has been so great, that it has destroyed the intent of his undertaking, and his books have been a means of hindering that knowledge they were intended to promote. It is a notion every child imbibes almost with his mother's milk, that Sir Isaac Newton has carried philosophy to the highest pitch it is capable of being carried, and established a system of physics upon the solid basis of mathematical demonstration.[9]

Such representative quotations disclose the creation, under Newton's leadership, of a new background in the minds of Europe's intelligentsia such that all problems must have been viewed afresh because they were seen against it.

A student of the history of physical science will assign to Newton a further importance which the average man can hardly appreciate. He will see in the English genius a leading figure in the invention of certain scientific tools necessary for fruitful further development such as the infinitesimal calculus. He will find in him the first clear statement of that union of the experimental and mathematical methods which has been exemplified in all subsequent discoveries of exact science. He will note the separation in Newton of positive scientific inquiries from questions of ultimate causation. Most important, perhaps, from the point of view of the exact scientist, Newton was the man who took vague terms like force and mass and gave them a precise meaning as quantitative continua, so that by their use the major phenomena of physics became amenable to mathematical treatment. It is because of these remarkable scientific performances that the history of mathematics and mechanics for a hundred years subsequent to Newton appears primarily as a period devoted to the assimilation of his work and the application of his laws to more varied

[9] *A Fair, Candid, and Impartial State of the Case between Sir Isaac Newton and Mr. Hutchinson,* Oxford, 1753, p. 72.

types of phenomena. So far as objects were masses, moving in space and time under the impress of forces as he had defined them, their behavior was now, as a result of his labours, fully explicable in terms of exact mathematics.

It may be, however, that Newton is an exceedingly important figure for still a third reason. He not only found a precise mathematical use for concepts like force, mass, inertia; he gave new meanings to the old terms space, time, and motion, which had hitherto been unimportant but were now becoming the fundamental categories of men's thinking. In his treatment of such ultimate concepts, together with his doctrine of primary and secondary qualities, his notion of the nature of the physical universe and of its relation to human knowledge (in all of which he carried to a more influential position a movement already well advanced)—in a word, in his decisive portrayal of the ultimate postulates of the new science and its successful method as they appeared to him, Newton was constituting himself a philosopher rather than a scientist as we now distinguish them. He was presenting a metaphysical groundwork for the mathematical march of mind which in him had achieved its most notable victories. Imbedded directly and prominently in the *Principia,* Newton's most widely studied work, these metaphysical notions were carried wherever his scientific influence penetrated, and borrowed a possibly unjustified certainty from the clear demonstrability of the gravitational theorems to which they are appended as *Scholia.* Newton was unrivalled as a scientist—it may appear that he is not above criticism as a metaphysician. He tried scrupulously, at least in his experimental work, to avoid metaphysics. He disliked hypotheses, by which he meant explanatory propositions which were not immediately deduced from phenomena. At the same time, following his illustrious predecessors, he does give or assume definite answers to such fundamental questions as the nature of space, time, and matter; the relations of man with the objects of his knowledge; and it is just such answers that constitute metaphysics. The fact that his treatment of these great themes—borne as it was over the educated world by the weight of his scientific prestige—was covered over by this cloak of positivism, may have become itself a danger. It may have helped not a little to insinuate a set of uncritically accepted ideas about the world into the common intellectual background of the modern man. What Newton did not distinguish, others were not apt carefully to analyse. The actual achievements of the new science were undeniable; furthermore, the old set of categories, involving, as it appeared, the now discredited medieval physics, was no longer an alternative to any competent thinker. In these circumstances it is easy to understand how modern philosophy might have been led into certain puzzles which were due to the unchallenged presence of these new categories and presuppositions.

Now a penetrating study of post-Newtonian philosophers quickly reveals the fact that they were philosophizing quite definitely in the light of his achievements, and with his metaphysics especially in mind. At the time of his death Leibniz was engaged in a heated debate on the nature of time and space with Newton's theological champion, Samuel Clarke. Berkeley's *Commonplace Book* and *Principles,* still more his lesser works such as *The Analyst, A Defence of Free Thinking in Mathematics,* and *De Motu,* show clearly enough whom he conceived to be his deadly foe.[10] Hume's *Enquiry Concerning Human Understanding* and *Enquiry Concerning the Principles of Morals* contain frequent references to Newton. The French Encyclopædists and materialists of the middle of the eighteenth century felt themselves one and all to be more consistent Newtonians than Newton himself. In his early years Kant was an eager student of Newton, and his first works[11] aim mainly at a synthesis of continental philosophy and New-

[10] The fullest edition of Berkeley's *Works* is that of A. C. Fraser, Oxford, 1871, 4 vols.

[11] See especially his *Thoughts on the True Estimation of Living Forces,* 1746; *General Physiogony and Theory of the Heavens,* 1755; *Monadologia Physica,* 1756; and *Inquiry into the Evidence of the Principles of Natural Theology and Morals,* 1764; in any edition of his works.

tonian science. Hegel wrote[12] an extended and trenchant criticism of Newton. Of course, these men do not accept Newton as gospel truth—they all criticize some of his conceptions, especially force and space—but none of them subjects the whole system of categories which had come to its clearest expression in the great *Principia* to a critical analysis. It may be that their failure to construct a convincing and encouraging philosophy of man is due in large part to this untested remainder. It may be that many of the terms and assumptions in which their thinking proceeded were in their unanalysed form essentially refractory to any such brilliant achievement.

The only way to bring this issue to the bar of truth is to plunge into the philosophy of early modern science, locating its key assumptions as they appear, and following them out to their classic formulation in the metaphysical paragraphs of Sir Isaac Newton. The present is a brief historical study which aims to meet this need. The analysis will be sufficiently detailed to allow our characters to do much speaking for themselves, and to lay bare as explicitly as possible the real interests and methods revealed in their work. At its close the reader will understand more clearly the nature of modern thinking and judge more accurately the validity of the contemporary scientific world-view.

Let us start our inquiry with certain questions suggested by the work of the first great modern astronomer and the founder of a new system of the celestial orbs, Nicholas Copernicus.

[12] Hegel, *Phenomenology of Mind* (Baillie trans.), London, 1910, Vol. I, pp. 124, ff., 233, ff.; *Philosophy of Nature, passim;* and *History of Philosophy* (Haldane trans.), Vol. III, 322, ff.

A. The Problem of the New Astronomy

Why did Copernicus and Kepler, in advance of any empirical confirmation of the new hypothesis that the earth is a planet revolving on its axis and circling round the sun, while the fixed stars remain at rest, believe it to be a true picture of the astronomical universe? This is historically the most convenient question with which to open our attack.

By way of preparing an answer to this question let us ask another, namely what ground a sane, representative thinker, contemporary to Copernicus, would have for rejecting this new hypothesis as a piece of rash and quite unjustified apriorism? We are so accustomed to think of the opposition to the great astronomer as being founded primarily on theological considerations (which was, of course, largely true at the time) that we are apt to forget the solid scientific objections that could have been, and were, urged against it.

First of all, there were no known celestial phenomena which were not accounted for by the Ptolemaic method with as great accuracy as could be expected without more modern instruments. Predictions of astronomical events were made which varied no more from the actual occurrence than did predictions made by a Copernican. And in astronomy, as elsewhere, possession is nine-tenths of the law. No sensible thinker would have abandoned a hoary, time-tested theory of the universe in favour of a new-fangled scheme unless there were important advantages to be gained, and in this case there was distinctly no gain in accuracy. The motions of the heavenly bodies could be charted according to Ptolemy just as correctly as according to Copernicus.

In the second place, the testimony of the senses appeared to be perfectly plain on the matter. It was before the days when one could actually see by the aid of a telescope the spots on the sun, the phases of Venus, the rough surface of the moon —could discover, in a word, fairly convincing proof that these bodies were made of essentially the same material as the earth, and could determine how vast their actual distances were. To the senses it must have appeared incontestable that the earth was a solid, immovable substance, while the light ether and the bits of starry flame at its not too distant limit floated easily around it day by day. The earth is to the senses the massive, stable thing; the heavens are by comparison, as revealed in every passing breeze and every flickering fire, the tenuous, the unresisting, the mobile thing.

In the third place, there had been built up on the basis of this supposedly unshakeable testimony of the senses a natural philosophy of the universe which furnished a fairly complete and satisfactory background for man's thinking. The four elements of earth, water, air, fire, in their ascending scale not only as to actual spatial relations, but also in dignity and value, were the categories in which men's thinking about the inanimate realm had become accustomed to proceed. There was necessarily involved in this mode of thinking the assumption that the heavenly bodies were more noble in quality and more mobile in fact than the earth, and when these prepossessions were added to the other fundamentals of the Aristotelian metaphysics, which brought this astronomical conception into general harmony with the totality of human experience to date, the suggestion of a widely different theory in astronomy would inevitably appear in the light of a contradiction of every important item of knowledge man had gained about his world.

Finally, there were certain specific objections to the new theory which in the state of astronomical observation and mechanical science reached at the time could not be satisfactorily answered. Some of them, such as the assertion that a body projected vertically in the air must fall considerably to the west of its starting-point if the Copernican theory be correct, had to wait for its refutation till Galileo laid the foundations of modern dynamics. Others, such as the objection that according to Copernicus the fixed stars ought to reveal an annual parallax, due to the 186,000,000-mile difference in the position of the earth every six months, were not answered till

Bessel's discovery of such a parallax in 1838. In Copernicus' day the non-appearance to the senses of any stellar parallax implied, if his theory be sound, the necessity of attributing to the fixed stars a distance so immense that it would have been dismissed by all but a few as ridiculously incredible. And these are but two of the many legitimate deductions from the new hypothesis which completely failed of empirical confirmation.

In the light of these considerations it is safe to say that even had there been no religious scruples whatever against the Copernican astronomy, sensible men all over Europe, especially the most empirically minded, would have pronounced it a wild appeal to accept the premature fruits of an uncontrolled imagination, in preference to the solid inductions, built up gradually through the ages, of men's confirmed sense experience. In the strong stress on empiricism, so characteristic of present-day philosophy, it is well to remind ourselves of this fact. Contemporary empiricists, had they lived in the sixteenth century, would have been first to scoff out of court the new philosophy of the universe.

Why, in the face of such weighty facts, did Copernicus propound the new theory as a true account of the relations between the earth and the heavenly bodies? He must have been moved by strong reasons, and if we can locate them with precision we shall have discovered the cornerstone and the foundation structure of the philosophy of modern physical science. For to oppose to these profoundly serious objections he could plead only that *his conception threw the facts of astronomy into a simpler and more harmonious mathematical order.* It was simpler, since in place of some eighty epicycles of the Ptolemaic system, Copernicus was able to "save the phenomena" with only thirty-four, all those which had been required by the assumption that the earth remained at rest being now eliminated. It was more harmonious, in that the major part of the planetary phenomena could now fairly well be represented by a series of concentric circles around the sun, our moon being the only irregular intruder. But what was this increased simplicity and harmony against the solid philosophical objections just advanced?

In answering this question, let us describe briefly the relevant circumstances in Copernicus' intellectual environment, and their influence upon him in this critical step. The answer, we shall discover, is to be found principally in the following four features of that environment.

First, of course, both ancient and medieval observers had noted that in many respects nature appeared to be governed by the principle of simplicity, and they had recorded the substance of their observations to this effect in the form of proverbial axioms which had become currently accepted bits of man's conception of the world. That falling bodies moved perpendicularly towards the earth, that light travelled in straight lines, that projectiles did not vary from the direction in which they were impelled, and countless other familiar facts of experience, had given rise to such common proverbs as: *"Natura semper agit per vias brevissimas"; "natura nihil facit frustra"; "natura neque redundat in superfluis, neque deficit in necessariis."* This notion, that nature performs her duties in the most commodious fashion, without extra labour, would have tended to decrease somewhat the repulsion which most minds must have felt at Copernicus; the cumbrous epicycles had been decreased in number, various irregularities in the Ptolemaic scheme were eliminated, and that was something to be expected if proverbs like these are true of nature. When Copernicus, in the name of this principle of simplicity, attacks certain complexities in the older view, such as the equants of Ptolemy and his inability to attribute uniform velocity to the planetary motions[1]; likewise when he praises his own system as representable by *"paucioribus et multo convenientioribus rebus"*; he rightly expects to decrease somewhat the prejudices which his revolutionary view is certain to awake.

The new astronomy involved, in the second place, the assertion that the correct point of reference in astronomy was not the earth, as had been taken for granted hitherto by all but a handful of ancient speculators, but the fixed stars and the sun. That such a tremendous shift in the point of reference could be legitimate was a suggestion quite beyond the grasp

[1]*Nicolai Coppernici de hypothesibus motuum cœlestium a se constitutis Commentariolus,* Fol. 1a.

of people trained for centuries to think in terms of a homocentric philosophy and a geocentric physics. No one whatsoever could be expected even to entertain such a notion a hundred years prior to Copernicus, save an occasional astronomer
skilled in the lore of his science and able to realize that at
least there was some recompense in the form of greater simplicity for considering the possibilities of a solar-centric system. But certain things had happened during these hundred
years that made it not quite so impossible to persuade people
who could appreciate the advantages of a new point of reference to give it some scope in their minds. The Renaissance
had happened, namely the shifting of man's centre of interest
in literature from the present to the golden age of antiquity.
The Commercial Revolution had begun, with its long voyages
and exciting discoveries of previously unknown continents and
unstudied civilizations; the business leaders of Europe and the
champions of colonialism were turning their attention from
petty local fairs to the great untapped centres of trade in Asia
and the Americas. The realm of man's previous acquaintance
seemed suddenly small and meagre; men's thoughts were becoming accustomed to a widening horizon. The earth was cir-
cumnavigated, which proved in more popular fashion its rotundity. The antipodes were found to be quite inhabited. It
seemed a possible corollary that the centre of importance in
the universe was perhaps not even in Europe. Further, the unprecedented religious upheaval of the times had contributed
powerfully to loosen men's thinking. Rome had been taken for
granted as the religious centre of the world for well over a
thousand years; now there appeared a number of distinct
centres of religious life besides Rome. The rise of vernacular
literatures and the appearance of distinctly national tendencies
in art added their bit to the same unsettlement; there was a
renouncement, in all these respects, of man's former centres of
interest and a fixation on something new. In this ferment of
strange and radical ideas, widely disseminated by the recent
invention of printing, it was not so difficult for Copernicus to
consider seriously for himself and suggest persuasively to
others that a still greater shift than any of these must now be
made, a shift of the centre of reference in astronomy from the

earth to the sun. That the way had already been paved to some extent for this most radical revolution is suggested by the free speculations of such a thinker as Nicholas of Cusa, who dared to teach that there is nothing at all without motion in the universe—the latter is infinite in all directions, possessing no centre—and that the earth travels its course in common with the other stars. That this widening of the intellectual horizon of the age, with the suggestion of new centres of interest, was a decisive factor in Copernicus' personal development, the brief biographical sketch which he gives of himself in the *De Revolutionibus* strongly suggests.[2] The argument used by Copernicus and other defenders of the new cosmography, like Gilbert of Colchester, in answer to the objection that objects on its surface would be hurled off like projectiles if the earth were really in such a rapid motion—the argument that rather would the supposed immense sphere of the fixed stars fly asunder—implies that these men were already venturing to think of the heavenly bodies as homogeneous with the earth, to which the same principles of force and motion apply. London and Paris had become like Rome; in the absence of evidence to the contrary it is to be conceived that the distant celestial bodies are like the earth.

B. Metaphysical Bearings of the
Pre-Copernican Progress in Mathematics

Thirdly, certain facts ordinarily confined to the histories of mathematics are of vital importance in this connexion. So significant are they for our study that we must pause upon them at somewhat greater length. It is a commonplace to mathematicians that save for the last two centuries, during which higher algebra has to a considerable extent freed men's

[2] Copernicus, *De Revolutionibus Cælestium Orbium,* Letter to Pope Paul III. Stray thinkers, of course, in the ancient world, such as Anaxagoras, and the late medieval period, such as Da Vinci, had regarded the stars as homogeneous with the earth.

minds from dependence on spatial representations in their mathematical thinking, geometry has always been the mathematical science *par excellence*. In it, as Kepler remarks,[3] the certainty possible in exact mathematical reasoning is allied at every step with visible extended images, hence many who are quite incompetent in abstract thinking readily master the geometrical method. In ancient times, as revealed by the literary works, as well as the special treatises in our possession, arithmetic developed in close dependence on geometry. Whenever Plato (as in the *Meno*) turns to mathematics for an illustration of some pet contention, his doctrine of reminiscence, for example, the proposition used is always one that can be presented geometrically. The famous Pythagorean doctrine that the world is made of numbers is apt to appear quite unintelligible to moderns till it is recognized that what they meant was *geometrical units, i.e.*, the sort of geometrical atomism that was taken over later by Plato in his *Timæus*. They meant that the ultimate elements of the cosmos were limited portions of space. Inasmuch as optics and mechanics were treated by the ancients as branches of mathematics, it was customary also to think by means of spatial images in these sciences, and to represent what was known of them geometrically.

Now when, in the later Middle Ages, there appeared a powerful revival of mathematical study, the same assumptions and methods were taken for granted, and enthusiastic expectations were expressed regarding the possibility of a fuller mathematical interpretation of nature. Roger Bacon[4] eagerly adopted these assumptions and shared to the full this enthusiasm; two centuries after Bacon, the great and many-sided thinker, Leonardo da Vinci, stands out as the leader in this development. The importance of mathematics in scientific inquiry is strongly stated: "He who is not a mathematician ac-

---

[3] *Joannis Kepleri Astronomi Opera Omnia*, ed. Ch. Frisch, Frankfurt and Erlangen, 1858, ff., Vol. 8, p. 148.

[4] W. W. R. Ball, *A Short Account of the History of Mathematics*, 4th ed., London, 1912, p. 175. Cf. also Robert Steele, *Roger Bacon and the State of Science in the Thirteenth Century* (in Singer, *Studies in the History and Method of Science*, Vol. 2, London, 1921).

cording to my principles must not read me" [5]; "Oh, students, study mathematics, and do not build without a foundation." He made extensive experiments in mechanics, hydraulics, and optics, in all of which he takes it for granted that sound conclusions are to be expressed mathematically and represented geometrically. During the next century, that marked by the appearance of Copernicus' epoch-making book, this geometrical method in mechanics and the other mathematico-physical sciences was assumed by all important thinkers. The *Nova Scienza* of Tartaglia, published in 1537, applies this method to certain problems of falling bodies and the maximum range of a projectile, while Stevinus (1548–1620) uses a definite scheme for the representation of forces, motions, and times by geometrical lines.

In view of these leading facts thus briefly summarized, it was natural that when in the fifteenth and sixteenth centuries a more extended use began to be made of algebraic symbols, mathematicians were able only very gradually to detach their thinking from continued dependence on geometrical representation. Let us study with some care the way in which this algebraic development took place. The popular objects of mathematical inquiry in these centuries dealt primarily with the theory of equations, and in particular with methods for the reduction and solution of quadratic and cubic equations. Pacioli, for example (died about 1510), was mainly interested in using the growing algebraic knowledge to investigate the properties of geometrical figures. He dealt with such problems as the following: *The radius of an inscribed triangle is four inches. The segments into which one side is divided by the point of contact are six inches and eight inches. Find the other two sides.* [6] A modern student would solve this problem at once by the aid of a simple algebraic equation; Pacioli finds it possible to do it only by an elaborate geometrical construction, using algebra merely to help him find the lengths of the various lines required. Similarly the solution of quadratic and cubic equations in the sixteenth century was always sought by

[5] H. Hopstock, *Leonardo as Anatomist* (Singer, Vol. 2).

[6] Ball, *Short Account,* p. 211, ff.

44

the geometrical method. W. W. R. Ball gives an interesting example of this cumbrous mode of reaching such results in Cardanus' solution of the cubic equation: $x^3 + qx = r$.[7] We can readily appreciate what a tremendous advance was in store for modern algebra when it finally succeeded in freeing itself from the shackles of spatiality. In the meantime, however, the vast possibilities hid in the algebraic symbols were rapidly opening up, and mathematicians were becoming familiar with more complicated processes, though still dependent on the aid of geometrical representations of their work. By the time of Cardanus men were occupied with problems complex enough to involve frequent transformations, especially the reduction of complex to simple terms, without any change of value. Put in the language of geometrical representation, this meant for such thinkers the reduction of complex to simple figures, a resultant simple triangle or circle being regarded as the equivalent of the more involved combination of figures which it replaced. This was often a rather complicated process, and various mechanical schemes were invented to aid the poor mathematician's endeavours. Galileo published in 1597 a geometrical compass, which consists of a detailed set of rules for reducing irregular to regular figures, and a combination of regular figures to a single one, with applications to such particular problems as extracting the square root, finding mean proportionals, and the like. This geometrical reduction, so characteristic of mathematics in the sixteenth century, is fundamental for our understanding of Copernicus. It is an essential factor in his doctrine of the relativity of motion.

Finally, throughout the ancient and medieval period to the time of Galileo, astronomy was considered a branch of mathematics, *i.e.,* of geometry. It was the geometry of the heavens. Our current conception of mathematics as an ideal science, of geometry in particular as dealing with an ideal space, rather than the actual space in which the universe is set, was a notion quite unformulated before Hobbes, and not taken seriously till the middle of the eighteenth century, though it was dimly felt after by a few Aristotelian opponents of Copernicus.

[7] *Ibid.,* p. 224, ff.

The space of geometry appears to have been the space of the real universe to all ancient and medieval thinkers who give any clear clue to their notion of the matter. In the case of the Pythagoreans and Platonists the identity of the two was an important metaphysical doctrine; in the case of other schools the same assumption seems to have been made, only its bearings were not thought out along cosmological lines. Euclid takes it for granted that physical space ($\chi\omega\rho\iota o\nu$) is the realm of geometry[8]; later mathematicians use his terminology, and there is no clear indication anywhere in the available works that anybody thought differently. When some, like Aristotle, defined space in a quite different manner,[9] it is noticeable that the definition is still such that the needs of geometers are fully met. The great issue among ancient astronomers was not on this fundamental point of the identity of the field of geometry and astronomical space, but on the question, whether a convenient set of geometrical figures that "saved the astronomical phenomena" could be appropriately used in case they implied the rejection of a speculative theory of the physical structure of the heavens.[10] It is possible that in the case of some who gave an affirmative answer to this question a vigorous touch of positivism had led to suspicion of all metaphysical assumptions about the matter, so that in their minds the relation of the world of geometry to that of astronomy was hardly more than methodological. Ptolemy, for example, in the first chapter of the *Almagest*, rejects the attempt to interpret the phenomena of astronomy physically (*i.e.*, metaphysically), but it is not cer-

[8] Euclid, *Elements*, Book I, Axioms 8 and 10, also Prop. IV; Book XI, Prop. III, VII; and especially Book XII, Prop. II. Sir Robert Heath, in his edition of the first book in Greek, doubts the genuineness of the second and third passages. If interpolations, however, they date from ancient times, and so far as I know no question has been raised about the other uses of the word in Euclid.

[9] The boundary of the enclosing body on the side of the enclosed. Phys. IV. 4. $\tau\acute{o}\pi o\varsigma$ is Aristotle's word.

[10] See a most interesting treatment of this whole matter in P. Duhem *Essai sur la notion de théorie physique de Platon à Galilée*, Paris, 1908.

tain whether this is mainly to brush aside those who would shackle his free geometrical procedure by speculations about homocentric spheres and the like, or whether it actually implied abstention from all assumptions about the ultimate nature of the astronomical realm. Certainly in the ancient world few were capable of such a degree of positivism as this implies, especially as to the senses the heavens appear to express the realm of geometry in its purest form. The sun and moon seem perfect circles, the stars but luminous points in pure space. To be sure, they were held to be physical bodies of some sort, and so possessed more than geometrical characteristics, but there was no way of investigating such, hence it must have been easy to raise no questions which would imply any difference between the realm of geometry and astronomical space. In fact, we know that, by many, astronomy was regarded as closer to the geometrical ideal of pure mathematics than arithmetic. Typical lists of the mathematical sciences offered by Alfarabi and Roger Bacon place them in the order: geometry, astronomy, arithmetic, music. Of course, this was in part due to the higher dignity ascribed to the heavenly bodies and the fact that the main uses of arithmetic were commercial. But not wholly. Astronomy, more than arithmetic, was like geometry. It was nothing essentially but the geometry of the heavens; men readily felt, therefore, that whatever was true in geometry must be necessarily and fully true of astronomy.

If, now, astronomy is but a branch of geometry, and if the transformation and reduction of algebraic equations is uniformly pursued by the geometrical method detailed above, indicating that such are still felt to be essentially geometrical problems, shall we have to wait long for a thinker to appear who will raise the question, why is not such reduction possible in astronomy? If astronomy is mathematics it must partake of the relativity of mathematical values, the motions represented on our chart of the heavens must be purely relative, and it makes no difference as far as truth is concerned what point be taken as the point of reference for the whole spatial system.

This position in part had been already taken in ancient times by Ptolemy himself; against the champions of this or that cosmology of the heavens he had dared to claim that it is legitimate to interpret the facts of astronomy by the simplest geometrical scheme which will "save the phenomena," no matter whose metaphysics might be upset.[11] His conception of the physical structure of the earth, however, prevented him from carrying through in earnest this principle of relativity, as his objections to the hypothesis that the earth moves amply show.[12] Copernicus was the first astronomer to carry it through in earnest, with full appreciation of its revolutionary implications.

Let us understand briefly what this principle of mathematical relativity in astronomy means. What astronomers observe is a set of regularly changing relations between their point of observation and the heavenly bodies. In the absence of any strong suggestion to the contrary they naturally take their point of observation as the point of reference in the science, and soon discovering, in the very infancy of astronomy, that the earth must be a globe, it becomes the *terra firma* in the charting of the celestial motions, it is the immovable centre to which all else is referred. Acting on this assumption, and supported by all the considerations mentioned earlier in the chapter, astronomers would have to express geometrically this system of changing relations substantially as Ptolemy did; his scheme of deferents and epicycles, excentrics, equants, and the rest, constitute about as simple a representation of the facts as is possible on this assumption. What Copernicus discovered was that exactly the same results could be attained by a mathematical reduction of Ptolemy's highly complex geometry of the planets. Let us take an illustration, oversimple as far as any actual fact about the celestial motions is concerned, but which will illustrate the point. From E as point of reference we observe the motion of a heavenly body D such that when it is opposite another body S, say at G, it appears very much larger than when it is on the other side of its orbit, at F. We can represent such a motion by a combination of

[11] In his *Mathematical Composition*, Book 13, Ch. 2.

[12] For example, "if there were motion, it would be proportional to the great mass of the earth and would leave behind animals and objects thrown into the air."

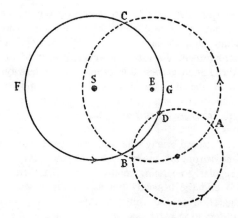

two circles ABC, with E as centre, and ABD, which has its centre on the circumference of the former. Let us suppose that each of these circles revolves as indicated by the arrows, a full revolution of each being completed in the same time. The point D on the circle ABD will then trace out a path DGCF, which, if the radii and velocities be properly chosen, will correspond fairly well with the observed facts. But it is obvious that there must be some point in the direction of the body S, which is the centre of the resulting circular path DGCF, and if it be taken as the point of reference, the facts can be represented by a single circle instead of two. Suppose that the facts do not negate locating that point at the centre of S. Suppose furthermore that, encouraged by this simplification of the charted motions, we note that certain irregularities in the motion of the planet D, which we had been able to represent only by additional circles, complete themselves in exactly the same time as the body S completes an important annual variation in its apparent motion around E. We regard S as at rest, with both our point of reference E and the planet D revolving around it, and lo, the irregularities in the planet and the annual variation in the motion of S cancel each other. Thus in place of a system around E as point of reference which had already begun to be involved and cumbrous, we have a simple system of two circular motions around S. This is exactly the way in which Copernicus thought out the new astronomy. As a result of his work, all the epicycles which had been demanded by the assumption that E is to be maintained as point of reference rather than S were eliminated. Mathematically, there is no question as to which is true. As far as astronomy is mathematics, both are true, because both represent the facts, but one is simpler and more harmonious than the other.

The particular event which led Copernicus to consider a new point of reference in astronomy was his discovery that the ancients had disagreed about the matter. Ptolemy's system had not been the only theory advanced.[13]

> When, therefore, I had long considered this uncertainty of traditional mathematics, it began to weary me that no more definite explanation of the movement of the world-machine established in our behalf by the best and most systematic builder of all, existed among the philosophers who had studied so exactly in other respects the minutest details in regard to the sphere. Wherefore I took upon myself the task of re-reading the books of all the philosophers which I could obtain, to seek out whether any one had ever conjectured that the motions of the spheres of the universe were other than they supposed who taught mathematics in the schools. And I found first, that, according to Cicero, Nicetas had thought the earth was moved. Then later I discovered, according to Plutarch, that certain others had held the same opinion. . . .
>
> When from this, therefore, I had conceived its possibility, I myself also began to meditate upon the mobility of the earth. And although the opinion seemed absurd, yet because I knew the liberty had been accorded to others before me of imagining whatsoever circles they pleased to explain the phenomena of the stars, I thought I also might readily be allowed to experiment whether, by supposing the earth to have some motion, stronger demonstrations than those of the others could be found as to the revolution of the celestial sphere.

[13] Copernicus, *De Revolutionibus,* Letter to Pope Paul III.

Thus, supposing these motions which I attribute to the earth later on in this book, I found at length by much and long observation, that if the motions of the other planets were added to the rotation of the earth and calculated as for the revolution of that planet, not only the phenomena of the others followed from this, but also it so bound together both the order and magnitude of all the planets and the spheres and the heaven itself, that in no single part could one thing be altered without confusion among the other parts and in all the universe. Hence for this reason in the course of this work I have followed this system. . . .

Likewise in the brief *Commentariolus,* written about 1530, after describing his dissatisfaction with the ancient astronomers for their inability to get a consistent geometry of the heavens that should not violate the postulate of uniform velocity,[14] he proceeds:

Hence this kind of theory did not seem sufficiently certain, nor sufficiently in accord with reason. So when I had noted these things, I often considered if perchance a more rational system of circles might be discovered, on which all the apparent diversity might depend, and in such a manner that each of the planets would be uniformly moved, as the principle of absolute motion requires. Attacking a problem obviously difficult and almost inexplicable, at length I hit upon a solution whereby this could be reached by fewer and much more convenient constructions than had been handed down of old, if certain assumptions, which are called axioms, be granted me. . . .

Accorded then these premises, I shall attempt to show briefly how simply the uniformity of motion can be saved. . . .[15]

These passages show clearly that to Copernicus' mind the question was not one of truth or falsity, not, does the earth

[14] A principle resting ultimately upon a religious basis. The cause (God) is constant and unremitting, hence the effect must be uniform. (*De Revolutionibus,* Bk. I, Ch. 8.)

[15] *Commentariolus,* Fol. 1a, b, 2a.

move? He simply included the earth in the question which Ptolemy had asked with reference to the celestial bodies alone; what motions should we attribute to the earth in order to obtain the simplest and most harmonious geometry of the heavens that will accord with the facts? That Copernicus was able to put the question in this form is ample proof of the continuity of his thought with the mathematical developments just recounted, and this is why he constantly appealed to mathematicians as those alone able to judge the new theory fairly. He was quite confident that they, at least, would appreciate and accept his view.

> Nor do I doubt that skilled and scholarly mathematicians will agree with me if, what philosophy requires from the beginning, they will examine and judge, not casually but deeply, what I have gathered together in this book to prove these things. "Mathematics is written for mathematicians, to whom these my labours, if I am not mistaken, will appear to contribute something. . . ." "What . . . I may have achieved in this, I leave to the decision of your Holiness especially, and to all other learned mathematicians." If perchance there should be foolish speakers who, together with those ignorant of all mathematics, will take it upon themselves to decide concerning these things, and because of some place in the Scriptures wickedly distorted to their purpose, should dare to assail this my work, they are of no importance to me, to such an extent do I despise their judgment as rash.[16]

And it is not surprising that for the sixty years that elapsed before Copernicus' theory was confirmed in more empirical fashion, practically all those who ventured to stand with him were accomplished mathematicians, whose thinking was thoroughly in line with the mathematical advances of the day.

[16] These quotations are all from his Letter to Pope Paul III in the *De Revolutionibus*. Cf. also Bk. I, Chs. 7 and 10.

c. Ultimate Implications of Copernicus' Step—Revival of Pythagoreanism

But now, of course, the question which Copernicus has thus easily answered carries with it a tremendous metaphysical assumption. Nor were people slow to see it and bring it to the forefront of discussion. *Is it legitimate to take any other point of reference in astronomy than the earth?* Mathematicians who were themselves subject to all the influences working in Copernicus' mind, would, so he hoped, be apt to say yes. But of course the whole Aristotelian and empirical philosophy of the age rose up and said no. For the question went pretty deep, it meant not only, is the astronomical realm fundamentally geometrical, which almost any one would grant, *but is the universe as a whole, including our earth, fundamentally mathematical in its structure?* Just because this shift of the point of reference gives a simpler geometrical expression for the facts, is it legitimate to make it? To admit this point is to overthrow the whole Aristotelian physics and cosmology. Even many mathematicians and astronomers might not be willing to follow the tendencies of their science to this extreme; the current of their general thinking flowed on another bed. To follow Ptolemy in ancient times meant merely to reject the cumbrous crystalline spheres. To follow Copernicus was a far more radical step, it meant to reject the whole prevailing conception of the universe. That Copernicus himself and some others were able to answer this ultimate question with a confident affirmative suggests a fourth contributory feature of Copernicus' environment; it suggests that for many minds of the age at least, there was an alternative background besides Aristotelianism, in terms of which their metaphysical thinking might go on, and which was more favourable to this astonishing mathematical movement.

As a matter of fact there was just such an alternative background. All students of philosophy are aware that during the early Middle Ages the synthesis of Christian theology and

Greek philosophy was accomplished with the latter in a predominantly Platonic, or rather Neo-Platonic cast. Now the Pythagorean element in Neo-Platonism was very strong. All the important thinkers of the school liked to express their favourite doctrines of emanation and evolution in terms of the number theory, following Plato's suggestion in the Parmenides that plurality unfolded itself from unity by a necessary mathematical process.

Now during this early period of medieval philosophy it is significant that the only original work of Plato in the hands of philosophers was the *Timæus,* which presents Plato more in the light of a Pythagorean than any other dialogue. It was largely because of this curious circumstance that the first return to a serious study of nature, under Pope Gerbert and his disciple Fulbert about 1000, was undertaken as a Platonic venture. Plato appeared to be the philosopher of nature; Aristotle, who was known only through his logic, seemed like a barren dialectician. It was no accident that Gerbert was an accomplished mathematician, and that William of Conches, a later member of the school, stressed a geometrical atomism which he had drawn from the *Timæus.*

When Aristotle captured medieval thought in the thirteenth century, Neo-Platonism was not by any means routed, but remained as a somewhat suppressed but still widely influential metaphysical current, to which dissenters from the orthodox Peripateticism were accustomed to appeal. The interest in mathematics evidenced by such freethinkers as Roger Bacon, Leonardo, Nicholas of Cusa, Bruno, and others, together with their insistence on its importance, was in large part supported by the existence and pervading influence of this Pythagorean stream. Nicholas of Cusa found in the theory of numbers the essential element in the philosophy of Plato. The world is an infinite harmony, in which all things have their mathematical proportions.[17] Hence "knowledge is always measurement," "number is the first model of things in the mind of the Creator"; in a word, all certain knowledge that is possible for man

[17] R. Eucken, *Nicholas von Kuss* (*Philosophische Monatshefte,* 1882).

must be mathematical knowledge. The same strain appears strongly in Bruno, though in him even more than in Cusa the mystico-transcendental aspect of the number theory was apt to be uppermost.

It was natural, then, that in the fifteenth and sixteenth centuries, after men's minds had become thoroughly restless but before they were independent enough to break more definitely with ancient traditions, there was a strong revival of Platonism in Southern Europe. An Academy was founded in Florence under the patronage of the Medicean family, and boasting as its scholarchs such names as Pletho, Bessarion, Marsilius Ficinus, and Patrizzi. In this Platonic revival it was again the Pythagorean element that assumed prominence, coming to striking expression in the thoroughgoing mathematical interpretation of the world offered by John Pico of Mirandola. The work of these thinkers penetrated to some extent every important centre of thought south of the Alps, including the University of Bologna, where their most important representative was Dominicus Maria de Novara, professor of mathematics and astronomy. Novara was Copernicus' friend and teacher during the six years of his stay in Italy, and among the important facts which we know about him is this, that he was a free critic of the Ptolemaic system of astronomy, partly because of some observations which did not agree closely enough with deductions from it, but more especially because he was thoroughly caught in this Platonic-Pythagorean current and felt that the whole cumbrous system violated the postulate that the astronomical universe is an orderly mathematical harmony.[18]

This was in fact the greatest point of conflict between the dominant Aristotelianism of the later Middle Ages and this somewhat submerged but still pervasive Platonism. The latter regarded a universal mathematics of nature as legitimate (though, to be sure, just how this was to be applied was not yet solved); the universe is fundamentally geometrical; its ultimate constituents are nothing but limited portions of

[18] Dorothy Stimson, *The Gradual Acceptance of the Copernican Theory of the Universe,* New York, 1917, p. 25.

space; as a whole it presents a simple, beautiful, geometrical harmony. On the other hand the orthodox Aristotelian school minimized the importance of mathematics. Quantity was only one of the ten predicaments and not the most important. Mathematics was assigned an intermediate dignity between metaphysics and physics. Nature was fundamentally qualitative as well as quantitative; the key to the highest knowledge must, therefore, be logic rather than mathematics. With the mathematical sciences alloted this subordinate place in his philosophy, it could not but appear ridiculous to an Aristotelian for any one to suggest seriously that his whole view of nature be set aside in the interest of a simpler and more harmonious geometrical astronomy. Whereas for a Platonist (especially as Platonism was understood at the time) it would appear a most natural, though still radical step, involving as it did a homogeneity of substance throughout the whole visible cosmos. However, Copernicus could take the step because, in addition to the motive factors already discussed, he had definitely placed himself in this dissenting Platonic movement. Already before he went to Italy in 1496 he had felt its appeal, and, while there, he found ample reinforcement for his daring leap in the energetic Neo-Platonic environment south of the Alps, and particularly in his long and fruitful intercourse with a bold and imaginative Pythagorean like Novara. It was no accident that he became familiar with the remains of the early Pythagoreans, who almost alone among the ancients had ventured to suggest a non-geocentric astronomy. His knowledge of Greek was first acquired while studying with Novara, perhaps with the explicit purpose of reading for himself the works of the Pythagorean astronomers. He had himself become convinced that the whole universe was made of numbers, hence whatever was mathematically true was really or astronomically true. Our earth was no exception—it, too, was essentially geometrical in nature—therefore the principle of relativity of mathematical values applied to man's domain just as to any other part of the astronomical realm. The transformation to the new world-view, for him, was nothing but a mathematical reduction, under the encouragement of the renewed Platonism of the day, of a complex geometrical labyrinth into a beautifully simple and harmonious system.

"We are taught all this [the motion of the earth on its axis and around the sun] by the order of succession, in which those phenomena (various planetary happenings) follow each other, and by the harmony of the world, if we will only, as the saying goes, look at the matter with both eyes." [19] Note the same strain in the quotations above.

D. Kepler's Early Acceptance of the New World-Scheme

Now during the half-century after Copernicus, no one was bold enough to champion his theory save a few eminent mathematicians like Rheticus and a few incorrigible intellectual radicals like Bruno. In the late eighties and early nineties, however, certain corollaries of Copernicus' work were seized upon by the youthful Kepler, then in his student days, and they form a helpful transition from the first great modern astronomer to the second. Copernicus had himself noted the greater importance and dignity which seemed to be attributed to the sun in the new world-scheme, and had been eager to find mystical as well as scientific justification for it. One passage is worth quoting by way of illustration. "Then in the middle of all stands the sun. For who, in our most beautiful temple, could set this light in another or better place, than that from which it can at once illuminate the whole? Not to speak of the fact that not unfittingly do some call it the light of the world, others the soul, still others the governor. Tremigistus calls it the visible God; Sophocles' Electra, the All-seer. And in fact does the sun, seated on his royal throne, guide his family of planets as they circle round him." [20] Also Copernicus had formed a rudimentary conception of scientific hypothesis, accommodated to his new astronomical method. A true hypothe-

[19] *De Revolutionibus,* Bk. I, Ch. 9.

[20] *De Revolutionibus,* Bk. I, Ch. 10.

sis is one which binds together rationally (*i.e.*, for him mathematically) things which had before been held distinct; it reveals the reason, in terms of that which unites them, why they are as they are. "We find then in this arrangement an admirable harmony of the world, and a dependable, harmonious interconnexion of the motion and the size of the paths, such as otherwise cannot be discovered. For here the penetrating observer can note why the forward and the retrograde movement of Jupiter appears greater than that of Saturn, and smaller than that of Mars, and again greater with Venus than with Mercury; and why such retrogression appears oftener with Saturn than with Jupiter, less often with Mars and Venus than with Mercury. Moreover, why Saturn, Jupiter, and Mars, when they rise in the evening, appear greater than when they disappear and reappear [with the sun] . . . And all this results from the same cause, namely the motion of the earth." [21]

These ideas were seized upon by the young Kepler, and they furnish in large part the motivation for his life-work. The specific reasons for his early adoption of the Copernican theory are in part obscure, but it is easy to show from his works that he felt vigorously all those general environmental influences that appealed so strongly to Copernicus. With him nature's simplicity and unity was a commonplace.[22] "*Natura simplicitatem amat.*" "*Amat illa unitatem.*" "*Numquam in ipsa quicquam otiosum aut superfluum exstitit.*" "*Natura semper quod potest per faciliora, non agit per ambages difficiles.*" The advantages of Copernicanism from this point of view were easily noted. Also the general broadening of men's outlook, now reinforced by Copernicanism, had become a powerful stimulus to every fertile and imaginative mind, and Kepler's profound attainments in the science of mathematics could not but lead him to feel with full force all those considerations which had influenced the mind of his predecessor. His teacher of mathematics and astronomy at Tübingen, Mästlin, who had been strongly attracted by the greater order and harmony attainable in the Copernican scheme, was an adherent of the

[21] *De Revolutionibus*, Bk. I, Ch. 10.

[22] *Opera*, I, 112, ff.

new astronomy at heart, though he had so far expressed himself only with the greatest caution. Kepler's achievements in mathematics would alone have been sufficient to win for him enduring fame; he first enunciated clearly the principle of continuity in mathematics, treating the parabola as at once the limiting case of the ellipse and the hyperbola, and showing that parallel lines can be regarded as meeting at infinity; he introduced the word "focus" into geometry; while in his *Stereometria Dolorum,* published 1615, he applied the conception to the solution of certain volumes and areas by the use of infinitesimals, thus preparing the way for Desargues, Cavalieri, Barrow, and the developed calculus of Newton and Leibniz. The Neo-Platonic background, which furnished the metaphysical justification for much of this mathematical development (at least as regards its bearing on astronomy) awoke Kepler's full conviction and sympathy. Especially did the æsthetic satisfactions gained by this conception of the universe as a simple, mathematical harmony, appeal vigorously to his artistic nature. "I certainly know that I owe it [the Copernican theory] this duty, that as I have attested it as true in my deepest soul, and as I contemplate its beauty with incredible and ravishing delight, I should also publicly defend it to my readers with all the force at my command." [23]

These elements were mingled in his thought in varying degree, but the most potent single factor in his early enthusiasm for Copernicanism appears to be found in its exaltation in dignity and importance of the sun. Founder of exact modern science though he was, Kepler combined with his exact methods and indeed found his motivation for them in certain long discredited superstitions, including what it is not unfair to describe as sunworship. In 1593, at the age of twenty-two, he defended the new astronomy in a disputation at Tübingen, which performance as a whole is apparently lost, at least Dr. Frisch does not present it in his complete edition of Kepler's works. However, there appears in Kepler's miscellaneous remains a small fragment of a disputation on the motion of the earth, which from its highly bombastic style and other internal

[23] *Opera,* VI, 116. Cf. also VIII, 693.

characteristics, may very likely be a portion of this adolescent effort. At any rate, the fragment is clearly a product of his early years, and the noteworthy fact about it is that the exalted position of the sun in the new system appears as the main and sufficient reason for its adoption.[24] A few quotations will reveal the tenor of this curious piece of exuberance.

In the first place, lest perchance a blind man might deny it to you, of all the bodies in the universe the most excellent is the sun, whose whole essence is nothing else than the purest light, than which there is no greater star; which singly and alone is the producer, conserver, and warmer of all things; it is a fountain of light, rich in fruitful heat, most fair, limpid, and pure to the sight, the source of vision, portrayer of all colours, though himself empty of colour, called king of the planets for his motion, heart of the world for his power, its eye for his beauty, and which alone we should judge worthy of the Most High God, should he be pleased with a material domicile and choose a place in which to dwell with the blessed angels. . . . For if the Germans elect him as Cæsar who has most power in the whole empire, who would hesitate to confer the votes of the celestial motions on him who already has been administering all other movements and changes by the benefit of the light which is entirely his possession? . . . Since, therefore, it does not befit the first mover to be diffused throughout an orbit, but rather to proceed from one certain principle, and as it were, point, no part of the world, and no star, accounts itself worthy of such a great honour; hence by the highest right we return to the sun, who alone appears, by virtue of his dignity and power, suited for this motive duty and worthy to become the home of God himself, not to say the first mover.

In his subsequently expressed reasons for accepting Copernicanism this central position of the sun is always included, usually first.[25] This ascription of deity to the sun was covered

[24] *Opera,* VIII, 266, ff.

[25] Cf., for example, *Opera,* VI, 313.

over by Kepler with such mystical allegorization as was necessary to give it a hearing in the prevailing theological environment, with especial reference to the doctrine of the Trinity.
The sun, according to Kepler, is God the Father, the sphere
of the fixed stars is God the Son, the intervening ethereal
medium, through which the power of the sun is communicated
to impel the planets around their orbits, is the Holy Ghost.[26]
To pronounce this allegorical trapping is not to suggest, of
course, that Kepler's Christian theology is at all insincere; it
is rather that he had discovered an illuminating natural proof
and interpretation of it, and the whole attitude, with its animism and allegorico-naturalistic approach, is quite typical of
much thinking of the day. Kepler's contemporary Jacob
Boehme, is the most characteristic representative of this type
of philosophy.

This aspect of his thought would have been, to say the least,
somewhat at variance with the exact mathematical method in
astronomy, of which Kepler was also the firm champion, as
revealed by his discovery, after long and arduous search such
as would have completely discouraged all but the most ardent
spirits, of the three great laws of planetary motion. But the
connexion between Kepler, the sun-worshipper, and Kepler,
the seeker of exact mathematical knowledge of astronomical
nature, is very close. It was primarily by such considerations
as the deification of the sun and its proper placing at the
centre of the universe that Kepler in the years of his adolescent
fervour and warm imagination was induced to accept the new
system. But, his mind immediately proceeded, and here his
mathematics and his Neo-Pythagoreanism come into play, if
the system is true, there must be many other mathematical
harmonies in the celestial order that can be discovered and
proclaimed as confirmation of Copernicanism, by an intensive
study of the available data. This was a task in exact mathematics, and it was very fortunate for Kepler that he was just
plunging into such profound labours at the time when Tycho
Brahe, the greatest giant of observational astronomy since
Hipparchus, was completing his life-work of compiling a vastly

[26] *Opera,* I, 11.

more extensive and incomparably more precise set of data than had been in the possession of any of his predecessors. Kepler had joined Tycho Brahe the year before the latter's death and had full access to his magnificent accumulations. It became the passion of his life to penetrate and disclose, for the "fuller knowledge of God through nature and the glorification of his profession," [27] these deeper harmonies, and the fact that he was not satisfied merely with mystical manipulation of numbers, or æsthetic contemplation of geometrical fancies, we owe to his long training in mathematics and astronomy, and in no small degree to the influence of the great Tycho, who was the first competent mind in modern astronomy to feel ardently the passion for exact empirical facts.

Thus Kepler joined with his speculative superstitions an eagerness to find precise formulae confirmed in the data; it was the observed world about which he was philosophizing, hence "without proper experiments I conclude nothing," [28] hence also his refusal to neglect variations between his deductions and the observations which would not have troubled the ancients. At one time he had a splendid theory of the planet Mars all ready to write off, but a discrepancy of eight minutes between certain of his conclusions and Tycho's results persuaded him to throw his labours overboard and begin anew. The difference between Kepler and the early philosophizers like Nicholas of Cusa who had taught that all knowledge is ultimately mathematical and that all things were bound together by proportion, is that the later thinker insists on exactly applying the theory to observed facts. Kepler's thinking was genuinely empirical in the modern sense of the term. The Copernican revolution and the star-cataloguing of Tycho were necessary to furnish an important new mathematical theory to be developed and confirmed and a fuller set of data, in which, if at all, the confirmation must be found. It was by this method and for this purpose that Kepler reached his epoch-making discoveries of the famous three laws. These were not especially important to Kepler's own mind, being only three

[27] *Opera*, VIII, 688.

[28] *Opera*, V, 224. Cf. also I, 143.

out of scores of interesting mathematical relations which, as he pointed out, were established between the observed motions if the Copernican hypothesis be true. The one of the three which delighted him most was the second, that the planet-vector, in its revolution round the sun, sweeps over equal areas in equal times, because it first solved the problem of the irregularity of planetary velocities, a prominent point of attack in Copernicus' treatment of the Ptolemaic system, but which he himself had been unable to solve. Both Copernicus and Kepler were firmly convinced for religious reasons of the uniformity of motion, *i.e.,* each planet in its revolution is impelled by a constant and never failing cause, hence Kepler's joy at being able to "save" this principle as regards the areas even though it had to be surrendered as regards the planet's path. But the discovery which yielded Kepler the most inordinate delight and to which he referred for many years as his most important achievement, was the discovery published in his first work, the *Mysterium Cosmographicum* (1597), that the distances between the orbits of the six planets then known bore a certain rough resemblance to the distances which would be obtained if the hypothetical spheres of the planets were inscribed in and circumscribed about the five regular solids properly distributed between them. Thus if a cube be inscribed in the sphere of Saturn, the sphere of Jupiter will approximately fit within it, then between Jupiter and Mars the tetrahedron, between Mars and the earth the dodecahedron, etc. Of course, this performance has remained entirely unfruitful—the correspondence is rough, and the discovery of new planets has quite upset its underlying assumptions—but Kepler never forgot the pristine enthusiasm which this achievement awoke in him. In a letter penned shortly after the discovery he wrote:

> The intense pleasure I have received from this discovery can never be told in words. I regretted no more the time wasted; I tired of no labour; I shunned no toil of reckoning, days and nights spent in calculation, until I could see whether my hypothesis would agree with the orbits of Copernicus or whether my joy was to vanish into air.[29]

[29] Oliver Lodge, *Pioneers of Science,* Ch. III.

Kepler's enunciation of his third law, in the *Harmonices Mundi*, 1619, is imbedded in a laborious attempt to determine the music of the spheres according to precise laws, and express it in our form of music notation.[30] These features of Kepler's work are commonly dismissed by puzzled historians of astronomy as relics of medievalism, a procedure hardly fair to the intelligence of the Middle Ages, and quite over-favourable to Kepler. For our purpose, however, it is essential to note them. They are decidedly of a piece with his central aim, namely to establish more mathematical harmonies in the Copernican astronomy quite irrespective of their fruitfulness for such further achievements as became the goal of later scientific labours. They grow directly out of his whole philosophy of the aim and procedure of science, and the new metaphysical doctrines which in rudimentary fashion he perceived to be implied in the acceptance of Copernicanism and in the adoption of such an aim.

E. First Formulation of the New Metaphysics—Causality, Quantity, Primary and Secondary Qualities

What are the fundamental features of Kepler's philosophy of scientific procedure? Let us work our way into them through a fuller understanding of the point we have just stressed. Kepler was convinced that there must be many more mathematical harmonies discoverable in the world which will amply serve to confirm the truth of the Copernican system. The connexion of this conviction with his background in mathematics and the Pythagorean metaphysics has already been noted. But he often speaks of his accomplishments as having *shown the necessary and rational ground* of the new structure of the world, as having penetrated to the mathematical con-

[30] Kepler did not suppose that the spheres emitted audible sounds; their mathematical relations, however, changed in ways analogous to the development of a musical harmony and similarly representable.

nexion of facts formerly held distinct.[31] In thus stating his aim and achievement he was carrying further and expressing more explicitly Copernicus' thought when the latter had declared that his new system solved such problems as why the retrograde motion of Jupiter is less frequent than that of Saturn, etc. Just what does he mean by stating his aim in this fashion?

First and centrally, he means that he has reached a new conception of *causality,* that is, *he thinks of the underlying mathematical harmony discoverable in the observed facts as the cause of the latter, the reason, as he usually puts it, why they are as they are.* This notion of causality is substantially the Aristotelian formal cause reinterpreted in terms of exact mathematics; it also has obvious close relations with the rudimentary ideas of the early Pythagoreans. The exactness or rigour with which the causal harmony must be verified in phenomena is the new and important feature in Kepler. Tycho had urged Kepler in a letter "to lay a solid foundation for his views by actual observation, and then by ascending from these to strive to reach the cause of things." [32] Kepler, however, preferred to let Tycho gather the observations, for he was antecedently convinced that genuine causes must always be in the nature of underlying mathematical harmonies. A typical example of this use of the word *cause* is in the preface to the *Mysterium Cosmographicum.* Kepler speaks of the system of the five regular solids, which can be inserted between the spheres of the six planets, as the cause of the planets being six in number. *"Habes rationem numeri planetarum."* [33] The centrality of the sun is the cause of the coincidence of the planetary excentrics according to the ancients within or near the sun.[34] God created the world in accordance with the principle of perfect numbers, hence the mathematical har-

---

[31] *Opera,* I, 239, ff.

[32] Sir David Brewster, *Memoirs of Sir Isaac Newton,* Vol. II, p. 401.

[33] *Opera,* I, 113. Cf. also I, 106, ff.

[34] *Opera,* III, 156; I, 118.

monies in the mind of the creator furnish the cause "why the number, the size, and the motions of the orbits are as they are and not otherwise." [35] Causality, to repeat, becomes reinterpreted in terms of mathematical simplicity and harmony.

Further, this conception of causality involves a corresponding transformation in the idea of scientific hypothesis. An explanatory hypothesis of observed effects being an attempt to express in simple form their uniform causes, a true hypothesis for Kepler must be a statement of the underlying mathematical harmony discoverable in the effects. Kepler includes an interesting treatment of astronomical hypothesis in a letter written partly to refute Reimarus Ursus' position on the same subject.[36] Kepler's thought is, that *of a number of variant hypotheses about the same facts, that one is true which shows why facts, which in the other hypotheses remain unrelated, are as they are, i.e., which demonstrates their orderly and rational mathematical connexion.* To put it in his own summary: "Therefore, neither this nor that supposition is worthy of the name of an astronomical hypothesis, but rather that which is implied in both alike." [37] To illustrate by his stock example, other theories of the heavens had been forced to rest content with the simple statement that certain planetary epicycles coincide in their time of completion with the time of the sun's apparent revolution around the earth. The Copernican hypothesis must be the true one, inasmuch as it reveals why these periods must be as they are. Such facts imply, in other words, that in the scheme of regularly changing mutual relations which makes up our solar system the sun is to be taken as at rest rather than the earth.[38] A true hypothesis is always a more inclusive conception, binding together facts which had hitherto been regarded as distinct; it reveals a mathematical order and harmony where before there had been unexplained diversity. And it is important to remember that this more inclusive math-

[35] *Opera,* I, 10.

[36] *Opera,* I, 238, ff.

[37] *Opera,* I, 241.

[38] Cf. *Opera,* I, 113.

ematical order is something discovered *in the facts* themselves. This is precisely stated in many passages,[39] and the constant insistence on exact verification from observations would otherwise lose its point.

Now such a mathematico-æsthetic conception of causality and hypothesis already implies a new metaphysical picture of the world; in fact, it is just these ideas that made Kepler so impatient with certain well-meaning Aristotelian friends who advised him to treat his own and Copernicus' discoveries as mathematical hypotheses merely, not necessarily true of the real world. Such hypotheses as these, Kepler maintained, are precisely what give us the true picture of the real world, and the world thus revealed is a bigger and far more beautiful realm than man's reason had ever before entered. We must not surrender that glorious and illuminating discovery of the true nature of reality. Let the theologians weigh their authorities; that is their method. But for philosophers the discovery of (mathematical) causes is the way to truth. "Indeed I reply in a single word to the sentiments of the saints on these questions about nature; in theology, to be sure, the force of authorities is to be weighed, in philosophy, however, that of causes. Therefore, a saint is Lactantius, who denied the rotundity of the earth; a saint is Augustine, who, admitting the rotundity, yet denied the antipodes; worthy of sainthood is the dutiful performance of moderns who, admitting the meagreness of the earth, yet deny its motion. But truth is more saintly for me, who demonstrate by philosophy, without violating my due respect for the doctors of the church, that the earth is both round and inhabited at the antipodes, and of the most despicable size, and finally is moved among the stars." [40]

We begin now to glimpse the tremendous significance of what these fathers of modern science were doing, but let us continue with our questions. What further specific metaphysical doctrines was Kepler led to adopt as a consequence of this notion of what constitutes the real world? For one thing, it

[39] As for example, *Opera*, V, 226, ff. II, 687.

[40] *Opera*, III, 156.

led him to appropriate in his own way the distinction between primary and secondary qualities, which had been noted in the ancient world by the atomist and sceptical schools, and which was being revived in the sixteenth century in varied form by such miscellaneous thinkers as Vives, Sanchez, Montaigne, and Campanella. Knowledge as it is immediately offered the mind through the senses is obscure, confused, contradictory, and hence untrustworthy; only those features of the world in terms of which we get certain and consistent knowledge open before us what is indubitably and permanently real. Other qualities are not real qualities of things, but only signs of them. For Kepler, of course, the real qualities are those caught up in this mathematical harmony underlying the world of the senses, and which, therefore, have a causal relation to the latter. *The real world is a world of quantitative characteristics only; its differences are differences of number alone.* In his mathematical remains there is a brief criticism of Aristotle's treatment of the sciences, in which he declares that the fundamental difference between the Greek philosopher and himself was that the former traced things ultimately to qualitative, and hence irreducible distinctions, and was, therefore, led to give mathematics an intermediate place in dignity and reality between sensible things and the supreme theological or metaphysical ideas; whereas he had found means for discovering quantitative proportions between all things, and therefore gave mathematics the pre-eminence. "Wherever there are qualities, there are likewise quantities, but not always *vice versa.*" [41]

Again, Kepler's position led to an important doctrine of knowledge. Not only is it true that we can discover mathematical relations in all objects presented to the senses; *all certain knowledge must be knowledge of their quantitative characteristics, perfect knowledge is always mathematical.* "There are, in fact, as I began to say above, not a few principles which are the special property of mathematics, such principles as are discovered by the common light of nature, require no demonstration, and which concern quantities primarily; then they are

[41] *Opera,* VIII, 147, ff.

applied to other things, so far as the latter have something in common with quantities. Now there are more of these principles in mathematics than in the other theoretical sciences because of that very characteristic of the human understanding which seems to be such from the law of creation, that nothing can be known completely except quantities or by quantities. And so it happens that the conclusions of mathematics are most certain and indubitable." [42] He notes certain practical illustrations of this fact in optics, music, and mechanics, which, of course, best afforded him the confirmation he sought. "Just as the eye was made to see colours, and the ear to hear sounds, so the human mind was made to understand, not whatever you please, but quantity." [43] Therefore, quantity is the fundamental feature of things, the *"primarium accidens substantiae,"* [44] "prior to the other categories." Quantitative features are the sole features of things as far as the world of our knowledge is concerned.

Thus we have in Kepler the position clearly stated that the real world is the mathematical harmony discoverable in things. The changeable, surface qualities which do not fit into this underlying harmony are on a lower level of reality; they do not so truly exist. All this is thoroughly Pythagorean and Neo-Platonic in cast, it is the realm of the Platonic ideas suddenly found identical with the realm of geometrical relationships. Kepler apparently has no affiliations with the Democritan and Epicurean atomism, whose revival was destined to play an important part in post-Keplerian science. So far as his thought dwells upon the elementary particles of nature it is the geometrical atomism of the *Timæus* and the ancient doctrine of the four elements that he inherited, but his interest is not in these; it is the mathematical relations revealed in the cosmos at large that arouse his enthusiasm and interest. When he says that God made the world according to number he is thinking

[42] *Opera,* VIII, 148.

[43] *Opera,* I, 31.

[44] *Opera,* VIII, 150.

not about minute figured portions of space, but about these vaster numerical harmonies.[45]

The reason why there exists this vast and beautiful mathematical order in the universe is not further explicable for Kepler except by way of the religious aspect of his Neo-Platonism. He quotes with approval the famous saying of Plato, that God ever geometrizes; he created the world in accordance with numerical harmonies,[46] and that is why he made the human mind such that it can only know by quantity.

We have here then, in Kepler's work, a second great event in

[45] The astrological affiliations of his doctrine of primary and secondary qualities bring this out very clearly. Kepler has usually been regarded as half insincere in his astrological labours, the passage cited to this end being so interpretable but not necessarily, nor, in the light of a host of other statements, justifiably. It is the statement that "God gives every animal the means of saving its life—why object if he gives astrology to the astronomer?" (*Opera*, VIII, 705). Like other poor astronomers of the time, Kepler found in astrology a kind of service he could render which people without astronomical zeal were willing to pay for, a situation which he regarded as quite providential. But this does not at all mean that he did not thoroughly believe in astrology. Those who so maintain can hardly have read his essay *De Fundamentis Astrologiae Certioribus* (*Opera*, I, 417, ff.), in which he advances for the criticism of philosophers seventy-five propositions, of varying generality, whose soundness he is prepared to defend. Those acquainted with the thought currents of Kepler's day know that there had been in the sixteenth century a powerful revival of interest and belief in astrology, and Kepler was prepared by his general philosophy of science to give it a comprehensive philosophical basis. When the planets in their revolutions happen to fall in certain unusual relations, portentous consequences might very well ensue for human life—mighty vapours are perhaps projected from them, penetrate the animal spirits of men, stir their passions to an uncommon heat, with the result that wars and revolutions follow. (Cf. *Opera*, I, 477, ff.) There is no question but that the suggestion of such possibilities harmonizes with his general philosophy—the interesting point here is the fact that the mathematical entities with which he is concerned are these larger astronomical harmonies rather than the elementary atoms.

[46] *Opera*, I, 31.

the development of the metaphysics of modern science. Aristotelianism had won out in the long preceding period of human thought because it seemed to make intelligible and rational the world of common-sense experience. Kepler early realized that the admission of validity to the Copernican world-scheme involved a radically different cosmology, a cosmology which could rest upon the revived Neo-Platonism for its general background, would find its historical justification in the remarkable developments in the sciences of mathematics and astronomy, and which could lay bare a marvellous significance and a new beauty in the observed events of the natural cosmos by regarding them as exemplifications of simple, underlying numerical relations. The task involved revising to this end the traditional ideas of causality, hypothesis, reality, and knowledge; hence Kepler offers us the fundamentals of a metaphysic based in outline upon the early Pythagorean speculations, but carefully accommodated to the new ideal and method. Fortunate indeed it was for Kepler's historical importance that his venture proved pragmatically successful. The acquisition of further empirical facts in astronomy by Galileo and his successors showed that the astronomical and physical universe was enough like what Copernicus and Kepler had dared to believe, for them to become established as fathers of the outstanding movement of human thought in modern times, instead of being consigned to oblivion as a pair of wild-minded apriorists. In particular, Kepler's method had just enough in common with the successful procedure of later science, so that out of a vast mass of painfully and laboriously won geometrisms in nature, three chanced to become fruitful foundations for the later stupendous scientific achievements of Newton. But only those who fix their attention on these three, forgetting the arduous amassing of quite useless numerical curiosities which to him were quite as significant, could make, without qualification, such claims for him as are made by Eucken and Apelt:

"Kepler is the first who ventured here an exact-mathematical treatment of the problems (of astronomical science), the first to establish natural laws in the specific sense of the new science." [47] "Kepler was the first to discover the art of successfully inquiring her laws of nature, since his predecessors merely constructed explanatory concepts which they endeavoured to apply to the course of nature." [48]

Such laudations, while not wholly false, obscure our genuine debt to Kepler. His solid and forward-looking achievement as a philosopher of science, is his insistence that valid mathematical hypotheses must be exactly verifiable in the observed world. He is entirely convinced on *a priori* grounds that the universe is basically mathematical, and that all genuine knowledge must be mathematical, but he makes it plain that the laws of thought innate in us as a divine gift, cannot come to any knowledge of themselves; there must be the perceived motions which furnish the material for their exact exemplification.[49] For this side of his thought we have to thank his training in mathematics and in particular his association with that giant of careful star-observation, Tycho Brahe. It is this, together with his reinterpretation, in terms set by the situation of his day, of such notions as causality, hypothesis, reality, and the like, that constitute the constructive portion of his philosophy. But his outlook and method were as fully dominated by an æsthetic as by a purely theoretic interest, and the whole of his work was overlaid and confused by crude inherited superstitions which the most enlightened people of his time had already discarded.

[47] R. Eucken, *Kepler als Philosoph* (*Philosophische Monatshefte*, 1878, p. 42, ff.).

[48] E. F. Apelt, *Epochen der Geschichte der Menscheit,* Vol. I, p. 243.

[49] *Opera,* V, 229.

Galileo was a contemporary of Kepler, his life overlapping that of the great German astronomer at both ends. After the two became acquainted through the publication of the *Mysterium Cosmographicum* in 1597, they remained firm friends and carried on a considerable and interesting correspondence, but it cannot be said that either influenced the philosophy of the other to any important extent. Each, of course, made use of the other's positive and fruitful scientific discoveries, but the metaphysics of each was conditioned primarily by general environmental influences and by intensive reflection on the ultimate bearings of his own achievements.

A. The Science of "Local Motion"

Galileo's father had destined his son for the study of medicine, but at the early age of seventeen the latter acquired a consuming interest in mathematics, and after securing his sire's reluctant consent, proceeded during the next few years to make himself master of the subject. Were it not for his more stupendous achievements he, like Kepler, would have won brilliant fame as a mathematician. He invented a geometrical calculus for the reduction of complex to simple figures, and wrote an essay on continuous quantity. The latter was never published, but such was his mathematical name that Cavalieri did not publish his own treatise on the *Method of Indivisibles*, as long as he hoped to see Galileo's essay printed. At the youthful age of twenty-five he was appointed professor of mathematics at the University of Pisa, largely because of the fame won by some papers on the hydrostatic balance, the properties of the cycloid, and the centre of gravity in solids. The direction of his early mathematical studies is sufficiently indicated by these works; it was the mechanical branch that absorbed his attention and interest from the very beginning. The famous event in the Cathedral of Pisa, when he observed that the swings of the great hanging lamp were apparently isochronous, had just preceded, and in part inspired, his first interest in mathematics, hence the mathematical study of mechanical motions became quite naturally the focus of his work. Furthermore, as soon as he became competent in this new field he eagerly embraced the Copernican system (though continuing for many years to teach Ptolemaism to his classes out of deference to popular feeling), and the Copernican attribution of motion to the earth gave him a powerful impetus to study more closely, *i.e.*, mathematically, such motions of small parts of the earth as occur in every-day experience, as we learn on the authority of his great English disciple, Hobbes.[1] Hence the birth of a new science, terrestrial dynamics, which presented itself to Galileo as a simple and natural extension of the exact mathematical method to a field of somewhat more difficult mechanical relations. Others before him had asked *why* heavy bodies fall; now, the homogeneity of the earth with the heavenly bodies having suggested that terrestrial motion is a proper subject for exact mathematical study, we have the further question raised: *how* do they fall? with the expectation that the answer will be given in mathematical terms.

As Galileo notes in the introduction to his science of dynamics or "local motion," [2] many philosophers had written on motion, "nevertheless I have discovered by experiments some properties of it which are worth knowing and which have not hitherto been either observed or demonstrated." Some, too,

[1] Epistle Dedicatory to the *Elements of Philosophy Concerning Body,* Works, Molesworth edition, London, 1839, Vol. I (English), p. viii.

[2] *Dialogues and Mathematical Demonstrations Concerning Two New Sciences,* by Galileo Galilei (Crew and De Salvio translation), New York, 1914, p. 153, ff.

had observed that the motion of a falling body was one of acceleration, "but to just what extent this acceleration occurs has not yet been announced." The same thought is again expressed with reference to the motion of projectiles—others had observed that a projectile followed a curved path, but none had demonstrated that the path must be a parabola. It was this reduction of terrestrial motions to terms of exact mathematics which, fully as much as the significant astronomical discoveries that empirically confirmed Copernicanism, measured his import to those of his contemporaries who were fitted to appreciate this stupendous advance in human knowledge. His friend and admirer Fra Paolo Sarpi reflected the opinion of such minds when he exclaimed, "To give us the science of motion God and Nature have joined hands and created the intellect of Galileo." [3] Galileo's practical mechanical inventions are themselves sufficiently remarkable. In his early years he invented a pulsimeter, operating by means of a small pendulum, and also a contrivance for measuring time by the uniform flow of water. Later he became the inventor of the first crude thermometer, and in the last year of his life sketched out complete plans for a pendulum clock. His achievements in the early development of the telescope are known to all students.

Now what are the main metaphysical conclusions that Galileo found implied in his work? Let us first consider briefly those in which his agreement with Kepler is most complete, passing then to a fuller treatment of his more novel suggestions. Our expectation that the reduction of the motions of bodies to exact mathematics must carry large metaphysical bearings to Galileo's mind will not be disappointed.

B. Nature as Mathematical Order—Galileo's Method

First of all, Nature presents herself to Galileo, even more than to Kepler, as a simple, orderly system, whose every proceeding is thoroughly regular and inexorably necessary. "Na-

[3] *Two New Sciences,* Editor's Preface.

ture . . . doth not that by many things, which may be done by few." [4] He contrasts natural science with law and the humanities, in respect that the conclusions of the former are absolutely true and necessary, not at all dependent on human judgment.[5] Nature is "inexorable," acts only "through immutable laws which she never transgresses," and cares "nothing whether her reasons and methods of operating be or be not understandable by men." [6]

Further, this rigorous necessity in nature results from her fundamentally mathematical character—nature is the domain of mathematics. "Philosophy is written in that great book which ever lies before our eyes—I mean the universe—but we cannot understand it if we do not first learn the language and grasp the symbols, in which it is written. This book is written in the mathematical language, and the symbols are triangles, circles, and other geometrical figures, without whose help it is impossible to comprehend a single word of it; without which one wanders in vain through a dark labyrinth." [7] Galileo is continually astonished at the marvellous manner in which natural happenings follow the principles of geometry,[8] and his favorite answer to the objection that mathematical demonstrations are abstract and possess no necessary applicability to the physical world, is to proceed to further geometrical demonstrations, in the hope that they will become their own proof to all unprejudiced minds.[9]

Mathematical demonstrations then, rather than the scholastic logic, furnish the key to unlock the secrets of the world. "Of course, logic teaches us to know, whether the conclusions and

[4] Dialogues Concerning the Two Great Systems of the World, Salusbury translation, London, 1661, p. 99.

[5] Two Great Systems, p. 40.

[6] Letter to the Grand Duchess Christina, 1615 (Cf. Salusbury, Vol. I).

[7] Opere Complete di Galileo Galilei, Firenze, 1842, ff., Vol. IV, p. 171.

[8] Two Great Systems, pp. 178, 181, ff.

[9] Two New Sciences, p. 52.

demonstrations which are already discovered and at hand are consistent, but it cannot be said that it teaches us how to find consistent conclusions and demonstrations." [10] "We do not learn to demonstrate from the manuals of logic, but from the books which are full of demonstrations, which are the mathematical and not the logical." [11] In other words, logic is the instrument of criticism, mathematics that of discovery. Galileo's chief criticism of Gilbert was that the father of the magnetic philosophy was not sufficiently well grounded in mathematics, particularly geometry.

Now this method of mathematical demonstration, being grounded as it is in the very structure of nature, presents itself occasionally in Galileo as being in large part independent of sensible verification—an exclusively *a priori* method of reaching truth. J. J. Fahie quotes him as having written that "ignorance had been the best teacher he ever had, since in order to be able to demonstrate to his opponents the truth of his conclusions, he had been forced to prove them by a variety of experiments, though to satisfy his own mind alone he had never felt it necessary to make any." [12] If this was seriously meant, it was extremely important for the advance of science that Galileo had strong opponents, and in fact there are other passages in his works which show that his confident belief in the mathematical structure of the world emancipated him from the necessity of close dependence on experiment.[13] He insists that from a few experiments valid conclusions can be drawn which reach far beyond experience because "the knowledge of a single fact acquired through a discovery of its causes prepares the mind to understand and ascertain other facts without need of recourse to experiment." [14] He illustrates the meaning of this principle in his study of projectiles; once we know that their path is a parabola, we can demonstrate by pure mathematics, without need of experiment, that their max-

[10] *Opere,* XIII, 134.

[11] *Opere,* I, 42.

[12] *The Scientific Works of Galileo* (Singer, Vol. II, p. 251).

[13] *Two Great Systems,* p. 82.

[14] *Two New Sciences,* p. 276.

imum range is 45°. In fact, confirmation through experiment
is only necessary in the case of conclusions, into whose necessary and rational basis we can have no immediate intuition.[15]
We shall return later to his use of this important word.

It is abundantly apparent, however, from the whole of Galileo's achievements and interests, that he never seriously
entertained the possible extreme of this mathematical apriorism,[16] and his meaning becomes fairly clear when we study
passages of a different tenor. After all, "our disputes are about
the sensible world, and not one of paper";[17] it is useless to
wrangle on general principles alone about what is fitting or not
in nature, we must "come to the particular demonstrations,
observations, and experiments." [18] This is just as true in astronomy as in physics. Experience is the "true mistress of
astronomy"; "the principal scope of astronomers is only to
render reason for the appearances in the celestial bodies." [19]
Sensible facts are before us to be explained; they cannot be
overridden or ignored. It was not merely for controversial
victories that Galileo found it frequently convenient to appeal
to the confirmation of the senses. His empiricism went pretty
deep. "Oh, my dear Kepler, how I wish that we could have one
hearty laugh together! Here at Padua is the principal professor of philosophy, whom I have repeatedly and urgently
requested to look at the moon and planets through my glass,
which he pertinaciously refuses to do. Why are you not here?
What shouts of laughter we should have at this glorious folly!
And to hear the professor of philosophy at Pisa labouring
before the Grand Duke with logical arguments, as if with
magical incantations, to charm the new planets out of the
sky." [20] Galileo could hardly have become the doughty figure

[15] *Opere*, IV, 189.

[16] Cf. *Two New Sciences*, p. 97.

[17] *Two Great Systems*, p. 96.

[18] *Two Great Systems*, p. 31.

[19] *Two Great Systems*, pp. 305, 308.

[20] Letter to Kepler, 1610, quoted in Lodge, *Pioneers of Science*, Ch. 4.

in the overthrow of Aristotelianism that he appeared to his contemporaries had it not been for his popularly verifiable discoveries, which showed clearly to men's senses that some of Aristotle's statements were false. The authority of the Stagyrite was profoundly shaken when people were empirically forced to admit that all bodies fall with uniform acceleration, that Venus presents phases like the moon, that the sun's face is spotted, and the like. Galileo himself remarks that Aristotle would change his opinion if he saw our new observations, for his method was essentially empirical. "I do believe for certain, that he first procured, by the help of the senses, such experiments and observations as he could, to assure him as much as was possible of the conclusion, and that he afterwards sought out the means how to demonstrate it; for this is the usual course in demonstrative sciences. And the reason thereof is, because when the conclusion is true, by the help of the resolutive method, one may hit upon some proposition before demonstrated, or come to some principle known *per se;* but if the conclusion be false, a man may proceed *in infinitum,* and never meet with any truth already known." [21]

This passage introduces us to Galileo's conception of the proper way of combining the mathematical and the experimental methods in science. With it in mind, let us study his other expressions on this point.

It is clear to start with that what our philosophy seeks to explain is nothing other than the world revealed by the senses. "In every hypothesis of reason, error may lurk unnoticed, but a discovery of sense cannot be at odds with the truth." "How could it be otherwise? Nature did not make human brains first, and then construct things according to their capacity of understanding, but she first made things in her own fashion and then so constructed the human understanding that it, though at the price of great exertion, might ferret out a few of her secrets." [22] But the world of the senses is not its own explanation; as it stands it is an unsolved cipher, a book written in a strange language, which is to be interpreted or

[21] *Two Great Systems,* p. 37.

[22] *Opere,* VII, 341; I, 288.

explained in terms of the alphabet of that language. After long wandering in false directions, man has at last discovered what the rudiments of this alphabet are—namely the principles and units of mathematics. We discover that every branch of mathematics always applies to the material world, physical bodies, for example, are always geometrical figures, even though they never reveal those exact shapes that we like to treat in pure geometry.[23] Hence when we seek to decipher an unfamiliar page of nature, obviously the method is to seek our alphabet in it, to "resolve" it into mathematical terms.

Galileo points out that this method of explaining the world of the senses often leads, strange though it may seem, to conclusions that do violence to immediate sensible experience. The prime example of this is the Copernican astronomy, which furnishes the supreme example of the victory of mathematical reason over the senses. "I cannot sufficiently admire the eminence of those men's wits, that have received and held it to be true, and with the sprightliness of their judgments offered such violence to their own senses, as that they have been able to prefer that which their reason dictated to them, to that which sensible experiments represented most manifestly to the contrary. . . . I cannot find any bounds for my admiration, how that reason was able in Aristarchus and Copernicus, to commit such a rape on their senses, as in despite thereof to make herself mistress of their credulity." [24] Reason even occasionally, by the invention of such instruments as the telescope, gives sense an opportunity to correct her own misjudgments.

Largely because of the acceptance of the Copernican astronomy and its substantiation by his own telescopic observations, Galileo was led to parade with all possible vigour the common facts of sense illusion, and for every fact that told against the trustworthiness of the senses he had many which tended to establish the validity of his mathematical solutions. On the one hand we cannot deny that it is the senses which offer us the world to be explained; on the other we are equally certain that they do not give us the rational order which alone

[23] *Two Great Systems*, p. 224, ff.

[24] *Two Great Systems*, p. 301.

supplies the desired explanation. The latter is always mathematical, to be reached only by the accepted methods of mathematical demonstration. "The properties belonging to uniform motion have been discussed in the preceding section; but accelerated motion remains to be considered. And, first of all, it seems desirable to find and explain a definition best fitting natural phenomena. For any one may invent an arbitrary type of motion and discuss its properties; thus, for instance, some have imagined helices and conchoids as described by certain motions, which are not met with in nature, and have very commendably established the properties which these curves possess in virtue of their definitions; but we have decided to consider the phenomena of bodies falling with an acceleration such as actually occurs in nature and to make this definition of accelerated motion exhibit the essential features of observed accelerated motions. And this, at last, after repeated efforts we trust we have succeeded in doing. In this belief we are confirmed mainly by the consideration that experimental results are seen to agree with and exactly correspond with those properties which have been, one after another, demonstrated by us. Finally, in the investigation of naturally accelerated motion we were led, by hand as it were, in following the habit and custom of nature herself, in all her various other processes, to employ only those means which are most common, simple, and easy." [25] Here the claim to have successfully applied mathematical demonstrations to physical motion is certainly central.

As with Kepler, so with Galileo, this mathematical explanation of nature must be in *exact* terms; it is no vague Pythagorean mysticism that the founder of dynamics has in mind. We might have gathered as much from his obvious achievements, but he tells us so explicitly. "Neither doth this suffice [knowledge that falling bodies descend with accelerating velocity], but it is requisite to know according to what proportion such acceleration is made; a problem that I believe was never hitherto understood by any philosopher or mathema-

[25] *Two Great Sciences,* p. 160, ff.

tician, although philosophers, and particularly the peripatetics, have writ great and entire volumes touching motion." [26]

Viewed as a whole, Galileo's method then can be analysed into three steps, *intuition* or *resolution, demonstration,* and *experiment;* using in each case his own favourite terms. Facing the world of sensible experience, we isolate and examine as fully as possible a certain typical phenomenon, in order first to intuit those simple, absolute elements in terms of which the phenomenon can be most easily and completely translated into mathematical form; which amounts (putting the matter in another way) to a resolution of the sensed fact into such elements in quantitative combinations. Have we performed this step properly, we need the sensible facts no more; the elements thus reached are their real constituents, and deductive demonstrations from them by pure mathematics (second step) must always be true of similar instances of the phenomenon, even though at times it should be impossible to confirm them empirically. This explains the bold tone of his more *a priori* passages. For the sake of more certain results, however, and especially to convince by sensible illustrations those who do not have such implicit confidence in the universal applicability of mathematics, it is well to develop where possible demonstrations whose conclusions are susceptible of verification by experiments. Then with the principles and truths thus acquired we can proceed to more complex related phenomena and discover what additional mathematical laws are there implicated. That Galileo actually followed these three steps in all of his important discoveries in dynamics is easily ascertainable from his frank biographical paragraphs, especially in the *Dialogues Concerning Two New Sciences.*[27]

A further question suggests itself at this point: is this remarkable mathematical structure of the world, which makes possible such stupendous conquests of science as the Copernican astronomy and the Galilean dynamics, something ultimate, or is it further explicable? If a religious basis be a further explication, the latter would appear to be the answer

[26] *Two Great Systems,* p. 144.

[27] Cf. especially p. 178.

for Galileo, as for Kepler. The Neo-Platonic background of the mathematical and astronomical development of the times has strongly penetrated the mind of the Italian scientist, as in the case of so many lesser figures. By his free use of the word "nature," he does not mean to deny an ultimately religious interpretation of things. God, by his immediate creative knowledge of nature, thinks into the world that rigorous mathematical necessity which we reach only laboriously through resolutions and demonstrations—God is a geometrician in his creative labours—he makes the world through and through a mathematical system. The distinction between his knowledge of things and ours is that his is complete, ours partial; his immediate, ours discursive. "As to the truth, of which mathematical demonstrations give us the knowledge, it is the same which the Divine Wisdom knoweth; but . . . the manner whereby God knoweth the infinite propositions, whereof we understand some few, is highly more excellent than ours, which proceedeth by ratiocination, and passeth from conclusion to conclusion, whereas his is done at a single thought or intuition." For God the apprehension of the essence of any thing means the immediate comprehension, without temporal reasoning, of all its infinite implications. "Now these inferences which our intellect apprehendeth with time and a gradual motion the Divine Wisdom, like light, penetrateth in an instant, which is the same as to say, hath them always present." [28] God knows infinitely more propositions than we, but yet in the case of those that we understand so thoroughly as to perceive the necessity of them, *i.e.*, the demonstrations of pure mathematics, our understanding equals the divine in objective certainty.

It was this religious basis of his philosophy that made Galileo bold to declare that doubtful passages of scripture should be interpreted in the light of scientific discovery rather than the reverse. God has made the world an immutable mathematical system, permitting by the mathematical method an absolute certainty of scientific knowledge. The disagreements of theologians about the meaning of scripture are ample testimony

[28] *Two Great Systems*, p. 86, ff.

to the fact that here no such certainty is possible. Is it not
obvious then which should determine the true meaning of the
other? "Methinks that in the discussion of natural problems,
we ought not to begin at the authority of places of scripture,
but at sensible experiments and necessary demonstrations. For,
from the Divine Word, the sacred scripture and nature did
both alike proceed. . . . Nature, being inexorable and immutable, and never passing the bounds of the laws assigned
her, . . . I conceive that, concerning natural effects, that
which either sensible experience sets before our eyes, or necessary demonstrations do prove unto us, ought not, upon any account, to be called into question, much less condemned upon
the testimony of texts of scripture, which may, under their
words, couch senses seemingly contrary thereto. . . . Nor does
God less admirably discover himself to us in Nature's actions,
than in the Scripture's sacred dictions." [29] He quoted by way
of orthodox support Tertullian's dictum that we know God
first by nature, then by revelation.

c. The Subjectivity of Secondary Qualities

Swept onward by the inherent necessities of this mathematical metaphysic, Galileo, like Kepler, was inevitably led
to the doctrine of primary and secondary qualities, only with
the Italian genius the doctrine appears in a much more pronounced and developed form. Galileo makes the clear distinction between that in the world which is absolute, objective,
immutable, and mathematical; and that which is relative, subjective, fluctuating, and sensible. The former is the realm of
knowledge, divine and human; the latter is the realm of
opinion and illusion. The Copernican astronomy and the
achievements of the two new sciences must break us of the
natural assumption that sensed objects are the real or mathematical objects. They betray certain qualities, which, handled
by mathematical rules, lead us to a knowledge of the true

[29] *Letter to the Grand Duchess,* 1615.

object, and these are the real or primary qualities, such as number, figure, magnitude, position, and motion, which cannot by any exertion of our powers be separated from bodies—qualities which also can be wholly expressed mathematically. The reality of the universe is geometrical; the only ultimate characteristics of nature are those in terms of which certain mathematical knowledge becomes possible. All other qualities, and these are often far more prominent to the senses, are secondary, subordinate effects of the primary.

Of the utmost moment was Galileo's further assertion that these secondary qualities are *subjective*. In Kepler there had been no clear statement of this position; apparently for him the secondary qualities were out there in the astronomical world, like the primary, only they were not so real or fundamental. Galileo fell definitely in line with the Platonic identification of the realm of changing opinion with the realm of sense experience, and became the heir to all the influences emanating from the ancient atomists which had been recently revived in the epistemology of such thinkers as Vives and Campanella. The confused and untrustworthy elements in the sense picture of nature are somehow the effect of the senses themselves. It is because the experienced picture has passed through the senses that it possesses all these confusing and illusive features. The secondary qualities are declared to be effects on the senses of the primary qualities which are alone real in nature. As far as the object itself is concerned, they are nothing more than names. This doctrine, too, was bolstered up by considerations derived from the Copernican astronomy. Just as the deceptive appearance of the earth, which makes us suppose it to be at rest, arises from the position and local motion of the onlooker, so these deceptive secondary qualities arise from the fact that our knowledge of objects is mediated by the senses.

This important and radical doctrine is most impressively presented by Galileo in a passage in the *Il Saggiatore* where the cause of heat offers itself for discussion. After asserting his conviction that motion is the cause sought, Galileo explains his meaning at considerable length.

But first I want to propose some examination of that which we call heat, whose generally accepted notion comes very far from the truth if my serious doubts be correct, inasmuch as it is supposed to be a true accident, affection, and quality really residing in the thing which we perceive to be heated. Nevertheless I say, that indeed I feel myself impelled by the necessity, as soon as I conceive a piece of matter or corporeal substance, of conceiving that in its own nature it is bounded and figured in such and such a figure, that in relation to others it is large or small, that it is in this or that place, in this or that time, that it is in motion or remains at rest, that it touches or does not touch another body, that it is single, few, or many; in short by no imagination can a body be separated from such conditions: but that it must be white or red, bitter or sweet, sounding or mute, of a pleasant or unpleasant odour, I do not perceive my mind forced to acknowledge it necessarily accompanied by such conditions; so if the senses were not the escorts, perhaps the reason or the imagination by itself would never have arrived at them. Hence I think that these tastes, odours, colours, etc., on the side of the object in which they seem to exist, are nothing else than mere names, but hold their residence solely in the sensitive body; so that if the animal were removed, every such quality would be abolished and annihilated. Nevertheless, as soon as we have imposed names on them, particular and different from those of the other primary and real accidents, we induce ourselves to believe that they also exist just as truly and really as the latter. I think that by an illustration I can explain my meaning more clearly. I pass a hand, first over a marble statue, then over a living man. Concerning all the effects which come from the hand, as regards the hand itself, they are the same whether on the one or on the other object—that is, these primary accidents, namely motion and touch (for we call them by no other names)—but the animate body which suffers that operation feels various affections according to the different parts touched, and if the sole of the foot, the kneecap, or the armpit be touched, it perceives besides the common sense of touch, another affection, to which we have given a particular name, calling it tickling. Now this affection is all ours, and does not belong to the hand at all. And it seems to me that they would greatly err who should say that the hand, besides motion and touch, possessed in itself another faculty different from those, namely the tickling faculty; so that tickling would be an accident that exists in it. A piece of paper, or a feather, lightly rubbed on whatever part of our body you wish, performs, as regards itself, everywhere the same operation, that is, movement and touch; but in us, if touched between the eyes, on the nose, and under the nostrils, it excites an almost intolerable tickling, though elsewhere it can hardly be felt at all. Now this tickling is all in us, and not in the feather, and if the animate and sensitive body be removed, it is nothing more than a mere name. Of precisely a similar and not greater existence do I believe these various qualities to be possessed, which are attributed to natural bodies, such as tastes, odours, colours, and others.[30]

The doctrine was further enlarged, as compared with Kepler, by Galileo's adoption of the atomic theory of matter. Kepler had needed no atomism; the mathematical harmonies in the world of astronomy which he was zealous to discover were vast geometrical relations among the celestial bodies. But Galileo, extending the mathematical idea to terrestrial motions, found it convenient to assume that matter is resoluble into "infinitely small indivisible atoms," [31] whereby he could explain the changes of solids into fluids and gases, and solve such problems as those of cohesion, expansion, and contraction, without the necessity of admitting the existence of empty spaces in solid bodies or the penetrability of matter.[32] These atoms possess none but mathematical qualities, and it is their varied motions operating upon the senses which cause the disturbing secondary experiences.[33] Galileo discusses in

[30] *Opere*, IV, 333, ff.

[31] *Two New Sciences*, p. 40.

[32] *Two New Sciences*, p. 48.

[33] *Opere*, IV, 335, ff.

some detail, in the case of taste, smell, and sound, how differences in number, weight, figure, and velocity on the part of these atoms may cause the experienced differences in the resulting sensation.

The question of the historical relations of Galileo's atomism is difficult to solve. He does not give the atoms prominence, and it is evident that their place in his work is more contributory than fundamental. Such remarks as he does make, however, appear to indicate that besides the geometrical atomism of the *Timæus*, which seems to underlie the notions of Copernicus and Kepler, his thought has taken on some affiliations with the philosophy of Democritus and Epicurus. Galileo does not always include weight among the primary qualities of the atoms. When he does so it is in a connexion which suggests that he was impelled to the addition by considerations arising from his own work rather than by an ancient tradition. "I desire, before passing to any other subject, to call your attention to the fact that these forces, resistances, moments, figures, etc., may be considered either in the abstract, dissociated from matter, or in the concrete, associated with matter. Hence the properties that belong to figures that are merely geometrical and non-material must be modified when we fill these figures with matter and give them weight." [34] He goes on to observe that when a geometrical figure is filled with matter it becomes *ipso facto* a "force" or a "moment," unphilosophical terms which he was struggling to endow for the first time with exact mathematical meaning. Yet the materialistic metaphysics of the ancient atomists was already being revived under influential auspices. The work of Gassendi and Magnenus did not appear till the middle of the seventeenth century, but Francis Bacon had already turned to Democritus as a possible substitute for Aristotelianism on some cosmological doctrines, and Löwenheim[35] has succeeded in discovering a few references to Democritus in Galileo himself.[36] The

[34] *Two New Sciences,* p. 112, ff.

[35] L. Löwenheim, *Der Einfluss Demokrits auf Galilei* (*Archiv für Geschichte der Philosophie,* 1894).

[36] For example, *Opere,* XII, 88.

Italian thinker had little use for some of the prominent features of Pythagoreanism, especially the notion of perfect figures, pointing out that perfection in any thing is wholly relative to the use to be made of it. It may be that to a considerable extent the Galilean atomism and its general mechanical corollaries were due to the percolation through the intervening ages of some fragmentary ideas from the great Greek materialist, especially as popularized by his Roman poet-follower. Certainly the doctrine of primary and secondary qualities, with causality lodged in the atoms as above portrayed, exhibits strong marks of a Democritanism brought up to date and fitted into the new mathematical programme. A quite similar subjectivism of secondary qualities had been taught by the ancient speculator, and it is to this feature of the doctrine that Galileo eagerly reverts.

But that external bodies, to excite in us these tastes, these odours, and these sounds, demanded other than size, figure, number, and slow or rapid motion, I do not believe; and I judge that, if the ears, the tongue, and the nostrils were taken away, the figure, the numbers, and the motions would indeed remain, but not the odours nor the tastes nor the sounds, which, without the living animal, I do not believe are anything else than names, just as tickling is precisely nothing but a name if the armpit and the nasal membrane be removed; . . . and turning to my first proposition in this place, having now seen that many affections which are reputed to be qualities residing in the external object, have truly no other existence than in us, and without us are nothing else than names; I say that I am inclined sufficiently to believe that heat is of this kind, and that the thing that produces heat in us and makes us perceive it, which we call by the general name fire, is a multitude of minute corpuscles thus and thus figured, moved with such and such a velocity; . . . But that besides their figure, number, motion, penetration, and touch, there is in fire another quality, that is heat—that I do not believe otherwise than I have indicated, and I judge that it is so much due to us that,

if the animate and sensitive body were removed, heat would
remain nothing more than a simple word.[37]

This form of the primary-secondary doctrine in Galileo is
worth a moment's pause, for its effects in modern thought
have been of incalculable importance. It is a fundamental
step toward that banishing of man from the great world of
nature and his treatment as an effect of what happens in the
latter, which has been a pretty constant feature of the philosophy of modern science, a procedure enormously simplifying the field of science, but bringing in its train the big
metaphysical and especially epistemological problems of modern philosophy. Till the time of Galileo it had always been
taken for granted that man and nature were both integral
parts of a larger whole, in which man's place was the more
fundamental. Whatever distinctions might be made between
being and non-being, between primary and secondary, man
was regarded as fundamentally allied with the positive and
the primary. In the philosophies of Plato and Aristotle this is
obvious enough; the remark holds true none the less for the
ancient materialists. Man's soul for Democritus was composed
of the very finest and most mobile fire-atoms, which statement
at once allied it to the most active and causal elements in the
outside world. Indeed, to all important ancient and medieval
thinkers, man was a genuine microcosm; in him was exemplified such a union of things primary and secondary as truly
typified their relations in the vast macrocosm, whether the
real and primary be regarded as ideas or as some material
substance. *Now, in the course of translating this distinction
of primary and secondary into terms suited to the new mathematical interpretation of nature, we have the first stage in
the reading of man quite out of the real and primary realm.*
Obviously man was not a subject suited to mathematical study.
His performances could not be treated by the quantitative
method, except in the most meagre fashion. His was a life of
colours and sounds, of pleasures, of griefs, of passionate loves,
of ambitions, and strivings. Hence the real world must be the
world outside of man; the world of astronomy and the world

[37] *Opere,* IV, 336, ff.

of resting and moving terrestrial objects. The only thing in common between man and this real world was his ability to discover it, a fact which, being necessarily presupposed, was easily neglected, and did not in any case suffice to exalt him to a parity of reality and causal efficiency with that which he was able to know. Quite naturally enough, along with this exaltation of the external world as more primary and more real, went an attribution to it of greater dignity and value. Galileo himself proceeds to this addition.[38] Sight is the most excellent of the senses, because it has relation to light, the most excellent object; but, as compared with the latter, it is as far inferior as the finite in comparison with the infinite, the temporal with the instantaneous, the divisible with the indivisible; it is even as darkness compared with light. Connexions are obvious with the ancient world in this respect also; Plato and Aristotle had taught that that which man is able to know and contemplate, in their case the realm of Ideas or Forms, is more exalted than man himself. But note again that in Galileo there is a far-reaching difference. The features of the world now classed as secondary, unreal, ignoble, and regarded as dependent on the deceitfulness of sense, are just those features which are most intense to man in all but his purely theoretic activity, and even in that, except where he confines himself strictly to the mathematical method. It was inevitable that in these circumstances man should now appear to be outside of the real world; man is hardly more than a bundle of secondary qualities. Observe that the stage is fully set for the Cartesian dualism—on the one side of primary, the mathematical realm; on the other the realm of man. And the premium of importance and value as well as of independent existence all goes with the former. Man begins to appear for the first time in the history of thought as an irrelevant spectator and insignificant effect of the great mathematical system which is the substance of reality.

[38] *Opere*, IV, 336.

D. Motion, Space, and Time

So far we have been studying in Galileo largely a further development of philosophical positions already reached in Kepler. But the fact that Galileo was devoting himself to the study of *bodies in motion,* including specifically physical bodies handled in daily experience on the surface of the earth, led to notable additions in his philosophy beyond anything distinctly suggested in the German astronomer. And first, his explicit abandonment of final causality as a principle of explanation. It is well to remind ourselves of the manner in which terrestrial or "local" motions had been analysed by Aristotle and the scholastics. The analysis, being intended to answer the question *why* they moved rather than *how* they moved, was developed in terms of the substances concerned in any given motion, hence the prominence of such words and phrases as action, passion, efficient cause, end, natural place. About the motion itself almost nothing was said, save that a few simple distinctions were drawn between natural and violent motion, motion in a right line and motion in a circle, and the like. The *why* of motion had been the object of study and the study had proceeded in qualitative and substantive terms; with Galileo now it is the *how* of motion that becomes the object of analysis, and that by the method of exact mathematics.

Obviously, the teleological terminology of the scholastics was no longer serviceable, and the lucid mind of Galileo perceived the necessity of developing a new terminology which would express the *process of motion itself* and that in such a manner as to give mathematics a foothold in the phenomena. This was to him, of course, an essential part of the first step in his scientific method, the intuitive perception in a group of facts, of such elements as, quantitatively combined, would produce the facts observed. In this gigantic task he found very little help offered in the labours of earlier and contemporary mathematicians. Astronomy, to be sure, had always been regarded as a branch of applied geometry, hence motion was recognized already as a geometrical conception. The work of Copernicus had intensified the mathematical study of motion, a result noticeable for example in the great interest excited among geometers of the time in various figures generated by curious observed motions. The properties of the cycloid were attacked by almost all the leading geometers of the period, those supposedly interested in pure mathematics as well as those, like Galileo and Torricelli, who were more particularly absorbed in mechanics. But Galileo's problem was nothing less than the creation of a new mathematical science to replace the idealistic physics of the scholastics. Naturally enough, the principle on which he developed the new terminology was the conservative one of taking terms of common parlance which as yet had had no precise significance, such as force, resistance, moment, velocity, acceleration, and the like, and giving them an exact mathematical meaning, *i.e.*, defining them in such a way that they could take their place beside the definitions of lines, angles, curves, and figures, that mathematicians were already familiar with. Of course, Galileo neither recognized this need nor satisfied it in the completely systematic fashion that we should like, even the great Newton was not above some confusion and error in this respect. Galileo offers the new definitions as he sees need for them, and in many cases the precise meaning must be gathered from his use rather than from any specific statement. But from his new terminology certain supremely important consequences follow for the metaphysics of modern science.

First of all, the mathematical study of the *how* of motion, inevitably thrusts into prominence the concepts of *space* and *time*. When we subject any case of motion to mathematical treatment we analyse it into certain units of distance covered in certain units of time. This had been recognized in a rudimentary fashion by the ancients as far as astronomy was concerned; to trace any planetary motion in the geometry of the heavens by mathematical methods meant correlating the successive positions of the planet on the celestial sphere with certain positions in the apparently regular succession of seasons, days, and hours, which were the accepted measure of time. But all this remained a thing apart from the metaphysical ideas of the ancients, for the latter, being shaped largely by considerations of man's life and interests, was worked out, as already noted, in quite a different terminology. The larger implications of the possibility of analysing motion quantitatively into space and time were not glimpsed, and ultimate questions about the nature of the latter were raised in other connexions. It must be remembered that the qualitative, as opposed to the quantitative method in the physics of Aristotle and scholasticism, not only made space and time very unimportant, but in the case of the former at least led to a definition fundamentally at variance with that given by the Platonists and Pythagoreans and rather more suited to the mathematical method. According to Aristotle space is not something underlying all objects so far as they are extended, something *occupied* by them; it is the boundary between any object and those which enclose it. The object itself was a qualitative substance rather than a geometrical thing. The habits of thinking encouraged by this aspect of the Aristotelian physics could be overcome only slowly by the new science; people could not at once accustom themselves to the thought that objects and their relations were fundamentally mathematical. For this, however, the revival of Neo-Platonism and the mathematical advances of the age culminating in the Copernican astronomy had contributed. Physical space was assumed to be identical with the realm of geometry, and physical motion was acquiring the character of a pure mathematical concept. Hence in the metaphysics of Galileo, space (or distance) and time become fundamental categories. *The real world is the world of bodies in mathematically reducible motions, and this means that the real world is a world of bodies moving in space and time.* In place of the teleological categories into which scholasticism had analysed change and movement, we now have these two formerly insignificant entities given new meanings as absolute mathematical continua and raised to the rank of ultimate metaphysical notions. The real world; to repeat, is a world of mathematically measurable motions in space and time.

With respect to time, there are features in Galileo's work of particular significance for modern metaphysics. To discuss events in terms of space or distance was to assign a new importance and dignity to a characteristic that had been regarded as merely accidental by the scholastics and to give it a new definition for those whose physical thinking had been controlled by Aristotle—to be sure, an important transformation enough because it made the world of nature infinite instead of finite—but in the case of time the thought-revolution went much deeper. Not that a new definition of it was particularly needed—the conception of time as the measure of motion, common to practically all parties among previous philosophers, was sufficiently serviceable still—but the substitution of the entity for the old categories of potentiality and actuality involved a radically new view of the universe, a view such that the very existence of a being like man became one enormous puzzle.

In the course of ancient philosophy previous to Aristotle, change (including, of course, motion) had been either denied, neglected, reluctantly admitted, or apotheosized; it had not been rationally explained. Aristotle offered his analysis of events in terms of potentiality and actuality as a means of reducing change to intelligibility. This signal achievement became the common possession of most important thought-movements since his day, especially when the victory of religious interests kept the mystical experience of the devout worshipper in the forefront of attention. Most remarkably did this method of analysis permit a logical continuity to appear between the transformation of the acorn into the oak or the oak into a table, and the union with God in the religious ecstasy, where man, the highest in the hierarchy of formed matter, came in blissful contact with Pure Form or Absolute Actuality. When medieval philosophers thought of what we call the temporal process it was this continuous transformation of potentiality into actuality that they had in mind, a transformation which culminated in those ravishing moments when the overpowering *visio Dei* was vouchsafed to some pious and trembling mortal. God was that One who eternally exists, and ever draws into movement by his perfect beauty all that is potentially the bearer of a higher existence. He is the divine harmony of all goods, conceived as now realized in ideal activity, eternally present, himself unmoved, yet the mover of all change. To put this in modern terms, the present exists unmoved and continually draws into itself the future. That this sounds absurd to our ears is because we have followed Galileo and banished man, with his memory and purpose, out of the real world. Consequently time seems to us nothing but a measurable continuum, the present moment alone exists, and that moment itself is no temporal quantity but merely a dividing line between the infinite stretch of a vanished past and the equally infinite expanse of the untrodden future. To such a view it is impossible to regard the temporal movement as the absorption of the future into the actual or present, for there really is nothing actual. All is becoming. We are forced to view the movement of time as passing *from* the past *into* the future, the present being merely that moving limit between the two. Time as something *lived* we have banished from our metaphysics, hence it constitutes for modern philosophy an unsolved problem. The fact that man can think in the present of a past happening seems a strange matter to modern speculators, requiring to be accounted for, and even M. Bergson, doughty champion though he is of time lived, can present it only in terms of an ever self-multiplying snowball, a notion which would make a modern physicist gnash his teeth and a medieval scholastic gasp in amazement.[39] We forget that we are no longer part of the real world of modern metaphysics and that time as a measurable continuum—the dividing line of the present moving in regular and solemn silence from the dead past into the unborn future—is a notion whose ultimate metaphysical validity is conditioned upon making our exclusion permanent. If we are a part of the world, then the *t* of physics must become but a partial element in real time, and a more inclusive philosophy thus rewon might again consider the evidence in favour of attributing movement to the future rather than to the present, while the idea of the past as dead and vanished might be consigned to oblivion with other curious relics of an over-mechanical age.

[39] Cf. Broad's attempt to introduce this notion into physics—*Scientific Thought*, Part I, Ch. 2. Some hints of a return to Aristotelianism are present.

But now we are observing the birth of that age. Instead of a process of actualization of potentiality we have time, a mathematically measurable duration. This further insistence, that the temporality of motion is reducible to terms of exact mathematics, has also been of fundamental importance—it means that time for modern physics becomes nothing more than an irreversible fourth dimension. Time, like a spatial dimension, can be represented by a straight line and co-ordinated with spatial facts similarly represented.[40] Galileo's exact study of velocities and accelerations forced him to devise a simple technique for the geometrical representation of time, which was fairly adequate to the truths he sought to illustrate. With him, the physical world begins to be conceived as a perfect machine whose future happenings can be fully predicted and controlled by one who has full knowledge and control of the present motions. With man eliminated from the real world, the latter appeared bound by mechanical necessity. Thinking was started on that current which led nearly two centuries later to the famous remark of Laplace, that a superhuman intelligence acquainted with the position and motion of the atoms at any moment could predict the whole course of future events. To hypothesize such an intelligence in a world whose present is nothing but a moving mathematical limit between past and future—in fact, the existence of any intelligence, reason, knowledge, or science in such a world—strikes one as something of an anomaly; however, modern metaphysicians, struggling desperately with the simpler difficulties presented by the new view of space, have had little time or energy to attack more perplexing scandals in the current notion of time. After all, it was a marvellous attainment for Galileo to have discovered that there was something in time that could be fully treated mathematically. In this aspect of his work there lay behind him the growing accuracy through the centuries of astronomical predictions, which had just made a marvellous leap in the labours of Tycho Brahe. Thinkers were now familiar enough with the idea of the exact measurement of motion for a genius to take the final step and discover mathematical time. Of Gal-

[40] *Two New Sciences*, p. 265.

ileo's own inventions for the more exact temporal measurement of motion, mention has already been made.

We have had occasion to note above how Galileo's dynamical investigations taught him that physical bodies possess qualities, other than the traditional geometrical ones, which are capable of mathematical expression. To be sure, these qualities only reveal themselves in differences of motion, but these differences are specific and themselves mathematical, hence it is advantageous to give them precise quantitative definitions. Thus appear the prime concepts of modern physics as distinct from geometry, such as force, acceleration, momentum, velocity, and the rest. The degree with which Galileo anticipated the full Newtonian conception of mass has been hotly debated by historians of science—for our purpose it is hardly necessary to enter the lists. His work with falling bodies would hardly have forced him to such a conception, for all bodies fall with the same acceleration. More probably his experiments on horizontal struts of various sizes and proportions, where differences of weight cause marked variations in the results, were the principal cause of his realization that bodies possess a characteristic, somehow connected with weight and with experienced resistance, that is capable of mathematical treatment.[41] This characteristic was not closely allied in his mind with the first law of motion, which (in his unsystematic statement of it) was a general corollary from the fact that forces always produce *accelerations* in bodies rather than simple velocities. Galileo was a pioneer in most of these matters—it is hardly fair to ask of him either much in achievement or unimpeachable consistency. In anticipation of Descartes, however, it is important to note in Galileo the realization that the exact mathematician can hardly be satisfied with motion as a blanket term of explanation, or with the general possibility of its mathematical expression. Bodies, geometrically equal, move differently when placed in the same position relative to the same other bodies. Galileo's thought was not clear on this point, but he perceived dimly that unless these differences can be so expressed that all motions become

[41] *Two New Sciences*, p. 2, ff., 89.

susceptible of exact quantitative treatment, our ideal of a complete mathematical physics has not been attained.

E. The Nature of Causality—God and the Physical World—Positivism

With what positive conception of causality did Galileo replace the rejected teleology of the scholastics? Here again we meet a doctrine of most profound significance for modern thought. We have noted in Kepler the translation into mathematical terms of the scholastic formal cause; the cause of the observed effects is the mathematical beauty and harmony discoverable in them. This idea of causality, however, could not satisfy Galileo. His thought moved in dynamical rather than formal terms; furthermore Kepler had been dealing with fairly simple and uniform motions, in whose case it was easy not to look for much more than a formal cause; whereas Galileo was primarily concerned with accelerated motions, and these always presuppose (according to his terminology) some force or forces as cause. Hence the cause of every motion which is not simple and uniform must be expressed in terms of *force*. But before we delve into this conception, it is imperative to note its relations with the doctrine of primary and secondary qualities, the elimination of man from the real world, and the change in the scientific notion of God which was encouraged by this whole revolution. Medieval philosophy, attempting to solve the ultimate *why* of events instead of their immediate *how,* and thus stressing the principle of final causality (for the answer to such a question could only be given in terms of purpose or use), had had its appropriate conception of God. Here was the teleological hierarchy of the Aristotelian forms, all heading up in God or Pure Form, with man intermediate in reality and importance between him and the material world. The final *why* of events in the latter could be explained mainly in terms of their use to man; the final *why* of human activities in terms of the eternal quest for union with God. Now, with the superstructure from man up banished from the primary

realm, which for Galileo is identified with material atoms in
their mathematical relations, the *how* of events being the sole
object of exact study, there had appeared no place for final
causality whatsoever. The real world is simply a succession of
atomic motions in mathematical continuity. Under these circumstances causality could only be intelligibly lodged in the
motions of the atoms themselves, everything that happens being regarded as the effect solely of mathematical changes in
these material elements. The connexion of this with the primary-secondary doctrine we have already observed, where
Galileo had some support for his position in Kepler's work
and in the views traditionally ascribed to the ancient atomists.
But what in the world should be done with God? With final
causality gone, God as Aristotelianism had conceived him was
quite lost; to deny him outright, however, at Galileo's stage
of the game, was too radical a step for any important thinker
to consider. The only way to keep him in the universe was
to invert the Aristotelian metaphysics and regard him as the
First Efficient Cause or Creator of the atoms. This view had
been already vaguely wandering about in some corners of
Europe, adopted probably from a few Arab speculators who
had thus endeavoured to reconcile atomism with Moham-
medan theism.[42] It also fitted admirably in many respects with
the popular Christian picture of God originally constructing
the world out of nothing. God thus ceases to be the Supreme
Good in any important sense; he is a huge mechanical inventor, whose power is appealed to merely to account for the
first appearance of the atoms, the tendency becoming more
and more irresistible as time goes on to lodge all further
causality for whatever effects in the atoms themselves. In Galileo, however, this step is not clearly taken. There seemed to
be some present invisible reality which produced the observed
acceleration of bodies. Atomic motions are treated merely as
secondary causes of events, the primary or ultimate causes
being conceived always in terms of force.[43]

[42] W. Windleband, *History of Philosophy* (Tufts translation), New York, 1907, p. 317.

[43] *Two Great Systems,* pp. 381, 407.

"There can be but one true and primary cause of the effects that are of the same kind," and between this primary cause and its various effects there is a firm and constant connexion. He means by these statements that for every distinct type of mathematically expressible motion there is some primary

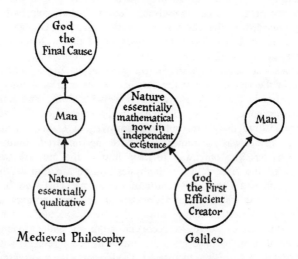

Medieval Philosophy   Galileo

cause, or indestructible force, which can always be depended on to produce its effects.[44] The chief tokens or characteristics of these ultimate causes are identity, uniformity, and simplicity, features essential to them if their effects are to be quantitatively treated. Gravity is an example of the most noticeable of these primary forces.

Secondary or immediate causes on the other hand are always themselves specific motions, which serve to set off or bring into play these more ultimate causes. Bodies at rest, for example, do not of themselves acquire motion; for that there must have been some prior motion or combination of motions as the cause. In this secondary and more specific sense of causality, "that and no other is in the proper sense to be called cause, at whose presence the effect always follows, and

[44] Cf. *Two New Sciences*, p. 95, ff.

at whose removal the effect disappears." [45] Furthermore any alteration in the effect can only be due to the presence of some new fact in the motion or motions which constitute the cause. This side of Galileo's doctrine of causality was destined for a most fruitful development; occasionally, in fact, in his own work he deprecated confusing the study of the properties of accelerated motions with discussions about the forces which cause them.[46] And when the concept of *work performed* became fundamental in physics, largely due to the achievements of Huyghens, all was ready for the final doctrine, already implicit in the whole movement, that causes and effects for science are both motions, and the cause is mathematically equivalent to the effect in terms of work. In more popular parlance we have the postulate of the conservation of energy, energy being always revealed in the form of motion. The conception of the world as a perfect machine is thus rendered inevitable, and it is no accident that first in Huyghens and (in a more philosophical form) in Leibniz we have this position unequivocally proclaimed. This was closely allied to the new idea of time as a mathematical continuum, and its contrast with the scholastic analysis of causality could hardly have been greater. Instead of causal explanation in terms not unsuited to a metaphysic which regarded man as a determinative part of nature and a link between matter and God, we now, after his banishment from the real world, explain causality solely in terms of forces revealing themselves in the mathematically expressible motions of matter itself.

But what, now, is the nature of these ultimate forces which reveal themselves in the vast system of motions constituting the real world? Can we find Galileo attempting to answer this question, much of the medieval metaphysics which has now been deported may be able to re-enter. But here is the last evidence of Galileo's revolutionary greatness. In an age when uncontrolled speculation was the order of the day we find a man with sufficient self-restraint to leave certain ultimate questions unsolved, as beyond the realm of positive science.

[45] *Opere*, IV, 216.

[46] *Two New Sciences*, p. 166, ff.

This touch of agnosticism in Galileo strikes one familiar with thought-currents of his generation as a mark of genius superior even to his marvellous constructive achievements. To be sure, it was not as thoroughgoing as agnosticism became later—Galileo never thought of denying an ultimately religious answer to the problems of the universe[47]—but it was enough to save science her opportunity for further stupendous victories in the mathematical interpretation of the world; it forbade man to gratify his animistic weaknesses at the expense of the rigorous mathematical character of reality, and it plunged modern metaphysics into the most curious embarrassments. According to Galileo, we know nothing about the inner nature or essence of force, we only know its quantitative effects in terms of motion.

> *Salv.* [Galileo's spokesman]. ". . . if he will but assure me, who is the mover of one of these movables [Mars and Jupiter], I will undertake to be able to tell him who maketh the earth to move. Nay, more; I will undertake to be able to do the same if he can but tell me, who moveth the parts of the earth downwards."
>
> *Simp.* "The cause of this is most manifest, and every one knows that it is gravity."
>
> *Salv.* ". . . you should say that every one knows that it is *called* gravity; but I do not question you about the name, but about the essence of the thing . . . not as if we really understood any more, what principle or virtue that is, which moveth a stone downwards, than we know who moveth it upwards, when it is separated from the projicient, or who moveth the moon round, except only the name, which more particularly and properly we have assigned to all motion of descent, namely gravity." [48]

In his discussion on the tides he severely criticizes Kepler for explaining the moon's influence on the tides in terms that sound like the occult qualities of the scholastics, judging it better for people "to pronounce that wise, ingenious, and

[47] *Two Great Systems*, pp. 385, 424.

[48] *Two Great Systems*, p. 210, ff.

modest sentence, 'I know it not,' " rather than to "suffer to
escape from their mouths and pens all manner of extrava-
gances." [49] Galileo was by no means consistent in this positivism. In some cases he allowed his own speculations to run
rampant. He did not hesitate to explain the spots on the sun
as black smoke given off by the ethereal pabulum which the
sun is continually devouring in constant supply in order to
continue spreading light and heat; nor to account for the miracle of Joshua[50] by supposing, with Kepler, that the planetary
revolutions on their axes were caused by the sun's revolution on
his, hence a temporary cessation of the latter might explain the
stoppage of the former. It is difficult to tell, however, whether
such a remark was meant for more than religious consumption.
Yet that this positivistic trend in his thought was something
vital is amply proved by the fact that at times even the fundamental questions of the creation of the universe and its first
cause he is tempted to relegate to the realm of the unknown,
at least until, on the basis of the positive achievements of
mechanics, we find it possible to proceed to their solution.
". . . Profound considerations of this sort belong to a higher
science than ours. We must be satisfied to belong to that class
of less worthy workmen who procure from the quarry the
marble out of which, later, the gifted sculptor produces those
masterpieces which lay hidden in this rough and shapeless ex-
terior." [51]

It is difficult indeed to leave Galileo without pausing a moment to reflect on the simply stupendous achievements of the
man. The space at our disposal forbids such supererogatory
disquisitions, but just consider that the history of thought must
turn to this single individual as the one who, by experimental
disproof, overthrew a hoary science, who confirmed by sensible
facts a new theory of the universe that hitherto had rested
on *a priori* grounds alone, who laid the foundations of the
most stupendous intellectual conquest of modern times, the

[49] *Two Great Sciences,* p. 406, ff.

[50] *Letter to the Grand Duchess.*

[51] *Two New Systems,* p. 194.

mathematical science of physical nature; and then, as if these accomplishments were not enough, we must turn to him like-wise as the philosopher who sufficiently perceived the larger implications of his postulates and methods to present in out-line a new metaphysic—a mathematical interpretation of the universe—to furnish the final justification for the onward march of mechanical knowledge. Teleology as an ultimate principle of explanation he set aside, depriving of their foun-dation those convictions about man's determinative relation to nature which rested upon it. The natural world was portrayed as a vast, self-contained mathematical machine, consisting of motions of matter in space and time, and man with his pur-poses, feelings, and secondary qualities was shoved apart as an unimportant spectator and semi-real effect of the great mathe-matical drama outside. In view of these manifold and radical performances Galileo must be regarded as one of the massive intellects of all time. In every single respect of importance he broke the ground or otherwise prepared the way for the only two minds in this advancing current of thought comparable to his own—Descartes and Sir Isaac Newton.

Descartes' importance in this mathematical movement was twofold; he worked out a comprehensive hypothesis in detail of the mathematical structure and operations of the material universe, with clearer consciousness of the important implications of the new method than had been shown by his predecessors; and he attempted both to justify and atone for the reading of man and his interests out of nature by his famous metaphysical dualism.

While still in his 'teens, Descartes became absorbed in mathematical study, gradually forsaking every other interest for it, and at the age of twenty-one was in command of all that was then known on the subject. During the next year or two we find him performing simple experiments in mechanics, hydrostatics, and optics, in the attempt to extend mathematical knowledge in these fields. He appears to have followed the more prominent achievements of Kepler and Galileo, though without being seriously affected by any of the details of their scientific philosophy. On the night of November 10th, 1619, he had a remarkable experience which confirmed the trend of his previous thinking and gave the inspiration and the guiding principle for his whole life-work.[1] The experience can be compared only to the ecstatic illumination of the mystic; in it the Angel of Truth appeared to him and seemed to justify, through added supernatural insight, the conviction which had already been deepening in his mind, that mathematics was the sole key needed to unlock the secrets of nature. The vision was so

[1] An admirable account of this event in the light of the available sources, with critical comments on the views of other Cartesian authorities, is given in Milhaud, *Descartes savant*, Paris, 1922, p. 47, ff.

vivid and compelling that Descartes in later years could refer
to that precise date as the occasion of the great revelation
that marked the decisive point in his career.

A. Mathematics as the Key to Knowledge

The first intensive studies into which he plunged after this
unique experience were in the field of geometry, where he was
rewarded within a very few months by the signal invention of a
new and most fruitful mathematical tool, analytical geometry.
This great discovery not only confirmed his vision and spurred
him on to further efforts in the same direction, but it was
highly important for his physics generally. The existence and
successful use of analytical geometry as a tool of mathematical
exploitation presupposes an exact one-to-one correspondence
between the realm of numbers, *i.e.*, arithmetic and algebra,
and the realm of geometry, *i.e.*, space. That they had been
related was, of course, a common possession of all mathematical science; that their relation was of this explicit and absolute
correspondence was an intuition of Descartes. He perceived
that the very nature of space or extension was such that its
relations, however complicated, must always be expressible in
algebraic formulae, and, conversely, that numerical truths
(within certain powers) can be fully represented spatially. As
one not unnatural result of this notable invention, the hope
deepened in Descartes' mind that the whole realm of physics
might be reducible to geometrical qualities alone. Whatever
else the world of nature may be, it is obviously a geometrical
world, its objects are extended and figured magnitudes in motion. If we can get rid of all other qualities, or reduce them to
these, it is clear that mathematics must be the sole and adequate key to unlock the truths of nature. And it was not a
violent leap from the wish to the thought.

During the following ten years, besides his numerous travels,
Descartes was engaged in further mathematical studies, which
were written down toward the end of this period, and he was
also working out a series of specific rules for the application

of his all-consuming idea. In these rules we find the conviction expressed that all the sciences form an organic unity,[2] that all must be studied together and by a method that applies to all.[3] This method must be that of mathematics, for all that we know in any science is the order and measurement revealed in its phenomena; now mathematics is just that universal science that deals with order and measurement generally.[4] That is why arithmetic and geometry are the sciences in which sure and indubitable knowledge is possible. They "deal with an object so pure and uncomplicated that they need make no assumptions at all that experience renders uncertain, but wholly consist in the rational deduction of consequences." [5] This does not mean that the objects of mathematics are imaginary entities without existence in the physical world.[6] Whoever denies that objects of pure mathematics exist, must deny that anything geometrical exists, and can hardly maintain that our geometrical ideas have been abstracted from existing things. Of course, there are no substances which have length without breadth or breadth without thickness, because geometrical figures are not substances but boundaries of them. In order for our geometrical ideas to have been abstracted from the world of physical objects, granted that this is a tenable hypothesis, that world would have to be a geometrical world—one fundamental characteristic of it is extension in space. It may turn out that it possesses no characteristics not deducible from this.

Descartes is at pains carefully to illustrate his thesis that exact knowledge in any science is always mathematical knowledge. Every other kind of magnitude must be reduced to mathematical terms to be handled effectively; if it can be reduced to extended magnitude so much the better, because extension can be represented in the imagination as well as dealt with by

[2] *The Philosophical Works of Descartes,* Haldane and Ross translation, Cambridge, 1911, Vol. I, p. 1, ff., 9.

[3] Vol. I, p. 306.

[4] Vol. I, p. 13.

[5] Vol. I, p. 4, ff.

[6] Vol. II, p. 227.

the intellect. "Though one thing can be said to be more or less white than another, or a sound sharper or flatter, and so on, it is yet impossible to determine exactly whether the greater exceeds the less in the proportion two to one, or three to one, etc., unless we treat the quantity as being in a certain way analogous to the extension of a body possessing figure." [7] Physics, as something different from mathematics, merely determines whether certain parts of mathematics are founded on anything real or not.[8]

What, now, is this mathematical method for Descartes in detail? Faced with a group of natural phenomena, how is the scientist to proceed? Descartes' answer early in the *Rules* is to distinguish two steps in the actual process, *intuition* and *deduction*. "By intuition I understand . . . the conception which an unclouded and attentive mind gives us so readily and distinctly that we are wholly freed from doubt about that which we understand." [9] He illustrates this by citing certain fundamental propositions such as the fact that we exist and think, that a triangle is bounded by three lines only, etc. By deduction he means a chain of necessary inferences from facts intuitively known, the certitude of its conclusion being known by the intuitions and the memory of their necessary connexion in thought.[10] As he proceeds further in the *Rules*, however, he realizes the inadequacy of this propositional method alone to yield a mathematical physics, and introduces the notion of *simple natures,* as discoveries of intuition in addition to these axiomatic propositions.[11] By these simple natures he means such ultimate characteristics of physical objects as extension, figure, motion, which can be regarded as producing the phenomena by quantitative combinations of their units. He notes that figure, magnitude, and impenetrability seem to be necessarily involved in extension, hence the latter and motion ap-

[7] Vol. I, 56.

[8] Vol. I, 62.

[9] Vol. I, 7.

[10] Vol. I, 8, 45.

[11] Vol. I, 42, ff.

pear to be the final and irreducible qualities of things. As he proceeds from this point he is on the verge of most far-reaching discoveries, but his failure to keep his thought from wandering, and his inability to work out the exceedingly pregnant suggestions that occur to him make them barren for both his own later accomplishments and those of science in general. Bodies are extended things in various kinds of motion. We want to treat them mathematically. We intuit these simple natures in terms of which mathematical deductions can be made. Can we formulate this process more exactly, with special reference to the fact that these simple natures must make *extension* and *motion* mathematically reducible? Descartes tries to do so, but at the crucial points his thought wanders, and as a consequence Cartesian physics had to be supplanted by that of the Galileo-Newton tradition. What are those features of extension, he asks, that can aid us in setting out mathematical differences in phenomena? Three he offers, dimension, unity, and figure. The development of this analysis is not clear,[12] but apparently a consistent solution of his idea would be that unity is that feature of things which enables simple arithmetic or geometry to gain a foothold in them, figure that which concerns the order of their parts, while dimension is any feature which it is necessary to add in order that no part of the facts shall have escaped mathematical reduction. "By dimension I understand not precisely the mode and aspect according to which a subject is considered to be measurable. Thus it is not merely the case that length, breadth, and depth are dimensions, but weight also is a dimension in terms of which the heaviness of objects is estimated. So, too, velocity is a dimension of motion, and there are an infinite number of similar instances." This conception of weight, velocity, etc., as further mathematical dimensions akin to length, breadth, and depth, except that they are dimensions of motion rather than of extension, harboured enormous possibilities which were entirely unrealized either in Descartes or in the work of later scientists. Had he succeeded in carrying the thought through, we might to-day think of mass and force as mathematical dimensions rather

[12] Vol. I, 61, ff.

110

than physical concepts, and the current distinction between mathematics and the physical sciences might never have been made. It might be taken for granted that *all* exact science is mathematical—that science as a whole is simply a larger mathematics, new concepts being added from time to time in terms of which more qualities of the phenomena become mathematically reducible. In this sense he might have converted the world to his doctrine at the end of the second book of the *Principles*,[13] that all the phenomena of nature may be explained by the principles of mathematics and sure demonstrations given of them. There are passages in his later works in which he still seems to be thinking of weight as a dimension of motion. He criticizes Democritus for asserting gravity to be an essential characteristic of bodies, "the existence of which I deny in any body in so far as it is considered by itself, because this is a quality depending on the relationship in respect of situation and motion which bodies bear to one another." [14] In general, however, he tended to forget this significant suggestion, and we find him denying weight as a part of the essence of matter because we regard fire as matter in spite of the fact that it appears to have no weight.[15] It has apparently slipped his mind that he once conceived of such differences as themselves mathematical.

The fact is, Descartes was a soaring speculator as well as a mathematical philosopher, and a comprehensive conception of the astronomico-physical world was now deepening in his mind, in terms of which he found it easy to make a rather brusque disposal of these qualities which Galileo was trying to reduce to exact mathematical treatment, but which could not be so reduced in terms of extension alone. This scheme was in effect to saddle such qualities upon an unoffending ether, or first matter, as Descartes usually calls it, thereby making it possible to view the bodies carried about in this ether as possessing no features not deducible from extension.

[13] *Principles of Philosophy*, Part II, Principle 64.

[14] *Principles*, Part IV, Principle 202.

[15] *Principles*, Part II, Principle 11.

Descartes' famous vortex theory was the final product of this vigorous, all-embracing speculation. Just how did he reach it?

B. Geometrical Conception of the Physical Universe

We have noted the biographical reasons for Descartes' hope that it would be possible to work out a physics which required no principles for its completion beyond those of pure mathematics; there were also certain logical prejudices operating, such as that *nothing* cannot possess extension, but wherever there is extension there must be some substance.[16] Furthermore, as for motion, Descartes had been able to account for it in a manner which fairly satisfied him; God set the extended things in motion in the beginning, and maintained the same quantity of motion in the universe by his "general concourse," [17] which, confirmed by more immediately conceived distinct ideas, meant that motion was just as natural to a body as rest, *i.e.*, the first law of motion. Since the creation then, the world of extended bodies has been nothing but a vast machine. There is no spontaneity at any point; all continues to move in fixed accordance with the principles of extension and motion. This meant that the universe is to be conceived as an extended *plenum,* the motions of whose several parts are communicated to each other by immediate impact. There is no need of calling in the force or attraction of Galileo to account for specific kinds of motion, still less the "active powers" of Kepler; all happens in accordance with the regularity, precision, inevitability, of a smoothly running machine.

How could the facts of astronomy and of terrestrial gravitation be accounted for in a way which would not do havoc with this beautifully simple hypothesis? Only by regarding the objects of our study as swimming helplessly in an infinite ether, or "first matter," to use Descartes' own term, which, being vaguely and not at all mathematically conceived, Des-

[16] *Principles,* Part II, Principles 8, 16.

[17] *Principles,* Part II, Principle 36.

cartes was able to picture as taking on forms of motion that rendered the phenomena explicable. This primary matter, forced into a certain quantity of motion divinely bestowed, falls into a series of whirlpools or vortices, in which the visible bodies such as planets and terrestrial objects are carried around or impelled toward certain central points by the laws of vortical motion. Hence the bodies thus carried can be conceived as purely mathematical; they possess no qualities but those deducible from extension and free mobility in the surrounding medium. Verbally, to be sure, Descartes made the same claim for the first matter itself, but it was the world of physical bodies that he was eager to explain, hence in terms of this hypothesis he imagined himself to have realized the great ambition of his life in the achievement of a thoroughly geometrical physics. What he did not appreciate was that this speculative success was bought at the expense of loading upon the primary medium those characteristics which express themselves in gravitation and other variations of velocity—the characteristics in a word which Galileo was endeavouring to express mathematically, and which Descartes himself in his more exact mathematical mood had conceived as dimensions. This procedure did not at all drive them out of the extended realm but merely hid under cover of vague and general terms the problem of their precise mathematical treatment. To solve that problem, Descartes' work had to be reversed, and the Galilean concepts of force, acceleration, momentum, and the like, reinvoked.

The unfortunate feature of the situation at this time was that thinkers were accepting the notion that *motion* was a mathematical concept, the object of purely geometrical study, whereas with the single exception of Galileo, they had not come to think of it seriously and consistently as *exactly reducible* to mathematical formulae. Galileo had caught this remarkable vision, that there is absolutely nothing in the motion of a physical body which cannot be expressed in mathematical terms, but he had discovered that this can be done only by attributing to bodies certain ultimate qualities beyond the merely geometrical ones, in terms of which this full mathematical handling of their motions can take place. Descartes

realized well enough the facts that underlie this necessity—
that bodies geometrically equivalent move differently when
placed in the same position relative to the same neighbouring
bodies—but thinking of motion as a mathematical conception in general and not having caught the full ideal of its exact
reduction in a way comparable to his treatment of extension,
he failed to work out to a clear issue his earlier suggestion of
weight and velocity as dimensions, and turned instead to the
highly speculative vortex theory, which concealed the causes
of these variations in the vague, invisible medium, and thereby
saved the purely geometrical character of the visible bodies.

The vortex theory was, none the less, a most significant
achievement historically. It was the first comprehensive attempt to picture the whole external world in a way fundamentally different from the Platonic-Aristotelian-Christian view
which, centrally a teleological and spiritual conception of the
processes of nature, had controlled men's thinking for a millen-
nium and a half. God had created the world of physical existence, for the purpose that in man, the highest natural end,
the whole process might find its way back to God. Now God
is relegated to the position of first cause of motion, the happenings of the universe then continuing *in æternum* as inci-
dents in the regular revolutions of a great mathematical
machine. Galileo's daring conception is carried out in fuller
detail. The world is pictured concretely as material rather than
spiritual, as mechanical rather than teleological. The stage is
set for the likening of it, in Boyle, Locke, and Leibniz, to a big
clock once wound up by the Creator, and since kept in orderly
motion by nothing more than his "general concourse."

The theory had an important practical value for Descartes
as well. In 1633 he had been on the point of publishing his
earliest mechanical treatises, but had been frightened by the
persecution of Galileo for his advocacy of the motion of the
earth in the *Dialogues on the Two Great Systems,* just published. As the impact, motion and vortex theory developed in
his mind, however, he perceived that place and motion must
be regarded as entirely relative conceptions, a doctrine which
might also save him in the eyes of the Church. As regards
place he had already reached this conviction, defining it in the

Rules as "a certain relation of the thing said to be in the place toward the parts of the space external to it." [18] This position was reaffirmed more strongly still in the *Analytical Geometry* and the *Dioptrics,* where he states categorically that there is no absolute place, but only relative; place only remains fixed so long as it is defined by our thought or expressed mathematically in terms of a system of arbitrarily chosen co-ordinates.[19] The full consequence of this for a true definition of motion is brought out in the *Principles,* in which, after noting the vulgar conception of motion as the "action by which any body passes from one place to another," [20] he proceeds to "the truth of the matter," which is that motion is "the transference of one part of matter or one body from the vicinity of those bodies that are in immediate contact with it, and which we regard as in repose, into the vicinity of others." [21] Inasmuch as we can regard any part of matter as in repose that is convenient for the purpose, motion, like place, becomes wholly relative. The immediate practical value of the doctrine was that the earth, being at rest in the surrounding ether, could be said in accordance with this definition to be unmoved, though it, together with the whole vortical medium, must be likewise said to move round the sun. Was this clever Frenchman not justified in remarking that "I deny the movement of the earth more carefully than Copernicus, and more truthfully than Tycho?" [22]

Now during these years in which Descartes was developing the details of his vortex theory and the idea of the extended world as a universal machine, he was occupying himself with still more ultimate metaphysical problems. The conviction that his mathematical physics had its complete counterpart in the structure of nature was being continually confirmed pragmat-

---

[18] *Philosophical Works,* Vol. I, p. 51.

[19] Cf. *Dioptrics,* Discourse 6 (*Oeuvres,* Cousin ed., Vol. V, p. 54, ff.).

[20] Part II, Principle 24.

[21] Part II, Principle 25.

[22] *Principles,* Part III, Principles 19–31.

ically, but Descartes was not satisfied with such empirical probabilism. He was eager to get an absolute guarantee that his clear and distinct mathematical ideas *must* be eternally true of the physical world, and he perceived that a new method would be required to solve this ultimate difficulty. A sense of the genuineness and fundamental character of this problem appears definitely in his correspondence early in 1629, and in a letter[23] to Mersenne, April 15, 1630, we learn that he has satisfactorily (to himself) solved it by conceiving the mathematical laws of nature as established by God, the eternal invariableness of whose will is deducible from his perfection. The details of this metaphysic are presented in the *Discourse,* the *Meditations,* and the *Principles,* where it is reached through the method of universal doubt, the famous *"cogito ergo sum,"* and the causal and ontological proofs of the existence and perfection of God. As regards the subjection of his mental furniture to the method of universal doubt, he had decided ten years earlier, as he tells us in the *Discourse,* to make the attempt as soon as he should be adequately prepared for it; now, however, the main motive that impels him to carry it through is no mere general distrust of his own early beliefs, but a consuming need to get a solution for this specific problem. We shall not follow him through these intricacies, but concentrate our attention upon one famous aspect of his metaphysics, the dualism of two ultimate and mutually independent entities, the *res extensa* and the *res cogitans.*

C. "Res extensa" and "res cogitans"

In Galileo the union of the mathematical view of nature and the principle of sensible experimentalism had left the status of the senses somewhat ambiguous. It is the sensible world that our philosophy attempts to explain and by the use of the senses our results are to be verified; at the same time when we com-

[23] *Oeuvres* (Cousin ed.), VI, 108, ff. Cf. an interesting treatment of this stage in Descartes biography in Liard, *Descartes,* Paris, 1911. p. 93, ff.

plete our philosophy we find ourselves forced to view the *real* world as possessed of none but primary or mathematical characteristics, the secondary or unreal qualities being due to the deceitfulness of the senses. Furthermore, in certain cases (as the motion of the earth) the immediate testimony of the senses must be wholly renounced as false, the correct answer being reached by reasoned demonstrations. Just what is, then, the status of the senses, and how are we specifically to dispose of these secondary qualities which are shoved aside as due to the illusiveness of sense? Descartes attempts to answer these questions by renouncing empiricism as a method and by providing a haven for the secondary qualities in an equally real though less important entity, the thinking substance.

For Descartes it is, to be sure, the sensible world about which our philosophizing goes on,[24] but the method of correct procedure in philosophy must not rest upon the trustworthiness of sense experience at all. "In truth we perceive no object such as it is by sense alone (but only by our reason exercised upon sensible objects)."[25] "In things regarding which there is no revelation, it is by no means consistent with the character of a philosopher . . . to trust more to the senses, in other words to the inconsiderate judgments of childhood, than to the dictates of mature reason."[26] We are to seek the "certain principles of material things . . . not by the prejudices of the senses, but by the light of reason, and which thus possess so great evidence that we cannot doubt of their truth."[27] Sensations are called "confused thoughts,"[28] and therefore sense, as also memory and imagination which depend on it, can only be used as aids to the understanding in certain specific and limited ways; sensible experiments can decide between alternative deductions from the clearly conceived first prin-

[24] *Philosophical Works,* Vol. I, p. 15.

[25] *Principles,* Part I, Principle 73.

[26] *Principles,* Part I, Principle 76. Cf. also Part II, Principles 37, 20.

[27] *Principles,* Part III, Principle 1.

[28] *Principles,* Part IV, Principle 197.

ciples; memory and imagination can represent extended corporeality before the mind as a help to the latter's clear conception of it.[29] It is not even necessary, as a basis for a valid philosophy, that we always have the sensible experience to proceed from; reasoning cannot of course alone suffice to give a blind man true ideas of colours, but if a man has once perceived the primary colours without the intermediate tints, it is possible for him to construct the images of the latter.[30]

Our method of philosophical discovery, then, is distinctly rational and conceptual; the sensible world is a vague and confused something, a quo philosophy proceeds to the achievement of truth. Why, now, are we sure that the primary, geometrical qualities inhere in objects as they really are, while the secondary qualities do not? How is it that "all other things we conceive to be compounded out of figure, extension, motion, etc., which we cognize so clearly and distinctly that they cannot be analysed by the mind into others more distinctly known?" [31] Descartes' own justification for this claim is that these qualities are *more permanent* than the others. In the case of the piece of wax, which he used for illustrative purposes in the second *Meditation,* no qualities remained *constant* but those of extension, flexibility, and mobility, which as he observes, is a fact perceived by the understanding, not by the sense or imagination. Now flexibility is not a property of all bodies, hence extension and mobility alone are left as the constant qualities of all bodies as such; they can by no means be done away with while the bodies still remain. But, we might ask, are not colour and resistance equally constant properties of bodies? Objects change in colour, to be sure, and there are varying degrees of resistance, but does one meet bodies totally without colour or resistance? The fact is and this is of central importance for our whole study, *Descartes' real criterion is not permanence but the possibility of mathematical handling;* in his case, as with Galileo, the whole course of his thought from his adoles-

[29] *Philosophical Works,* Vol. I, p. 35, 39, ff. *Discourse,* Part V.
[30] Vol. I, p. 54.
[31] Vol. I, p. 41.

cent studies on had inured him to the notion that we know objects only in mathematical terms, and the sole type for him of clear and distinct ideas had come to be mathematical ideas, with the addition of certain logical propositions into which he had been led by the need of a firmer metaphysical basis for his achievements, such as the propositions that we exist, that we think, etc. Hence the secondary qualities, when considered as belonging to the objects, like the primary, inevitably appear to his mind obscure and confused[32]; they are not a clear field for mathematical operations. This point cannot be stressed too strongly, though we shall not pause over it now.

But now the addition of such logical propositions as the above to the mathematical definitions and axioms, as illustrations of clear and distinct ideas, is quite important. It occurs as early as the *Rules,* and shows already the beginnings of his metaphysical dualism. No mathematical object is a more cogent item of knowledge than the *"cogito ergo sum";* we can turn our attention inward, and abstracting from the whole extended world, note with absolute assurance the existence of a totally different kind of entity, a thinking substance. Whatever may be the final truth about the realm of geometrical bodies, still we *know* that we doubt, we conceive, we affirm, we will, we imagine, we feel. Hence when Descartes directed his energies toward the construction of a complete metaphysic, this clean-cut dualism was inescapable. On the one hand there is the world of bodies, whose essence is extension; each body is a part of space, a limited spatial magnitude, different from other bodies only by different modes of extension—a geometrical world—knowable only and knowable fully in terms of pure mathematics. The vortex theory provided an easy disposal of the troublesome questions of weight, velocity, and the like; the whole spatial world becomes a vast machine, including even the movements of animal bodies and those processes in human physiology which are independent of conscious attention. This world has no dependence on thought whatever, its whole machinery would continue to exist and operate if

[32] *Philosophical Works.* Vol. I, p. 164, ff.

there were no human beings in existence at all.[33] On the other hand, there is the inner realm whose essence is thinking, whose modes are such subsidiary processes[34] as perception, willing, feeling, imagining, etc., a realm which is not extended, and is in turn independent of the other, at least as regards our adequate knowledge of it. But Descartes is not much interested in the *res cogitans,* his descriptions of it are brief, and, as if to make the rejection of teleology in the new movement complete, he does not even appeal to final causes to account for what goes on in the realm of mind. Everything there is a mode of the thinking substance.

In which realm, then, shall we place the secondary qualities? The answer given is inevitable. We can conceive the primary qualities to exist in bodies as they really are; not so the secondary. "In truth they can be representative of nothing that exists out of our mind." [35] They are, to be sure, caused by the various effects on our organs of the motions of the small insensible parts of the bodies.[36] We cannot conceive how such motions could give rise to secondary qualities *in the bodies;* we can only attribute to the bodies themselves a disposition of motions, such that, brought into relation with the senses, the secondary qualities are produced. That the results are totally different from the causes need not give us pause:

> The motion merely of a sword cutting a part of our skin causes pain (but does not on that account make us aware of the motion or figure of the sword). And it is certain that this sensation of pain is not less different from the motion that causes it, or from that of the part of our body that the

[33] *Oeuvres,* Cousin ed., Paris, 1824, ff., Vol. X, p. 194.

[34] In his *Traité de l'homme* Descartes had asserted that these subsidiary processes can be performed by the body without the soul, the sole functions of the latter being to think. Cf. *Oeuvres,* XI, pp. 201, 342: *Discourse* (Open Court ed.), p. 59, ff.; Kahn, *Metaphysics of the Supernatural,* p. 10, ff. His mature view, however, as expressed in the *Meditations* and *Principles,* is as above stated. Cf., for example, Meditation 11.

[35] *Principles,* Part I, Principles 70, 71.

[36] *Oeuvres* (Cousin), Vol. IV, p. 235, ff.

sword cuts, than are the sensations we have of colour, sound, odour, or taste.[37]

Hence all qualities whatever but the primary can be lumped together and assigned to the second member of the metaphysical wedding. We possess a clear and distinct knowledge of pain, colour, and other things of this sort, when we consider them simply as sensations or thoughts; but

. . . when they are judged to be certain things subsisting beyond our minds, we are wholly unable to form any conception of them. Indeed, when any one tells us that he sees colour in a body or feels pain in one of his limbs, this is exactly the same as if he said that he there saw or felt something of the nature of which he was entirely ignorant, or that he did not know what he saw or felt.[38]

We can easily conceive, how the motion of one body can be caused by that of another, and diversified by the size, figure, and situation of its parts, but we are wholly unable to conceive how these same things (size, figure, and motion), can produce something else of a nature entirely different from themselves, as, for example, those substantial forms and real qualities which many philosophers suppose to be in bodies. . . .[39]

But since we know, from the nature of our soul, that the diverse motions of body are sufficient to produce in it all the sensations which it has, and since we learn from experience that several of its sensations are in reality caused by such motions, while we do not discover that anything besides these motions ever passes from the organs of the external senses to the brain, we have reason to conclude that we in no way likewise apprehend that in external objects which we call light, colour, smell, taste, sound, heat, or cold, and the other tactile qualities, or that which we call their substantial forms, unless as the various dispositions of these

[37] *Principles,* Part IV, Principle 197.

[38] *Principles,* Part I, Principle 68, ff.

[39] Part IV, Principles 198, 199.

objects which have the power of moving our nerves in various ways. . . .

Such, then, is Descartes' famous dualism—one world consisting of a huge, mathematical machine, extended in space; and another world consisting of unextended, thinking spirits. And whatever is not mathematical or depends at all on the activity of thinking substance, especially the so-called secondary qualities, belongs with the latter.

D. Problem of Mind and Body

But the Cartesian answer raises an enormous problem, how to account for the interrelation of these diverse entities. If each of the two substances exists in absolute independence of the other, how do motions of extended things produce unextended sensations, and how is it that the clear conceptions or categories of unextended mind are valid of the *res extensa?* How is it that that which is unextended can know, and, knowing, achieve purposes in, an extended universe? Descartes' least objectionable answer to these difficulties is the same answer that Galileo made to a similar though not so clearly formulated problem—the appeal to God. God has made the world of matter such that the pure mathematical concepts intuited by mind are forever applicable to it. This was the answer that the later Cartesians attempted to work out in satisfactory and consistent form. The appeal to God was, however, already beginning to lose caste among the scientific-minded; the positivism of the new movement was above everything else a declaration of independence of theology, specifically of final causality, which seemed to be a mere blanket appeal to a kind of answer to scientific questions as would make genuine science impossible. It was an answer to the ultimate *why,* not to the present *how.* Descartes himself had been a powerful figure in just this feature of the new movement. He had categorically declared it impossible for us to know God's purposes.[40] Hence this answer

[40] *Principles,* Part III, Principle 2.

had little weight among any but his metaphysically-minded
followers, whose influence lay quite outside the main current
of the times; and those passages in which he appeared to offer
a more immediate and scientific answer to these overwhelming
difficulties, especially when capitalized by such a vigorous
thinker as Hobbes, were the ones which proved significant.
In these passages Descartes appeared to teach that the obvious
relationships between the two entities of the dualism implied
after all the real localization of mind, *but it was of the utmost
importance for the whole subsequent development of science
and philosophy that the place thus reluctantly admitted to the
mind was pitifully meagre, never exceeding a varying portion
of the body with which it is allied.* Descartes never forswore
the main philosophical approach which had led to his out-
spoken dualism. All the non-geometrical properties are to be
shorn from *res extensa* and located in the mind. He asserts in
words that the latter "has no relation to extension, nor dimensions," [41] we cannot "conceive of the space it occupies";
yet, and these were the influential passages, it is "really joined
to the whole body and we cannot say that it exists in any one
of its parts to the exclusion of the others"; we can affirm that
it "exercises its functions" more particularly in the conarion,
*"from whence it radiates forth through all the remainder of
the body by means of the animal spirits, nerves, and even the
blood."* With such statements to turn to in the great philosopher of the new age, is it any wonder that the common run of
intelligent people who were falling into line with the scientific
current, unmetaphysically minded at best, totally unable to
appreciate sympathetically the notion of a non-spatial entity
quite independent of the extended world, partly because such
an entity was quite unrepresentable to the imagination, partly
because of the obvious difficulties involved, and partly because
of the powerful influence of Hobbes, *came to think of the mind
as something located and wholly confined within the body?*
What Descartes had meant was that through a part of the

[41] *Passions of the Soul,* Articles 30, 31 (*Philosophical Works,*
Vol. I, 345, ff.). Italics ours. In his later writings Descartes
was much more guarded in his language. Cf. *Oeuvres* (Cousin
ed.), X, 96, ff.

brain a quite unextended substance came into effective relation with the realm of extension. The net result of his attempts on this point for the positive scientific current of
thought was that the mind existed in a ventricle of the brain.
The universe of matter, conceived as thoroughly geometrical
save as to the vagueness of the "first matter," extends infinitely
throughout all space, needing nothing for its continued and
independent existence; the universe of mind, including all experienced qualities that are not mathematically reducible,
comes to be pictured as locked up behind the confused and
deceitful media of the senses, away from this independent extended realm, in a petty and insignificant series of locations
inside of human bodies. This is, of course, the position which
had been generally accorded the "soul" in ancient times, but
not at all the "mind," except in the case of those philosophers
of the sensationalist schools who made no essential distinction
between the two.

Of course, the problem of knowledge was not solved by
this interpretation of the Cartesian position, but rather tre-
mendously accentuated. How is it possible for such a mind to
know anything about such a world? We shall postpone for the
present, however, considerations of this sort; all the men with
whom we are immediately occupied either failed to see this
enormous problem, or else evaded it with the easy theological
answer.

Note, however, the tremendous contrast between this view
of man and his place in the universe, and that of the medieval
tradition. The scholastic scientist looked out upon the world
of nature and it appeared to him a quite sociable and human
world. It was finite in extent. It was made to serve his needs.
It was clearly and fully intelligible, being immediately present
to the rational powers of his mind; it was composed fundamentally of, and was intelligible through, those qualities which
were most vivid and intense in his own immediate experience—
colour, sound, beauty, joy, heat, cold, fragrance, and its plas-
ticity to purpose and ideal. Now the world is an infinite and
monotonous mathematical machine. Not only is his high place
in a cosmic teleology lost, but all these things which were the
very substance of the physical world to the scholastic—the

things that made it alive and lovely and spiritual—are lumped together and crowded into the small fluctuating and temporary positions of extension which we call human nervous and circulatory systems. The metaphysically constructive features of the dualism tended to be lost quite out of sight. It was simply an incalculable change in the viewpoint of the world held by intelligent opinion in Europe.

The work of Descartes had an enormous influence throughout all Europe during the latter half of the seventeenth century, largely because he was not only a great mathematician
and anatomist, but also a powerful philosophical genius, who
treated afresh, and with a remarkably catholic reach, all the
big problems of the age by hitching them up in one fashion
or another to the chariot of victorious mathematical science.
In England especially, he aroused widespread interest mixed
with considerable keen criticism. Among the thinkers flourish-
ing there in the third quarter of the century who were
sympathetic with the big task that Descartes was trying to
accomplish though severely critical of him in certain important
details, were Thomas Hobbes and Henry More. The work of
the former has been already briefly referred to; we shall now
describe his significance in the mathematical current of the
times by locating it in a somewhat wider context as indicated
by the above title.

During the preceding century thought had been relatively
freer of theological trammels in England than elsewhere in
Europe, and in the first quarter of the seventeenth century
secular learning had been mightily advanced by the championship of a man than whom there was none higher in the political
counsels of the realm, Lord Chancellor Bacon. It is impossible
to trace any direct influence of Bacon on the metaphysics of
Boyle or Newton, but the former's conception of science as
an exalted co-operative enterprise, his empirical stress on the
necessity and cogency of sensible experiments, his distrust of
hypothesis and general analysis of inductive procedure, all
penetrated the leading scientific minds of the middle of the

century, especially Robert Boyle, through whom they exercised a notable influence on Newton. We shall discuss Boyle in some detail in the chapter following.

A. Hobbes' Attack on the Cartesian Dualism

Thomas Hobbes was a trusted friend of Bacon, but his philosophical powers were not seriously awakened until he acquired an interest in geometry at the advanced age of forty, and under the urge of that interest familiarized himself with all the new developments which had been set in such vigorous motion by the astronomical revolution. Especially did he acquire a profound respect for Galileo, whom he visited at length on his third journey to the continent (1634–37) and from whom he received helpful confirmation of the notion already simmering in his own mind, that the sole and adequate explanation of the universe is to be found in terms of body and motion. He never succeeded, however, in giving precise mathematical meanings to these terms in the way of the great Italian; his shift to the new terminology of space, time, force, momentum, etc., was somewhat superficial and in many important respects he always remained a scholastic.

On his next journey to France Hobbes became acquainted with the *Meditations* of Descartes through the medium of their common friend Mersenne, and penned for the author's benefit the third set of *Objections* to the proposed work. In these objections Hobbes appears as an uncompromising opponent of Descartes' dualism and the conception of "idea" by which it was justified. According to Hobbes, all activity and change whatever are *motion;* now thinking in all its forms is an activity, therefore thinking is a kind of motion. Mind is simply a name for the sum of an individual's thinking activities, is thus nothing but a series of motions in an animal organism. "If this be so, reasoning will depend on names, names on the imagination, and imagination, perchance, as I think, on the motion of the corporeal organs. Thus mind will be nothing but the motions in certain parts of an organic body." [1] To set up mind as a separate substance, wholly different in kind from corporeal substance or its activities appeared to Hobbes a mere relic of the scholastic occult qualities. "If M. Descartes shows that he who understands and the understanding are identical, we shall lapse back into the scholastic mode of speaking. The understanding understands, the vision sees, will wills, and by exact analogy, walking, or at least the faculty of walking, will walk." [2] This, Hobbes holds, will hardly do for a philosophical presentation of the situation. Away with this unjustified dualism. Mental processes, including reasoning itself, are but kinds of activity, and activity is always motion. Let us carry forward the new method consistently, reduce these things, too, frankly to motion, and study them in terms of the recently established principles of motion. It is because of this position that Hobbes regards geometry, "the science of simple motion," [3] and geometrical mechanics, which he took over from Galileo, as the indispensable prerequisite for all further accomplishments in science or philosophy.

Now motion implies a something which moves, and that something can only be conceived in corporeal fashion; we must think of it as a *body*. "We can conceive no activity whatsoever apart from its subject, *e.g.*, we cannot think of leaping apart from that which leaps, of knowing apart from a knower, or of thinking without a thinker. And hence it seems to follow that that which thinks is something corporeal; for, as it appears, the subject of all activities can be conceived only after a corporeal fashion, or as in material guise, as M. Descartes himself afterwards shows, when he illustrates by means of wax." [4] Why, we ask, must it be so conceived? The answer is that for Hobbes an idea is always an *image*,[5] and an image,

[1] *The Philosophical Works of Descartes* (Haldane and Ross), Vol. II, p. 65.

[2] Haldane and Ross, Vol. II, p. 65.

[3] Hobbes, *Works,* Vol. I (English), p. 71, ff.

[4] Haldane and Ross, Vol. II, p. 62.

[5] Haldane and Ross, Vol. II, p. 65.

of course, must always be of something possessing corporeal characteristics. "Hence we have no idea, no image of God; we are forbidden to worship him in the form of an image, lest we should think we could conceive him who is inconceivable. Therefore it appears that we have no idea of God." [6] We merely give the name God to the object which we reach by a reasoned search for the first cause of things.[7] Inasmuch as images are always of particular objects, we find Hobbes quite in line with the strong nominalistic tendency of the later Middle Ages, vigorous especially in England, which regarded individual things as the only real existences. This nominalistic aspect of his philosophy led him to see no reality in universal essences or natures. They are just *names,* nothing more. For example a triangle: "If the triangle exists nowhere at all, I do not see how it can have any nature . . . The triangle in the mind comes from the triangle we have seen, or from one imaginatively constructed out of triangles we have beheld. Now when we have once called the thing by the name triangle, although the triangle itself perishes, yet the name remains. . . . But the nature of the triangle will not be of eternal duration, if it should chance that that triangle perished. In like manner the proposition, man is an animal, will be eternally true, because the names it employs are eternal, but if the human race were to perish there would no longer be a human nature. Whence it is evident that essence in so far as it is distinguished from existence, is nothing else than a union of names by means of the verb *is.* And thus essence without existence is a fiction of our mind." [8]

Nothing exists then but particular objects in motion, which we have to think in terms of images and hence must conceive as corporeal; further, reasoning is nothing but a stringing together of images or the names which we have arbitrarily assigned to them[9]; it is the motion of these images succeeding

[6] Haldane and Ross, Vol. II, p. 67.

[7] Haldane and Ross, Vol. II, p. 71.

[8] Haldane and Ross, Vol. II, p. 76, ff.

[9] Hobbes, *Leviathan,* Bk. I, Chs. 3, 5. (*Works,* Vol. 3.)

one another in a certain way. Therefore Hobbes sees no justification for a metaphysical dualism. Nothing without us but
bodies in motion, nothing within us but organic motions. In
this peremptory conclusion he not only sets the fashion for the
popular interpreters of the Cartesian dualism, in holding that
the mind is something confined to a portion of the brain and
circulatory system, but more radical still, he swallows up the
res cogitans by treating it as a combination of certain types
of motion possessed by *res extensae*. We have in his work the
first important attempt to apply the new assumptions and
method of Galileo universally.

Now Hobbes recognizes that he has obligated himself to
give an explanatory account, in terms of body and motion, of
these images, inasmuch as they do not obviously present themselves as either bodies, or motions, or located in the brain.
This explanation, which appears first in the *Treatise of Human
Nature,* is of profound significance in the early development
of the new doctrine of the human mind, and represents
Hobbes' chief importance in the current which leads on to the
metaphysics of Newton. Much of his naturalism, especially in
psychology and political theory, was too upsetting to influence
greatly the thought of his generation except counteractively,
but his contribution here was too much in line with the
victorious scientific march of the times to fail of profound
effect. He attacks the problem by way of an attempt to show
how it is that although secondary qualities are not really in
bodies ("an image or colour is but an apparition unto us of
the motion, agitation, or alteration, which the object work-
eth in the brain, or spirits, or some internal substance of the
head" [10]), yet they seem to us to be there just as much as the
primary.

[10] Hobbes, *Treatise of Human Nature* (English Works, Vol.
IV), Ch. 2, Par. 4.

B. Treatment of Secondary Qualities and Causality

Hobbes' position is that images are simply gradually decaying sense experiences, or phantasms, as he calls them, and that the latter arise from a conflict of motions produced in the human organism; the motion coming in from the object clashes with certain vital motions proceeding outward from the heart,

> which endeavour because outward, seemeth to be some matter without. And this seeming, or fancy, is that which men call Sense; and consisteth, as to the eye, in a light, or colour figured; to the ear, in a sound; to the nostril, in an odour; to the tongue and palate, in a savour; and to the rest of the body, in heat, cold, hardness, softness, and such other qualities, as we discern by feeling. All which qualities called sensible, are in the object which causeth them but so many several motions of the matter, by which it presseth our organs diversely. Neither in us that are pressed are they any thing else but diverse motions (for motion produceth nothing but motion). But their appearance to us is Fancy, the same waking that dreaming. And as pressing, rubbing, or striking the eye, makes us fancy a light; and pressing the ear produceth a din; so do the bodies also we see or hear produce the same by their strong, though unobserved actions. For if those colours or sounds were in the bodies or objects which cause them, they could not be severed from them, as by glasses, and in echoes by reflection, we see they are; where we know the thing we see is is in one place, the appearance in another. And though at some certain distance the real and very object seem invested with the fancy it begets in us; yet still the object is one thing, the image or fancy another.[11]
>
> And from hence also it followeth, that whatsoever accidents or qualities our senses make us think there be in the world, they be not there, but are seeming and appari-

[11] Hobbes, *Leviathan*, Bk. I, Ch. 1.

tions only; the things that really are in the world without us, are those motions by which these seemings are caused. And this is the great deception of sense, which also is to be by sense corrected: for as sense telleth me, when I see directly, that the colour seemeth to be in the object; so also sense telleth me, when I see by reflection, that colour is not in the object.[12]

Hobbes thus adds to his materialistic reduction of the Cartesian dualism and his conviction that man is to be adequately explained in the same terms that have been found so successful in treating *res extensae* (which was possible for him because he had failed to appreciate the exact-mathematical ideal of the new movement in the minds of his more scientific contemporaries), a specific explanation of the big difficulty which would naturally occur to any one suddenly taught that secondary qualities were really not in the object but in himself. According to Hobbes, all sense qualities appear to be without, because "there is in the whole organ, by reason of its own internal natural motion, some resistance or reaction against the motion which is propagated from the object to the innermost part of the organ; there is also in the same organ an endeavour opposite to the endeavour which proceeds from the object; so when that endeavour inwards is the last action in the act of sense, then from the reaction, how little soever the duration of it be, a phantasm or idea hath its being; which by reason that the endeavour is now outward, doth always appear as something situate without the organ. . . . For light and colour, and heat and sound, and other qualities which are commonly called sensible, are not objects, but phantasms in the sentients." [13] It is no more true that fire heateth, therefore it is itself hot; than that fire causeth pain, therefore it is itself in pain.[14]

Now, we might ask, does not this line of reasoning apply

[12] *Treatise of Human Nature,* Ch. 2, Par. 10.

[13] *Elements of Philosophy* (English Works, Vol. I), Bk. IV, Ch. 25, Par. 2.

[14] *Elements of Philosophy,* Bk. IV, Ch. 27, Par. 3.

to the primary qualities as much as to the secondary—are not they also mere phantasm in the sentients? Apparently there is no difference between them in this respect. Hobbes answers this objection by a frank affirmative, and proceeds to make a distinction between space and geometrical extension, a distinction which, as we saw, may have been felt by some ancient scientists and which ultimately became important in modern thought but only in post-Newtonian times. Space, for Hobbes, is itself a phantasm, "the phantasm of a thing existing without the mind simply; that is to say, that phantasm, in which we consider no other accident, but only that it appears without us." [15] Extension, however, is an essential characteristic body, as we learn by the geometrical study of motion. There are always such extended bodies in motion external to us, which cause by their motions the phantasms within, including that "withoutness" of the phantasms, which is space. Time is likewise a phantasm, "of before and after in motion." "The present only has a being in Nature; things past have a being in the memory only; but things to come have no being at all; the future being but a fiction of the mind, applying the sequels of actions past to the actions that are present." [16] In nature there is motion but no time; time is a phantasm of the before-and-afterness of memory and anticipation. Thus the entire perceived image, however contrary to appearances, is within the body. Mind is organic motion, and sense is appearance of outness taking place really within the organs. The big epistemological difficulty in such a position Hobbes apparently does not notice. He assumes without critical examination the essentials of Galileo's mechanical cosmology.

Now Hobbes' combination of materialism and nominalism as thus developed has prepared him to proclaim quite frankly and without the qualifications and exceptions in Galileo and Descartes the doctrine of causality which has become accepted more and more fully and clearly in modern times, deserving for that reason to be set over against the medieval

[15] *Elements of Philosophy,* Bk. II, Ch. 7, Par. 2, ff. Cf. also quotation 11, p. 130, ff. above.

[16] *Leviathan,* Bk. I, Ch. 3.

principle of final causality by the Supreme Good as its contrasting modern conception. Hobbes insists very strongly on interpreting causality always in terms of particular motions of particular bodies. The vast, hidden forces, which were for Galileo the primary or ultimate causes of effects, disappear in Hobbes, who has followed Descartes in denying the existence of a vacuum in nature. "There can be no cause of motion, except in a body contiguous and moved." [17] "For if those bodies be not moved which are contiguous to a body unmoved, how this body should begin to be moved is not imaginable; as has been demonstrated . . . to the end that philosophers might at last abstain from the use of such unconceivable connections of words." [18] The latter passage occurs in the midst of a criticism of Kepler for calling in such occult powers as magnetic attraction as causes for motion. Hobbes held, of course, that magnetic virtue itself can be nothing but a motion of body. Everything that exists is a particular body; everything that happens a particular motion.

Finally, Hobbes' nominalism together with his mechanical account of the genesis of the deceitful phantasms, expressed itself in a feature of his philosophy that has been subsequently most influential. We should note that in a certain respect Hobbes represented a counter-tendency to the work of Galileo and Descartes; he is trying to reunite the sundered halves of the Cartesian dualism and bring man back into the world of nature as a part of her domain. But the contrary logic of the movement was too much for him. He was unable to introduce the exact-mathematical method into his biology or psychology, with the result that the allied astronomy and physics became inexact and uncertain, and were for that reason of no use whatever to later scientists. Couple this fact with the extreme radicalism of his endeavour to reduce mind to bodily motion, and his failure to convert science to complete materialism is quite understandable. A remnant of the *res cogitans* still remained; even Hobbes' phantasms had to be explained rather than denied. But someone might have carried over the teleo-

[17] *Elements of Philosophy,* Bk. II, Ch. 9, Par. 7.

[18] *Elements,* Book IV, Ch. 26, Pars. 7, 8.

logical method of explanation, discredited now in physics, to the modern analysis of the human mind; nature might have been abandoned to mathematical atomism while the other side of the dualism might have been accounted for mainly in terms of purpose or use. That this did not happen in the dominant current of modern thought we likewise owe largely to Hobbes. Having carried through the new conception of causality to a decisive statement, having also, in his doctrine of the relation of the human mind to nature, made such a strong bid for a consistent materialism, there was no temptation for him to return to teleology in his psychological analysis. He was not able to develop a psychology in terms of mathematical atoms, but he strayed no farther from this method than was necessary; he described the mind as a compound of the elementary parts or phantasms above referred to, produced in the vital organs by the clash of inrushing and outpushing motions, and combined according to simple laws of association. Purpose and reasoning are admitted, but they appear not as ultimate principles of explanation, which had been their significance for the scholastic psychologist; they represent merely a certain type of phantasm or group of phantasms within the total compound. This treatment, aided by the decline of the notion of God as Supreme Good, set the fashion for almost the whole modern development of psychology. Locke, the next great psychologist, followed Hobbes' method still more explicitly and in greater detail, with the result that after him only an occasional idealist ventured to write a psychology in terms of different main assumptions. Spinoza, though without influence till much later, is interesting to mention in contrast with Hobbes. His main interests would have been favourable to an ultimate teleology in explaining the attribute of thought; only being able, as he thought, to apply the mathematical method here also, he conceived it, like the realm of extension, in terms of mathematical implication rather than in terms of ends and means. From now on it is a settled assumption for modern thought in practically every field, that to explain anything is to reduce it to its elementary parts, whose relations, where temporal in character, are conceived in terms of efficient causality solely.

c. More's Notion of Extension as a Category of Spirit

Henry More, the Cambridge Platonist, was also powerfully stimulated by the philosophy of Descartes and was eager to get beyond the dualism of the French thinker, but being a deeply religious spirit, he sensed serious difficulties in Hobbes' smashing way of disposing of the problem. The general account of man's cognitive relation to nature which had developed by this time he took over (very significantly) without noticing any serious difficulty with it. "I say in general, that sensation is made by the arrival of motion from the object to the organ, where it is received in all the circumstances we perceive it in, and conveyed by virtue of the soul's presence there, assisted by her immediate instrument the spirits, by virtue of whose continuity to those of the common sensorium, the image or impress of every object is faithfully transmitted thither." [19] These phrases "the soul's presence there," "her immediate instrument the spirits," "the common sensorium," will need elucidation later; let us proceed to note here that More accepts the general structure of the primary-secondary doctrine, though on Galileo-Cartesian rather than Hobbesian lines; the latter's dismissal of the "soul" as merely a name for the unconceivable cause of vital motions More would not at all admit. For him it was as real a substance as corporeal matter. But for the rest he is quite orthodox. "The diversity there is of sense or perception does necessarily arise from the diversity of the magnitude, position, figure, vigour, and direction of motion in parts of the matter . . . there being a diversity of perception, it must imply also a diversity of modification of reaction; and reaction being nothing but motion in matter, it cannot be varied but by such variations as are compatible to matter, namely such as are magnitude, figure, posture, local motion, . . . direction . . .

[19] More, *Immortality of the Soul* (*A Collection of Several Philosophical Writings*, 4th ed., London, 1712). Bk. II, Ch. 11, Par. 2.

and a vigour thereof. These are the first conceivables in matter, and therefore diversity of perception must of necessity arise from these." [20] As regards the ultimate structure of matter, too, the common notions of the day were accepted uncritically, with the exception that there appear certain added idiosyncracies, such as the contention that the atoms, though extended, have no figure. Matter is composed "of homogeneous atoms, impenetrable as regards each other, without figure, though extended, filling all space, and by their own nature inert, though movable by spirit." [21] The reason, such as it is, for this curious notion, is given in the preface to the *Immortality of the Soul:* "those indiscerptible particles of matter have no figure at all; as infinite greatness has no figure, so infinite littleness has none also." The Cartesian doctrine of the conservation of the quantity of motion was likewise accepted. God originally impressed the same quantity of motion on matter as exists in it now.

But More was in trouble because he, no more than Hobbes, could conceive it possible that anything could exist without extension, "it being the very essence of whatsoever is, to have parts or extension in some measure or other. For, to take away all extension, is to reduce a thing only to a mathematical point, which is nothing else but pure negation or nonentity, and there being no medium betwixt extended and nonextended, no more than there is betwixt entity and nonentity, it is plain that if a thing be at all it must be extended." [22] It was just this consideration, however, that led More boldly to refuse to join Descartes and Hobbes in assigning extension solely to matter as its essential quality, and made him a vigorous protestant against certain assumptions of the new ontology. For him, spirit too must be extended, though its other qualities are widely different from those of matter. Spirit is freely penetrable, and itself able to penetrate and impart motion to matter; [23]

[20] *Immortality of the Soul,* Bk. II, Ch. 1, Axiom 22.

[21] *Enchiridion Metaphysicum,* London, 1671, Ch. 9, Par. 21.

[22] *Immortality of the Soul,* Preface. Cf. also *Divine Dialogues,* 2nd edition, London, 1713, p. 49, ff.

[23] *Enchiridion,* Ch. 9, Par. 21.

it has absolute powers of contraction and dilation, which means that it can occupy greater or less space at will. "The chief seat of the soul, where she perceives all objects, where she imagines, reasons, and invents, and from whence she commands all the parts of the body, is those purer animal spirits in the fourth ventricle of the brain," [24] but he adds that it is not by any means confined there, it is able to spread throughout the whole body on occasion, and even slightly beyond the limits of the body, as a kind of spiritual effluvium.[25] The notion of these extended spirits possessing powers of contraction and dilation led More to a curious doctrine of a fourth dimension which he calls *essential spissitude*—as we might put it, a kind of spiritual density. "I mean nothing else by spissitude, but the redoubling or contracting of substance into less space than it does sometimes occupy." [26] When the soul, for example, is contracted principally in the fourth ventricle, the space occupied possesses not only the three normal dimensions, but also this fourth dimension or spissitude. There are no distinctions of degree in the latter, however, its dilation into more space leaves it essentially the same. To appreciate to the full More's speculations along this line, it is necessary to read his portrayal of the life of the soul after death, where it occupies an ethereal body, the motions of whose particles it can completely control. It adds and diminishes motion, alters the temper and shape of the body, quite according to its fancy.[27]

Is this just loose-reined imagination, or does More feel confident that he can point to facts which are only thus explicable? In a letter to Boyle, December 4, 1665, he writes as the sum and substance of his doctrine that "the phenomena of the world cannot be solved merely mechanically, but that there is the necessity of the assistance of a substance distinct from

[24] *Immortality of the Soul,* Bk. II, Ch. 7, Par. 18.

[25] *Divine Dialogues,* p. 75, ff.

[26] *Immortality of the Soul,* Bk. I, Ch. 2, Par. 11.

[27] *Immortality of the Soul,* Bk. III, Ch. 1, Pars. 7, 8, 10, 11.

matter, that is, of a spirit, or being incorporeal," [28] and again he declares his fundamental disagreement with Descartes' philosophy to be due to "its pretense of solving, though but the easiest and simplest phenomena merely mechanically; [a refutation of which] I think I have done irrefutably, nay I am unspeakably confident of it; and have therewithal ever and anon plainly demonstrated the necessity of incorporeal beings; which is a design, than which nothing can be more seasonable in this age; wherein the notion of a spirit is hooted at by so many for nonsense."

What are these irrefutable demonstrations of the existence of incorporeal beings, which, of course, for More, mean extended spiritual substances? Are the new doctrines of the nature of the world riding roughshod over certain important facts?

Most obviously, of course, the immediate experience of volition, in which we move, in accordance with our own purposes, both the limbs and other organs of our bodies, and likewise parts of the material world around us. "I regard this gland [the pineal] in accordance with your principles, as the seat of the common sense, and as the fortress of the soul. I question, however, if the soul does not occupy the whole body. Otherwise, I beg you, how can it happen that the soul, not being possessed of hooked or branching parts, can be so exactly united to the body? I ask you further, if there are not effects in nature, of which one would be unable to offer a mechanical reason? Whence this natural sense that we have of our own existence? And this empire which our soul has over the animal spirits, whence it also? How does it make them flow through all parts of the body?" [29] We have the immediate testimony for such powers "when we find it possible at our will to set in motion or arrest our animal spirits; to despatch them or to draw them back, as we please. Whence, I ask if it be unworthy of a philosopher to inquire if there be not in nature an in-

[28] Boyle, *Works* (Birch edition), Vol. VI, p. 513, ff. Cf. *Divine Dialogues*, p. 16, ff.

[29] Second Letter to Descartes (*Oeuvres de Descartes*, Cousin ed., Vol. X, p. 229, ff.). Cf. also *Immortality of the Soul*, Bk. II, Chs. 17, 18; Bk. I, Ch. 7.

corporeal substance, which, while it can impress on any body all the qualities of body, or at least most of them, such as motion, figure, position of parts, etc. . . . would be further able, since it is almost certain that this substance removes and stops bodies, to add whatever is involved in such motion, that is, it can unite, divide, scatter, bind, form the small parts, order the forms, set in circular motion those which are disposed for it, or move them in any way whatever, arrest their circular motion, and do such similar further things with them as are necessary to produce according to your principles light, colours, and the other objects of the senses. . . . Finally, incorporeal substance having the marvellous power of cohering and dissipating matter, of combining it, dividing it, thrusting it forth and at the same time retaining control of it, by mere application of itself without bonds, without hooks, without projections or other instruments; does it not appear probable that it can enter once more in itself, since there is no impenetrability to frustrate it, and expand itself again, and the like?"

In this passage More extends his reasoning from the conclusion of an incorporeal substance in human beings to the assumption of a similar and greater incorporeal substance in nature as a whole, for he was convinced that the facts of science showed nature to be no more a simple machine than is a human being. The facts cited in this further connexion are the facts which had become the subject-matter of the most eager scientific study of the time, such as the ultimate cause of motion, cohesion, magnetism, gravity, and the like.[30] More notes that, although the sufficient *immediate* causes of motion can be described in mechanical terms, the ultimate reason of why the parts of the universe are in motion rather than in rest cannot be accounted for mechanically. Furthermore, many of the particular qualities or motions exhibited by the parts of matter had not been mechanically reduced, such as the phenomena of cohesion and magnetism. Why do the parts of a solid body cohere so powerfully together, and yet when once sundered that cohesion is lost? What is the cause of the

[30] *Enchiridion,* Chs. 9–15.

curious motions set up by the loadstone? How, finally, is his challenge to the adherents of a universal mechanical view of nature, is it possible to reconcile the facts of gravitation with the principles of mechanical motion as revealed in the laws of motion expressed by Descartes and Hobbes?

According to mechanical principles, by which he means the doctrine that all motion is by impact, More holds that a stone let loose above the surface of the earth ought to fly off at a tangent, or at most, by the theory of the Cartesian vortices, be carried around continually by the earth's diurnal motion at the same distance from it.[31] It would never, by mechanical principles, fall in a straight line towards the earth. "So that in all nature there can be nothing more certain or well tested than that the phenomenon of gravity is repugnant to mechanical laws; and further that its explanation cannot be resolved into causes purely mechanical and corporeal; but that it is necessary here to admit certain additional causes which are immaterial and incorporeal." [32] Such causes More finds in the conception of a "spirit of nature," which holds the different parts of the material universe together in a unitary system which is distinctly not mechanical.

D. The "Spirit of Nature"

This "spirit of nature," as More describes it, bears obvious similarities with the ancient, especially Platonic notion of the *anima mundi,* a living hylarchical principle which penetrates matter and whose active powers are expressed in the larger astronomical and physical phenomena of nature. In fact More occasionally calls it the "universal soul of the world." [33] The idea was quite common throughout the later Middle Ages, being appealed to frequently by mystics, theosophists and speculative natural philosophers; in Kepler, for example, we find

[31] *Enchiridion,* Ch. II, Par. 14.

[32] *Immortality of the Soul,* Bk. III, Ch. 13.

[33] As in *Immortality,* Bk. III, Ch. 13, Par. 7.

each planet, including the earth, endowed with a soul, whose constant powers are shown in the planetary whirlings. More's main purpose, however, was to reinterpret this vagrant idea in terms which would give it better standing in the new scientific current, and, of course, without prejudice to his religious views. In the preface to the *Immortality of the Soul* he calls the spirit of nature "the vicarious power of God upon the matter," that is, the immediate plastic agent of God through which his will is fulfilled in the material world. It corresponds in nature as a whole to the animal spirits supposed to pervade the nervous and circulatory systems of an individual, through whose agency the purpose of the soul is transmitted to the various organs and limbs. Its functions are vital, vegetative, and directive, but it is not itself conscious. More defines it more carefully as "a substance incorporeal, but without sense and animadversion, pervading the whole matter of the universe, and exercising a plastic power therein, according to the sundry predispositions and occasions in the parts it works upon (note his contentment with vague and general statements here), raising such phenomena in the world, by directing the parts of the matter, and their motion, as cannot be resolved into mere mechanical powers." [34] He adds more specifically still in a note that it possesses life, but not sense, animadversion, reason, or free-will. However, More is eager to guard against the charge that by invoking as causes incorporeal spiritual substances he is weakening the zest for exact scientific treatment of natural phenomena and the growing faith in the possibility of their reduction to regular, orderly principles. This spirit of nature, he says, is to be held a genuine cause, yet it is dependable and uniform in its manifestations, hence the careful scientific study of the *how* of things is not superseded or prejudiced. "I affirm with Descartes, that nothing affects our sense but such variations of matter as are made by differences of motion, figure, position of parts, etc., but I dissent from him in this, that I hold it is not mere and pure mechanical motion that causes all these sensible modifications in matter, but that many times the immediate director thereof

[34] *Immortality of the Soul,* Bk. III, Ch. 12, Par. 1.

is this spirit of nature, one and the same everywhere, and *acting always alike upon the like occasions, as a clearminded man, and of a solid judgment, gives always the same verdict in the same circumstances.*" [35] It is chiefly in this respect that More wishes to distinguish his conception from that of the ancient and medieval *anima mundi* (an interest which itself reveals the widespread influence of the exact ideal of the new science), and hopes thereby to obviate the objection of those who, like Descartes, opposed the injection of such a principle into natural philosophy while it seemed still possible that all the phenomena might be explained on a purely mechanical basis. In effect, his position is that mechanical causes produce types of motion that are not exhaustive of all motion—they produce only the kind of motion that obeys the basic laws of motion. But there are also these phenomena of gravity, cohesion, magnetism, etc., revealing other forces and motions not mechanical, but yet without which the universe that we know and live in could not exist. Since these forces are not mechanical they must be spiritual (*e.g.,* the Cartesian dualism), and something akin to the spirit of nature offers itself as the most suitable explanatory entity. More thus sums up his fundamental conclusions on this subject: "I have . . . from mechanical principles, granted on all sides, and confirmed by experience, demonstrated that the descent . . . of a stone, or a bullet, or any such like heavy body, is enormously contrary to the laws of mechanics; and that according to them they would necessarily, if they lie loose, recede from the earth and be carried away out of our sight into the farthest parts of the air, if some power more than mechanical did not curb that motion, and force them downwards towards the earth. . . . Nor . . . needs the acknowledgment of this principle to dampen our endeavours in the search of the mechanical causes of the phenomena of nature, but rather make us more circumspect to distinguish what is the result of the mere mechanical powers of matter and motion, and what of a higher principle. For questionless this secure presumption in some, that there is nothing but matter in the world, has emboldened

[35] *Immortality of the Soul,* Bk. III, Ch. 13, Par. 7. Italics ours.

them too rashly to venture on mechanical solutions where they would not hold." [36]

But finally, for More, this all-pervading order and harmony in the world itself implies the existence of incorporeal substance of a yet higher order than the spirit of nature, a spiritual substance rational, purposive, supremely worthy of obedience and worship. "We have discovered out of the simple phenomenon of motion [*i.e.,* its ultimate cause] the necessity of the existence of some incorporeal essence distinct from the matter. But there is a further assurance of this truth, from the consideration of the order and admirable effect of this motion in the world. Suppose matter could move itself, could mere matter, with self-motion, amount to that admirable wise contrivance of things which we see in the world? Can a blind impetus produce such effects, with that accuracy and constancy, that the more wise a man is, the more he will be assured, that no wisdom can add, take away, or alter anything in the works of nature, whereby they may be bettered? How can that therefore which has not so much as sense, arise to the effects of the highest reason or intellect?" [37] More is convinced by such teleological proofs that there exists a supremely wise creator and governor of the universe, whose agent and subordinate medium in the execution of his purposes is this lower incorporeal being, the spirit of nature.

E. Space as the Divine Presence

Now since every thing real is extended, God too, for More, must be an extended being. To deny him extension would be to reduce him to a mathematical point; it would read him out of the universe altogether. More's devout religious interest, coupled with his keen appreciation of the scientific current of

[36] *Immortality of the Soul,* Preface.

[37] *Immortality of the Soul,* Bk. I, Ch. 12. Cf. also *Antidote to Atheism* (same collection) Bk. II, Chs. 1, 2; *Divine Dialogues,* p. 29, ff., etc.

the day, led him to feel instinctively that the only way to save a proper place for God in the new metaphysical terminology of the times was to declare boldly for the divine extension throughout all space and all time. This was one of the significant points at issue between More and Descartes. In his first letter to the latter More declared: "You define matter or body in too broad a fashion, for it seems that not only God, but even the angels, and everything which exists by itself, is an extended being; whence extension appears to possess no narrower limits than the absolute essence of things, though it can nevertheless be diversified in accordance with the variety of the same essences. Now the reason which makes me believe that God is extended in his fashion, is that he is omnipresent, and fills intimately the whole universe and each of its parts; for how could he communicate motion to matter, as he has done betimes, and as he is actually doing according to you, if he did not have immediate contact with matter. . . . God is therefore extended and expanded after his fashion; whence God is an extended being." [38] Descartes' reply[39] to this contention was that God is indeed extended *in power,* that is, he is able to move matter at any point, but that this was essentially different from the exact geometrical extension attributable to matter. More, however, was not satisfied. "By true extension you understand that which is accompanied with the faculty of being touched and possesses impenetrability. I admit with you that this is not the case with God, with an angel, and with the soul, which are devoid of matter; but I maintain that there is in angels, and in souls, just as true an extension, however little acknowledged by the run of the schools." [40] Hence in the case of the vase emptied of air, an illustration used by Descartes, who asserted that either some other material must enter the vase or else its sides would fall into mutual contact, More was prepared stoutly to maintain that this was no necessary conclusion—the divine extension

---

[38] *Oeuvres de Descartes* (Cousin), Vol. X, p. 181.

[39] *Oeuvres,* X., p. 195, ff.

[40] Second Letter, *Oeuvres,* X, p. 212, ff.

might fill the vase and hold its sides apart.[41] At the same time More, no more than Descartes or Hobbes, seriously entertained the idea of a vacuum in nature. Matter is doubtless infinite, because "the divine creative activity, never idle at any point, has created matter in all places, without leaving the least minute space void." [42]

The suggestion of the vase, however, filled with naught but the divine extension, leads to More's interesting and important conception of space and its relation to the divine being. For Descartes, space and matter were the same thing, a material body being nothing but a limited portion of extension. Hobbes, in his struggles with the doctrine of primary and secondary qualities, had been led to distinguish between space and extension. You can suppose all bodies of matter annihilated, but you cannot succeed in thinking away space. Therefore space is a phantasm, an imaginary thing of the mind, while extension remains an essential quality of bodies which exist, of course, quite independently of those motions in human brains which make up the mind. More agrees with Hobbes that matter can be thought away without thereby space being successfully eliminated, but he draws an entirely different conclusion from the fact.[43] If space cannot be thought away, it must be a real existence underlying all extended substances in the universe, and posssesing a list of most remarkable qualities. Matter may be infinite, but none the less it is thoroughly distinct from this limitless immobile substratum or space against which its varied movements become measurable. More attacked Descartes' doctrine of the relativity of motion, holding that an absolute, homogeneous, unchanging space was presupposed by motion and its measurability. Otherwise, he maintained, one is forced into self-contradiction.[44] Take, for example, three bodies AB, CD, and EF

[41] First Letter, *Oeuvres,* X, p. 184.

[42] Second Letter, *Oeuvres,* X, p. 223.

[43] *Enchiridion,* Ch. 8.

[44] *Enchiridion,* Ch. 7, Par. 5. Cf. an argument involving similar premises in *Divine Dialogues,* p. 52, ff.

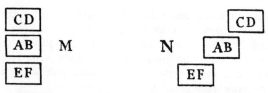

in the position M, and let them change their relations so as to appear as at N. Now, then, AB has moved to the right in relation to EF, and to the left in relation to CD, that is, it has moved in opposite directions at the same time. More holds that the only way out of this contradiction is to affirm an absolute space in which AB has remained at rest. This is, of course, a failure to appreciate fully the doctrine of relativity, and the contradiction results only because the point of reference in the bodies is changed; but what More is concerned to maintain is really something deeper, namely that the fact and the measurability of motion imply the assumption of an infinite geometrical system as a real existent background of the world of nature, in terms of which the measurement is made. What sensible body we take to be at rest in this system as the centre of our coordinates is a matter of complete indifference as far as the principle of absolute space is concerned.

This absolute space thus defended, More finds to be a most marvellous being. It must be a real existence, because it is infinitely extended, yet being absolutely distinguished from matter, it has no corporeal characteristics whatever except extension.[45] Therefore, according to his premises, it must be a genuine spiritual substance, and as More reflects further about it it becomes more and more exalted to his mind. He lists no fewer than twenty attributes which can be applied both to God and to space: each is "one, simple, immobile, eternal, perfect, independent, existing by itself, subsisting through itself, incorruptible, necessary, immense, uncreated, uncircumscribed, incomprehensible, omnipresent, incorporeal, permeating and embracing all things, essential being, actual being, pure actuality." The ascription of this remarkable list of epithets to space is a significant illustration of how religious spirits in sympathy with the new mathematical movement

[45] *Enchiridion,* Ch. 8, Par. 7.

found in infinite space the true substitute, in terms of the geometrical view of the universe, for the Pure Form or Absolute Actuality of Aristotelianism. On the continent this religious corollary of the new order found its great champion in Malebranche, to whom space became practically God himself.

More did not go quite as far as this. In the *Antidote against Atheism*, written prior to 1662, he suggests three possible views of space, evidently uncertain which to adopt.[46] One is that space is the immensity or omnipresence of the divine essence; the second, that it is simply the possibility of matter, distance being no real or physical property, but merely the negation of tactual union, etc.; and the third, that space is no other than God himself. In his last important work, the *Enchiridion Metaphysicum*, published in 1671, More is prepared to tell us his final choice between these possibilities.[47]

---

[46] *Antidote against Atheism*, Appendix, Ch. 7. "If there were no matter, but the immensity of the divine essence only, occupying all by his ubiquity, then the reduplication, as I may so speak, of his indivisible substance, whereby he presents himself everywhere, would be the subject of that diffusion and mensurability. And I add further, that the perpetual observation of this infinite amplitude and mensurability, which we cannot disimagine in our fancy . . . may be a more rude and obscure notion offered to our mind of that necessary and self-existent essence which the idea of God does with greater fulness and distinctness represent to us."
"There is also another way of answering this objection, which is this; that this imagination of space is not the imagination of any real thing, but only of the large and immense capacity of the potentiality of the matter, which we cannot free our minds from. . . ."
"If, after the removal of corporeal matter out of the world, there will be still space and distance, in which this very matter, while it was there, was also conceived to lie, and this distant space cannot but be something, and yet not corporeal because neither impenetrable nor tangible, it must of necessity be a substance incorporeal, necessarily and eternally existent of itself; which the clearer idea of a Being absolutely perfect will more fully and punctually inform us to be the self-subsisting God."

[47] *Enchiridion*, Ch. 8, Par. 8, ff.

The second that of space as potentiality, he rejects as definitely unsatisfactory, but he does not quite venture to say that space is itself God without considerable qualification from the first position. He expresses his conclusion thus: "I have clearly shown that this infinite extension, which commonly is held to be mere space, is in truth a certain substance, and that it is incorporeal or a spirit. . . . This immense *locus internus* or space really distinct from the matter, which we conceive in our understanding, is a certain rather rude ὑπογραφή, . . . a certain rather confused and vague representation of the divine essence or essential presence, in so far as it is distinguished from his life and activities. For none of these attributes which we have been recounting [*i.e.*, the twenty listed above] appear to concern the divine life and activity, but simply his bare essence and existence." [48] Elsewhere he presents the same thought in a somewhat more worshipful mood: "That spiritual object, which we call space, is only a passing shadow, which represents for us, in the weak light of our intellect, the true and universal nature of the continuous divine presence, till we are able to perceive it directly with open eyes and at a nearer distance." [49] In other words, space is God so far as he is omnipresent merely, abstracting from the other characteristics which concern his life and power. But its spiritual character is something essential. Space is divine. A mechanical world alone would inevitably fly into pieces, by the unhampered operation of the laws of motion. All continuity in the universe—this immobile, incorporeal space as well as those invisible forces such as gravity and cohesion, which hold together in one system the different parts of the cosmic frame— is fundamentally spiritual.[50] "The prop and stay of things is God's benignity." [51]

Ralph Cudworth, the second most influential of the Cambridge thinkers, did not venture to adopt More's bold hypoth-

[48] *Enchiridion*, Ch. 8, Par. 14, ff.

[49] *Opera Omnia*, London, 1675–9, Vol. I, p. 171, ff.

[50] Compare with the pre-Socratic notion of the world as the product of the opposite forces Love and Strife.

[51] *A Platonic Song of the Soul*, Part II, Canto 4, Stanza 14.

esis of the spatiality of God; in his case a thorough familiarity with the ancient philosophers and a consuming zeal to confute atheists kept him from developing such a scientific interest in the detailed progress of the mechanical philosophy, as had been also an obvious motive in More. Hence his religious interest expresses itself not in an attempt to force a theistic metaphysics into the categories of the new science at any cost, but rather by a return to Platonic and Aristotelian thought. But it is interesting to observe how, even in a thinker essentially conservative and failing to share the dominant interests of the main current of his day, certain of its significant results had taken firm root. He adopts the doctrine of the mechanical structure of the material universe and the notion of primary and secondary qualities approvingly, observing that the real difficulty is not to explain forms and qualities in terms of magnitudes, figures, motions, and the like, but how to account for souls and minds on any such basis. He is confident that a consistent pursuit of the mechanical philosophy would inevitably lead to the admission of incorporeal beings, especially one supreme spiritual Deity. Cudworth brings forward five reasons for this assurance.[52] First, the atomical hypothesis, allowing nothing to body but extension and its modes, "cannot possibly make life and cogitation to be qualities of body; since they are neither contained in those things . . . nor can result from any conjugation of them. Wherefore it must needs be granted, that life and cogitation are the attributes of another substance distinct from body, or incorporeal. Again . . . since no body could ever move itself, it follows undeniably, that there must be something else in the world besides body, or else there could never have been any motion in it. Moreover, according to this philosophy, the corporeal phenomena themselves cannot be solved by mechanism alone without fancy (reference to Hobbes' theory). Now fancy is no mode of body, and therefore must needs be a mode of some other kind of being in ourselves, that is cogitative and incorporeal. Furthermore, . . . sense itself is not a mere

[52] Cudworth, *The True Intellectual System of the Universe*, Bk. I, Ch. 1, Pars. 27, 28, 38, 39.

corporeal passion from bodies without, in that . . . there is nothing really in bodies like to those fantastic ideas that we have of sensible things, as of hot and cold, red and green, bitter and sweet, and the like, which therefore must needs owe their being to some activity of the soul itself; and this is all one as to make it incorporeal. Lastly . . . sense is not the κριτήριον of truth concerning bodies themselves . . . from whence it plainly follows, that there is something in us superior to sense, which judges of it, detects its fantastry, and condemns its imposture, and determines what really is and is not, in bodies without us, which must needs be a higher self-active vigour of the mind, that will plainly speak it to be incorporeal." [53] At the same time, the mechanical philosophy does offer an adequate and satisfactory explanation of the material world, and hence for Cudworth it definitely supersedes the scholastic forms and qualities, an explanation in terms of which "is nothing else but to say, that it is done we know not how; or, which is yet more absurd, to make our very ignorance of the cause, disguised under those terms of forms and qualities, to be itself the cause of the effect."

Cudworth is thus thinking in general conformity with the main outlines of the Cartesian dualism, and for him, as for every one else in the century with the possible exception of Hobbes, all ultimate difficulties, metaphysical or epistemological, are resolved by the appeal to God.

F. Barrow's Philosophy of Method, Space, and Time

Isaac Barrow (1630–77), Newton's intimate friend, teacher, and predecessor in the Lucasian chair of mathematics at Cambridge, is usually counted important in the history of his century as a mathematician and theologian only. In his mathematical and geometrical lectures, however, he offers some remarks on mathematical method, space, and time, which have significant metaphysical bearings; also he, like More, influ-

[53] He speaks of the soul as extended, however. Cf. Bk. III, Ch. 1, Sect. 3.

enced strongly the metaphysical thinking of Newton. Hence it seems appropriate to consider his importance in the present chapter. Newton was a student at Cambridge during the entire period of Barrow's mathematical interest, and it is known that he attended the latter's lectures. After 1664 their friendship became quite intimate, and in 1669 Newton revised and edited Barrow's geometrical lectures, adding the last lecture himself, with perhaps parts of the others. It is hardly possible, however, that the discussion of time, in which we are principally interested, should have been the work of Newton, inasmuch as it covers practically the entire first lecture, and had Newton been the author we should certainly have record of the fact.

Barrow's views on mathematical method and on space appear most prominently in his *Lectiones mathematicae,* delivered in the years 1664–66. With regard to the former he comes as near as any philosopher of the century to a clear perception and statement of just what the method of the victorious mathematical physicists was, but his failure to see all the way through and to propound a coherent and consistent programme, for the use of scientific enquirers, of mathematical units, hypothesis, experiment, etc., is most tantalizing.

After a few preliminary remarks on the history of mathematics, Barrow observes that the object of the science is *quantity,* which may be considered either in its pure form, as in geometry and arithmetic, or in its mixed form, united with non-mathematical qualities.[54] For example, a straight line may be considered in its pure and absolute form, as in geometry, or it may be considered as the distance between the centres of two bodies, or as the path of the centre of a body, as in astronomy, optics, or mechanics. The geometer simply abstracts magnitude in general as his object, just as any other scientist abstracts that which appears to be the essential nature of whatever portion of phenomena he is studying. The attempt to speak of the mathematician as dealing with an ideal or intelligible realm as opposed to the realm of sensible objects is mistaken: it is the sensible realm, so far as it is intelligible,

[54] *The Mathematical Works of Isaac Barrow D.D.* (Whewell edition), Cambridge, 1860, Vol. I, p. 30, ff.

especially so far as it reveals quantitative continuity, that is the object of all science.[55] Thus physics, so far as it is a science, is wholly mathematical, likewise all of mathematics is applied in physics, hence we may say that the two sciences are co-extensive and equal.[56] Similarly in astronomy, once its special postulates are laid down, all the reasoning is purely geometrical. In fact, Barrow regards geometry as distinctly the type science in mathematics (following his predecessors); algebra is not a part of mathematics but a kind of logic used in it, while arithmetic is included in geometry, numbers only possessing mathematical significance when the units of which they are composed are equal, *i.e.,* when they are equal parts of a continuous homogeneous quantity.[57] Now it is such a quantity that is the object of geometry, and mathematical numbers are thus nothing more than marks or signs of geometrical magnitudes.[58] Barrow here appears a true English nominalist, and is evidently maintaining (in agreement with Hobbes and More) that everything genuinely existent must be conceived as extended. Weights, forces, and times, Barrow holds, are extended in some sense, inasmuch as they are treated as geometrical quantities.[59]

Next, Barrow attempts a description of the method of geometrical investigation and demonstration.[60] His first statement of it is exceedingly vague and general,[61] but his summary a few pages later is somewhat better. Mathematicians "take up for contemplation those features of which they have in their minds clear and distinct ideas, they give these appropriate, adequate and unchanging names; then, for the investigation of their properties and the construction of true conclusions about them, they apply *a priori* only certain axioms which are ex-

[55] Barrow, p. 38, ff.

[56] Barrow, p. 44, ff.

[57] Barrow, p. 53, ff.

[58] Barrow, p. 56.

[59] Barrow, p. 134, ff.

[60] Barrow, p. 65, ff.

[61] Barrow, p. 75, ff. Cf. also p. 89, 115, ff.

ceedingly familiar, indubitable, and few in number. Similarly the hypotheses which they set up *a priori* are very few, in the highest degree consonant with reason, and undeniable by any sane mind." In this manner mathematical science becomes unique in its cogency.[62] Barrow, somewhat repetitive here, lists eight specific reasons for the certainty of geometry; the clearness of the conceptions involved, the unambiguous definitions of mathematical terms, the intuitive assurance and universal truth of its axioms, the clear possibility and easy imaginability of its postulates and hypotheses, the small number of its axioms, the clear conceivability of the mode by which magnitudes are supposed to be generated, the easy order of the demonstrations, and finally the fact that mathematicians pass by what they do not know, or are not certain of, "preferring to acknowledge their ignorance than rashly to affirm any thing." Even the positivism of the new movement had touched Barrow.

How, now, we may ask, are we sure of the truth of those principles by which we confidently apply geometry to the study of nature? Barrow holds that these are ultimately derived from reason, sensed objects being merely the occasion which awakens them.[63] "Who ever saw, or distinguished by any sense, an exact straight line, or a perfect circle?" Reason perceives, however, thus stimulated by sense, that geometrical figures really exist in the sensible world, though not visibly or tangibly; they are like the statue which exists in the block of marble upon which the sculptor is working. At the same time, Barrow affirms, if you prefer to believe with Aristotle that all general propositions are derived by induction, you must still admit the universal validity of mathematical principles, because they have been confirmed by constant experience, and God is immutable. Mathematics is thus the perfect and certain science.[64] The way to get the fullest knowledge possible is always to define your object in terms of those properties from which mathematical deductions can be drawn in the simplest

[62] Barrow, p. 66, ff.
[63] Barrow, p. 82, ff.
[64] Barrow, p. 90, ff.

fashion. Barrow reaches this conclusion rather hazily and without perceiving its full import for physical science; later on in the course of lectures, however, he attacks the problem from another angle and appears to make a somewhat closer approximation to clarity.

Mathematics is fundamentally, Barrow observes, a science of measurement.[65] Now anything whatever may be used as a measure—we may measure our distance from a fire by the degree of heat experienced, or from a flower by its odour, just as we may measure a longer distance by the time employed by a traveller or a ship.[66] But we hardly speak of such measurement as mathematical. Now, wherever possible, mathematical measurement is the simplest and easiest manner of such determination, because it measures in terms of a definite unit which is homogeneous with the thing measured, and thus gives the resulting measure an exact numerical form.[67] Hence that is said to be known in a peculiar sense which is expressed by numerical relation to some definite, known quantity which we thus take as a unit.[68] Till quantities are reduced to such numerical expressions they are judged unknown, inasmuch as immediate judgments of sense about its world lack the clearness of number, they cannot be conceived so easily by the mind, nor held so well in the memory because of their fickle, changeable character; and only by numbers can the quantities of all things be reduced to a few familiar and commonly adopted measures.

The only omission in this discussion is definite direction how to disentangle among those characteristics of an object that have been hitherto unreduced to mathematics, a unit in terms of which they can be numerically expressed. Perhaps we should not blame Barrow too heavily for this failure, however, since for that science has still to wait.

Barrow's religious interest appears above in his postulate of the constancy of nature; he goes on to affirm that all demon-

[65] Barrow, p. 216.
[66] Barrow, p. 223.
[67] Barrow, p. 226, ff.
[68] Barrow, p. 239, ff.

stration presupposes the existence of God. "I say that all demonstration assumes the truth of hypotheses [postulates, we should say]; the truth of an hypothesis attributes to the thing which is assumed a possible existence; this possibility involves an efficient cause of the thing (otherwise it would be impossible for it to exist); the efficient cause of all things is God." [69] This religious reference appears more strongly, however, in his discussion of space and time.

One of the important attributes of geometrical magnitudes is, that they occupy space.[70] What is space? It is impious, Barrow observes, to regard space as a real existence independent of God; likewise to regard matter as infinitely extended is contrary to scripture. But, if we discover the proper relation between space and God, we can truthfully ascribe a real existence to the former. God can create worlds beyond this world, hence God must extend beyond matter, and it is just this superabundance of the divine presence and power that we mean by space.[71] Apart from this religious reference, however, space cannot be described as anything actually existing[72]; it is "nothing else than pure simple potency, mere capacity, ponibility, or . . . interponibility of some magnitude."

Here is an interesting combination of ideas about space with which More was playing at the same time; in fact, inasmuch as both men were resident in Cambridge, it is likely that the thinking of each was directly influenced by the other. More was not much interested in time, however, whereas Barrow, having come to conceive of geometrical magnitudes as generated by motion, and being zealously engaged in the attempt to construct a geometrical calculus on the basis of this conception, was just as much interested in time as in space. And in his views on time, which are offered in the *Lectiones geometricae*, probably written before the above discourses on method and space, he appears in a somewhat more original light.

After noting some of the interesting features of time, es-

[69] Barrow, p. 111.
[70] Barrow, p. 149, ff.
[71] Barrow, p. 154.
[72] Barrow, p. 158, ff.

pecially its quantitative character, Barrow asks whether there was time before the creation of the world, and whether it flows now beyond the limits of the world, where nothing persists.[73] His answer is:

Just as there was space before the world was founded, and even now there is an infinite space beyond the world (with which God co-exists) . . . so before the world and together with the world (perhaps beyond the world) time was, and is; since before the world arose, certain beings were able continually to remain in existence [God and the angels presumably], so now things may exist beyond the world capable of such permanence. . . . Time, therefore, does not denote an actual existence, but simply a capacity or possibility of permanent existence; just as space indicates the capacity of an intervening magnitude. . . . But does time not imply motion? Not at all, I reply, as far as its absolute, intrinsic nature is concerned; no more than rest; the quantity of time depends on neither essentially; whether things run or stand still, whether we sleep or wake, time flows in its even tenor. Imagine all the stars to have remained fixed from their birth; nothing would have been lost to time; as long would that stillness have endured as has continued the flow of this motion. Before, after, at the same time (as far as concerns the rise and disappearance of things), even in that tranquil state would have had their proper existence, and might by a more perfect mind have been perceived. But although those magnitudes are quantities absolutely, independent of all reference to measure, yet we cannot perceive their quantities except by the application of measures; thus time is in itself a quantity, although, that the quantity of time may be distinguished by us, the aid of motion must be called in as a measure by which we judge temporal quantities and compare them with each other; and so time as something measurable implies motion, since if all things had remained unmoved, in no way would we be able to distinguish how much time had flowed past;

[73] Barrow, Vol. II, p. 160, ff.

the age of things would have been indistinguishable to us and its growth would have been undiscoverable.[74]

. . . It is not apparent to those aroused from sleep how much time has intervened; but from this it is not rightly deduced that, "It is clear, that apart from motion and change there is no time." We do not perceive it clearly, hence it does not exist—a piece of deceptive inference—and sleep is deceptive, which causes us to connect two distant instants of time. . . . Moreover, since we conceive time as flowing past always in an even channel, not now more slowly, then more rapidly in turn (if indeed such disparity be granted, time would in no wise admit of computation or dimension), on that account not all motion is judged equally suited for determining and distinguishing the quantity of time, but chiefly that which, being in the highest degree simple and uniform, proceeds always in an even tenor; the mobile preserving always the same force, and being borne through a uniform medium. Wherefore to determine time some such mobile must be chosen as at least so far as concerns the periods of its motion, keeps constantly an equal impulse and covers an equal distance.

Barrow notes that the motions of the stars, and especially of the sun and moon, are generally accepted for this purpose, and then takes up the question how, if the measurement of time be thus dependent on motion, time may itself be, as defined, the measure of motion.

[74] The intervening part of the quotation shows again how far the Cartesian-Hobbesian philosophy was influencing even pious minds who were interested in science. "Do I say that we would not perceive the flow of time? Most certainly not, nor would we perceive anything else, but bound in a continued stupor we would remain stock still like posts or rocks. For we notice nothing except so far as some change affecting the sense disturbs us, or an internal operation of the mind stimulates our consciousness and excites it. It is from the extension or intension of motion pressing inward or raising a disturbance within us, that we judge the different degrees and quantities of things. So the quantity of motion, in so far as it can be noted by us, depends on the extension of motion."

But how, say you, do we know that the sun is carried by an equal motion, and that one day, for example, or one year, is exactly equal to another, or of equal duration? I reply that in no other way is this known to us (excepting what may be gathered from the divine testimony) than by comparing the motion of the sun itself with other equal motions. Certainly if the motion of the sun as registered in the sundial . . . be perceived to agree with the motions of any time-measuring instrument which is constructed with sufficient accuracy[75] . . . From which reasoning it seems to follow, which perchance may appear astonishing to some, that strictly speaking the celestial bodies are not actually the first and original measures of time; but rather those motions which are observed near us by the senses, and are subject to our experiments; since by their aid we judge the regularity of the celestial motions. Not even is Sol himself a worthy judge of time, or to be accepted as a veracious witness, except so far as time-measuring instruments attest his veracity by their votes.

Barrow adds that there is no way at all of comparing the periods of the celestial revolutions now with those many centuries ago, hence it is not possible to declare for certain that Methusaleh was really longer lived than a modern who failed of his hundredth year. He then answers the specific problem of the ultimate relation of time and motion, as had his predecessors the ultimate relation of space and extension.

Nor let anyone object that time is commonly regarded as the measure of motion, and that consequently differences of motion (swifter, slower, accelerated, retarded) are defined by assuming time as known; and that therefore the quantity of time is not determined by motion but the quantity of motion by time: for nothing prevents time and motion from rendering each other mutual aid in this respect. Clearly, just as we measure space, first by some magnitude, and learn how much it is, later judging other congruent magnitudes by space; so we first reckon time from some

[75] The sentence is incomplete in the original.

motion and afterwards judge other motions by it; which is plainly nothing else than to compare some motions with others by the mediation of time; just as by the mediation of space we investigate the relations of magnitudes with each other. . . . Further, since time, as has been shown, is a quantity uniformly extended, all of whose parts correspond to the respective parts of an equable motion, or proportionately to the parts of space traversed by an equable motion, it can be represented, that is, proposed to our mind or fantasy, in a most successful manner by any homogeneous magnitude; especially by the simplest, such as a straight or circular line; between which and time there are also not a few similarities and analogies.[76]

This lengthy disquisition has been presented almost entire, because it represents beautifully a natural and logical step in the development of a philosophy of time comparable to that of space common in England at the time of More and Barrow, and it clearly leads up to the conception of time advanced in Newton. In the case of both space and time Barrow admits the validity of More's religious approach; considered as real and absolute existences they are nothing but the omnipresence and the eternal duration of God. But Barrow was likewise inter-

[76] The balance of the passage elucidates this point somewhat further. "For besides the fact that time has parts which are wholly similar, it accords with reason to consider it as a quantity endowed with a single dimension; for we conceive it constituted either by the simple addition of successive moments, or by the (so to speak) continued flow of a single moment, whence we are accustomed to attribute to it length alone; nor do we determine its quantity in any other way than by the length of a traversed line. Just as I say, a line is regarded as the path of a moving point, possessing from the point a certain indivisibility, but from the motion divisibility of one kind, that is according to length; so time is conceived as the path of an instant continually flowing, possessing a certain indivisibility from the instant, but divisible in so far as it is a successive flow. And just as the quantity of a line depends on length alone, the result of motion, so the quantity of time follows from a single succession spread out, as it were, in length; which the length of the traversed space proves and determines. So we shall always represent time by a straight line . . ."

ested in another approach, that of positive mathematical science. From this point of view they are nothing really existing, but merely express potentialities of magnitude and duration. Why, then, when discussing them from the scientific point of view, does Barrow not drop the absolutistic terminology and treat space and time as purely relative to magnitude and motion, inasmuch as practically that is how they must always be treated? In part, doubtless, because Barrow has evidently formed a clearer and more definite conception of the meaning of time as a distinct mathematical dimension, but mainly because the validity of the other approach never disappears from sight. Time is not a metaphysically independent entity. Barrow never forgot that there was an infinite and everliving God, whose existence beyond the world involved space, and whose continued life before the creation of things in motion involved time. It was just because they were caught up in the unchangeable divine nature that space and time possessed that clarity and fixity which made it possible to compare with exactness by their aid sensible magnitudes and motions. Hence even when he no longer notes the specifically religious reference it is implicitly present; he can speak of time as "flowing in its even tenor," as "independent of motion as far as its absolute and intrinsic nature is concerned," as "an absolute quantity, independent of all reference to measure," and the like. We shall find these remarks on time a helpful introduction to the portrayal of it in the chief work of his illustrious pupil.

In the meantime let us not forget our larger bearings. Galileo's mathematical analysis of motion had thrust upon the attention of the philosophically-minded two strange new entities, which had to be taken account of, and for those in the onward march of the times used as basic categories in place of the old scholastic substances, essences, and the like. Space and time acquired new meanings, and became of central importance in men's thinking. What should be done with them philosophically? Descartes, bold metaphysician that he was, had an answer ready as regards space—he seized upon it as the very substance of the material universe, crowding into the immaterial world of thought whatever could not be fully treated geometrically. Pious English thinkers like More and Barrow sensed the religious danger of this summary dualism, and attempted to bring the conception of God up to date so that space would no longer appear independent of the deity; likewise, following Hobbes, they made a more fundamental distinction between space and matter. It took somewhat longer, however, for a philosophy of time to develop. Descartes had been unable to do it, partly because time was obviously a mode of thinking substance as well as of *res extensa*, but more because he considered motion as a mathematical conception in general and had failed to appreciate Galileo's ideal of its detailed quantitative formulation. When men gradually attempted, however, to make more precise the notions and interrelations of force, acceleration, momentum, velocity, etc., it was natural that they found themselves compelled to an exact statement of what they meant by time. As they grew more confident on this point, time came gradually to seem as natural and self-justifying a continuum as space, quite as independent of human perception and knowledge, and to be metaphysically disposed of on the same principles. This stage in the development of a philosophy of time we reach first distinctly in Barrow. Just as space had ceased to appear accidental to objects and relative to magnitudes, and became a vast, infinite substance existing in its own right (except for its relation to God) so time ceased to be regarded merely as the measure of motion, and became a mysterious something ultimately of religious significance, but quite independent of motion, in fact measured now by it, flowing on from everlasting to everlasting in its even mathematical course. From being a realm of substances in qualitative and teleological relations the world of nature had definitely become a realm of bodies moving mechanically in space and time.

CHAPTER VI. GILBERT AND BOYLE

Hobbes' classic works had appeared in the forties and fifties of the seventeenth century; Newton's *Principia* was finished in 1687. During the intervening generation English thought was affected to a considerable extent by the writings of men like More, Cudworth, and Barrow, but more powerfully moved by the discoveries and publications of the great physicist and chemist Robert Boyle. Newton's thinking on ultimate problems bears as obvious marks of his lucid and many-sided mind as it does of the religious metaphysic of the Cambridge leader. For Boyle, although not commonly recognized as such, was a thinker of genuine philosophical calibre.

But before we attempt a presentation of the fundamentals of Boyle's philosophy, it will be helpful to bring together a few threads which should now be united in our minds as we pass on to Newton via the metaphysics of the father of modern atomic chemistry.

More's conception of a "spirit of nature," an active, nourishing, generating, directing agent, through whom the will of God becomes expressed in the world of matter, is apt to be somewhat puzzling to modern students, though in essence the notion is simple and it came to play a quite understandable part in the newly-evolving philosophy of science. Its connexions with the ancient idea of the "soul of the world" and its similarity of function in the world at large to the "animal spirits" within the nervous and circulatory system of an individual have been already remarked upon. More, it will be remembered, had insisted that this spirit of nature is an incorporeal, spiritual being, though without conscious intelligence or purpose, and had pounced upon it to explain such phenomena as gravity and magnetism, which seemed to him obvious evidence of non-mechanical forces in nature. Boyle, too, is convinced that clear thinking must admit something of the sort, and it is of central importance in Newton. We need a somewhat larger background for this conception.

A. The Non-Mathematical Scientific Current

Back in the days of Kepler and Galileo, besides the exact mathematical movement in science, so powerfully advanced by their achievements and bringing in its train the remarkable metaphysical revolution which it seemed to imply, there was another scientific current under way, flowing by slower and more tentative steps, but none the less scientific in interest and fruitfulness. Its method was wholly empirical and experimental rather than mathematical, and it was primarily in connexion with this other current that attempts to give science a correct metaphysical groundwork made a quite positive and definite appeal to this "spirit of nature," or, as it was more commonly called, "ethereal spirit."

William Gilbert, the father of scientific magnetism, whose classic work *On the Loadstone and Magnetic Bodies* appeared in the year 1600, was one of the luminaries of this non-mathematical scientific current. We shall not pause for a study of the details of his work, but the conviction into which he was led by the phenomena of magnetism, that the earth is fundamentally a huge magnet,[1] is of interest and importance. Gilbert conceives the interior of the earth as composed of a homogeneous magnetic substance[2]; the earth's cohesion and likewise its diurnal revolution about its poles being thus accounted for, since "a spherical loadstone, floated in water, moves circularly on its centre to become conformed to the earth on the plane of the equator."[3] Moreover, as all but the

[1] William Gilbert of Colchester, *On the Loadstone and Magnetic Bodies*, Mottelay translation, New York, 1893, p. 64, ff.

[2] Gilbert, p. 313, ff.

[3] Gilbert, p. 331.

very surface of the earth is of a homogeneous structure, the geometrical centre of the earth is also the centre of its magnetic movements.[4] Gilbert was one of the earliest champions in England of the Copernican theory as regards the diurnal revolution of the earth[5]; he did not accept the more radical position that the earth also revolves around the sun, though holding that the latter is the first mover and inciter of the planetary motions. Further, it is to Gilbert's experiments on magnetism that we owe the first beginnings of the use and conception of the word "mass" as we find it later matured in Newton. According to Gilbert, the strength and reach of a loadstone's magnetism varies according to its quantity or mass,[6] that is, if it be of uniform purity and from a specified mine. Galileo and Kepler borrowed the notion of mass from Gilbert in this sense and connexion.

Now Gilbert, like the other fathers of modern science, was not content simply to note and formulate the results of his experiments; he sought ultimate explanations of the phenomena. How can a loadstone attract a piece of iron that is separated from it in space? His answer in essence was one which had been current in ancient times; magnetism is interpreted animistically. Magnetic force is something "animate," [7] it "imitates a soul," nay, it "surpasses the human soul while united to an organic body," because though the latter "uses reason, sees many things, investigates many more; but however well equipped, it gets light and the beginnings of knowledge from the outer senses, as from beyond a barrier—hence the very many ignorances and foolishnesses whereby our judgments and our life-actions are confused, so that few or none do rightly and duly order their acts." [8] But the magnet sends forth its energy "without error . . . quick, definite, constant, directive,

[4] Gilbert, p. 150.

[5] Gilbert, p. 344.

[6] Gilbert, p. 152, ff.

[7] Gilbert, p. 308, ff.

[8] Gilbert, p. 311.

motive, imperant, harmonious." [9] Thus the earth, since it is itself a great magnet, has a soul, which is none other than its magnetic force. "As for us, we deem the whole world animate, and all globes, all stars, and this glorious earth, too, we hold to be from the beginning by their own destinate souls governed and from them also to have the impulse of self-preservation. Nor are the organs required for organic action lacking, whether implanted in the homogenic nature or scattered through the homogenic body, albeit these organs are not made up of viscera as animal organs are, nor consist of definite members." [10] The power of this magnetic soul to act at a distance, which especially interested Gilbert, he explained by the conception of a magnetic effluvium emitted by the loadstone. This effluvium he supposes to reach out around the attracted body as a clasping arm and draw it to itself[11]; yet it is nothing corporeal at all; it "must needs be light and spiritual so as to enter the iron"; it is a breath or vapour which awakens within the attracted body a responding vapour. It is thus apparent that although Gilbert calls this magnetic effluvium incorporeal and spiritual, he does not mean that it is unextended or absolutely non-material in the Cartesian sense, but only that it is extremely thin like a rare atmosphere.[12] It is unlike matter in being penetrable and a motive power. The earth and every other astronomical body send out these magnetic effluvia to certain spatial limits, and the surrounding incorporeal ether thus composed shares the diurnal rotation of the body.[13] Beyond this ethereal vapour there is void space, in which the suns and planets, meeting no resistance, move by their own magnetic force. In his posthumous work, *De mundo nostro sublunari Philosophia Nova*, Gilbert discusses the relation between the earth and the moon in magnetic terms,[14] the earth

[9] Gilbert, p. 349.

[10] Gilbert, p. 309.

[11] Gilbert, p. 106, ff.

[12] Gilbert, p. 121, ff.

[13] Gilbert, p. 326.

[14] Book II, Chs. 18, 19, Amsterdam, 1651.

exercising the greater effect of the two because of its greater mass, but he is unable to make clear the principles which prevent the two from falling together.

William Harvey, discoverer of the circulation of the blood, in spite of his strong insistence on empiricism, admitted the conception of ethereal spirits to explain the passage of heat and nourishment from the sun to the heart and blood of living creatures[15]; and we are already aware how Descartes, whose physiology was greatly influenced by Harvey,[16] surreptitiously transferred to the ether those qualities which express themselves in the weight and varied velocity of bodies, in order that he might regard the bodies themselves as purely geometrical. In so doing Descartes gave the cue for the further harmonious development of the theory of an ethereal medium and the mathematico-mechanical interpretation of the universe. Secondary qualities of things had been banished to the realm of man; now those qualities which went beyond pure geometry but whose effects in motion Galileo had been reducing to mathematical formulae, or Gilbert and Harvey had been studying by sensible experiments, came to be thought of as somehow explicable through this ethereal medium, which was regarded by most as pervading all space. In it and by its determinate forces, the visible and tangible bodies moved. It was this distinction between solid bodies and the ether that More at once seized upon. Descartes' doctrine of the all-sufficiency of simple impact motion to account for every happening in the *res extensa,* More pronounced an unjustified assumption. The ethereal medium, whatever may be said about tangible bodies, was not a mere machine. If it were, the universe would rapidly dissipate, by the first law of motion. Qualities

[15] William Harvey, *On the Motion of the Heart and Blood in Animals* (Everyman edition), p. 57.

[16] Hobbes was also profoundly influenced by Harvey. In the Preface to the *Elements of Philosophy* he refers to Harvey as the founder of scientific physiology, forsooth because it was developed in terms of *motion.* He notes with envy that Harvey was the only man he knew of who was able to conquer prejudice sufficiently to achieve the complete revolution of a science within his lifetime.

and powers were assumed in it which were not mechanical. Therefore it must be spiritual, incorporeal, the active executor of the divine will, holding the frame of the world together in the phenomena of cohesion, magnetism, and gravity. At the same time its effects are regular and orderly, doubtless reducible to exact scientific law. All this complex of ideas was shared by Boyle, and passed from More and Boyle to Newton, in whose philosophy it played a distinctive part.

B. Boyle's Importance as Scientist and Philosopher

Robert Boyle exemplifies in most interesting fashion all the leading intellectual currents of his day; every important or prevalent interest and belief occupied some place in his thinking and the conglomeration was harmonized with considerable success around the foci of his two most dominant enthusiasms, experimental science and religion. Boyle defines philosophy as "a comprehension of all those truths or doctrines, which the natural reason of man, freed from prejudices and partiality, and assisted by learning, attention, exercise, experiments, etc., can manifestly make out, or by necessary consequence deduce from clear and certain principles." [17] His conception of the leading note of the scientific current of which he formed a part appears at the end of an attack on the highly dogmatic and metaphysical character of the scholastic philosophy. "Our great Verulam attempted with more skill and industry (and not without some indignation) to restore the more modest and useful way practised by the ancients, of inquiry into particular bodies without hastening to make systems, into the request it formerly had; wherein the admirable industry of two of our London physicians, Gilbert and Harvey, had not a little assisted him. And I need not tell you that since him Descartes, Gassendi, and others, having taken in the application of geometrical theorems for the explanation of physical problems; he

[17] *The Works of the Honourable Robert Boyle,* Birch edition, 6 Vols., London, 1672, Vol. IV, p. 168.

168

and they, and other restorers of natural philosophy, have
brought the experimental and mathematical way of inquiry
into nature, into at least as high and growing an esteem, as it
ever possessed when it was most in vogue among the naturalists that preceded Aristotle." [18] Boyle frequently mentions as
his three leading predecessors Bacon, Descartes, and Gassendi;
he remarks that he did not in his youth read them seriously
"that I might not be prepossessed with any theory or principles, till I had spent some time in trying what things themselves
would incline me to think" [19]; but now that he has begun to
examine their writings carefully he realizes that his essays
might have been enriched and some things better explained
had he read them before. As for Bacon, Boyle early joined a
small group of scientific inquirers pledged to the Baconian
spirit and purpose—an embryo Salomon's house—and he always
shared those many features of the chancellor's philosophy
which were in harmony with the other significant developments
of the time. In particular he carried forward the interest in
practical control of nature through knowledge of causes, which
had been such a prominent feature in Bacon, and which he
regards as closely related to the empirical method. If your
ultimate aim is to know, deductions from the atomical or
Cartesian principles are likely to give you most satisfaction;
if your aim is control of nature in the interest of particular
ends, you can often discover the necessary relations between
qualities immediately experienced, without ascending to the
top in the series of causes.[20] Gassendi's revival of Epicurean
atomism seemed to Boyle especially important, although he
never made significant use of its specific points of difference
from Descartes' cosmology, so that one suspects that the feeling of kinship was due more to Gassendi's empiricism than to
his atomic speculations. Boyle notes that the Cartesians and
atomists agree in explaining phenomena by small bodies variously figured and moved, the difference being on metaphysical rather than physical points, whence "their hypotheses

[18] Boyle, Vol. IV, p. 59.
[19] Boyle, I, 302.
[20] Boyle, I, 310.

might, by a person of reconciling disposition, be looked upon as . . . one philosophy which, because it explicates things by corpuscles, or minute bodies, may (not very unfitly) be called corpuscular." [21] Frequently, too, following More, though with a somewhat broader meaning for the phrase, he calls it the mechanical philosophy, because its characteristics appear in obvious and powerful form in mechanical engines. Boyle's chief points of disaffection with Descartes were the latter's banishment of final causes on the ground that we cannot know God's purposes, and his main postulates about motion.[22] The English thinker holds it obvious that some of the divine ends are readable by all, such as the symmetry of the world and the marvellous adaptation of living creatures, hence it is foolish to reject teleological proofs for the existence of God. As for the laws of motion, they appear to him clearly evident neither to experience nor to reason.[23] In particular, the doctrine of the permanence of the quantity of motion in the world rests upon too *a priori* and speculative a proof, that from the immutability of God. Some experiments do not seem to bear it out, and in any case we have no means of investigating its truth in the remote regions of the universe. Boyle was likewise a prominent figure in the overthrow of Hobbes' physical philosophy and its method. After his experimental refutation of Hobbes' theory of the nature of the air, no important thinker dared again to promulgate a physics composed of deductions from general principles without careful and exact experimental verification. The element of faithfulness to fact in the method of the new movement found a most powerful champion in Boyle. Besides these affiliations with the recent past, Boyle carried on an enormous correspondence with various prominent contemporary scientists and philosophers, including Locke, Newton, More, Hobbes, Sydenham, Hooke, Glanvill; and even Spinoza offered criticisms of some of his experimental conclusions.

[21] Boyle, I, 355.

[22] Boyle, V, 401.

[23] Boyle, V, 140, 397.

How, specifically, did he conceive his own function in this advancing movement? "Since the mechanical philosophers have brought so few experiments to verify their assertions, and the chemists are thought to have brought so many on behalf of theirs, that of those that have quitted the unsatisfactory philosophy of the schools . . . the greater number have embraced their doctrines . . . for these reasons, I say, I hoped I might at least do no unseasonable piece of service to the corpuscular philosophers, by illustrating some of their notions with sensible experiments, and manifesting that the things by me treated of may be at least plausibly explicated without having recourse to inexplicable forms, real qualities, the four peripatetic elements, or so much as the three chemical principles." [24] In other words, Boyle notes that the new assumptions lacked as yet extensive experimental verification, and that in particular the subject-matter of chemistry had not yet been successfully explained atomically; the prevailing method was largely mystical and magical; the three principles supposed to be ultimate constituents were the highly complex substances salt, sulphur, and mercury. Chemistry had not moved forward with astronomy and mechanics, and Boyle is eager to see it raised to their exact level by trying whether the principles of atomism may not be successfully applied in this other field. Astronomers and geographers "have hitherto presented us rather a mathematical hypothesis of the universe than a physical, having been careful to show us the magnitudes, situations, and motions of the great globes, without being solicitous to declare what simpler bodies, and what compounded ones, the terrestrial globe we inhabit does or may consist of." [25] It is this chemical analysis of things right before our eyes that Boyle is eager to further, and the method he champions, following Gilbert's practice more than Bacon's theory, is that of reasoned analysis of sensible facts, confirmed by exact experiment. The new philosophy, he observes, is built upon two foundations, reason and experience, of which the latter has only

[24] Boyle, I, 356.

[25] Boyle, III, 318.

recently come into its own.[26] Does this unduly subordinate reason to experience? Not at all, Boyle answers. "Those that cry up abstracted reason, as if it were self-sufficient, exalt it in words; but we that address reason to physical and theological experience, and direct it how to consult them and take its information from them, exalt it in effect; and reason is much less usefully served by the former sort of men than by the latter; since while those do but flatter it, these take the right way to improve it." [27] In the last analysis, moreover, our criterion of truth is rational. "Experience is but an assistant to reason, since it doth indeed supply informations to the understanding, but the understanding still remains the judge, and has the power or right to examine and make use of the testimonies that are presented to it." [28]

[26] Boyle, V, 513, ff. "But now the virtuosi I speak of (. . . by whom . . . I mean those that understand and cultivate experimental philosophy) make a much greater and better use of experience in their philosophical researches. For they consult experience both frequently and heedfully; and not content with the phenomena that nature spontaneously affords them, they are solicitious, when they find it needful, to enlarge their experience by trials purposely devised."

[27] Boyle, V, 540.

[28] Boyle, V, 539. Boyle remarks further: "The outward senses are but the instruments of the soul . . . the sensories may deceive us . . . it is the part of reason, not sense, to judge whether none of the requisites of sense be wanting . . . and also it is the part of reason to judge what conclusions may, and what cannot, be safely grounded on the information of the senses and the testimony of experience. So when it is said that experience corrects reason, it is somewhat an improper way of speaking; since it is reason itself that upon the information of experience, corrects the judgments she had made before."

c. Acceptance and Defence of the Mechanical World View

Boyle was not himself a profound mathematician, but he readily perceived the fundamental importance of mathematics in an atomistic interpretation of the chemical world, according to the now prevalent principle. "It is true that matter, or body, is the subject of the naturalist's speculation; but if it be also true that most, if not all, the operations of the parcels of that matter . . . one upon another, depend upon those modifications which their local motion receives from their magnitude and their figure, as the chief mechanical affections of the parts of matter; it can scarcely be denied that the knowledge of what figures are, for instance, more or less capacious and advantaged or disadvantaged for motion or for rest, for penetrating or for resisting penetration, for being fastened to one another, etc., must be of constant use in explaining many of the phenomena of nature." [29] This is, of course, just the business of geometry, it is the science of magnitude, figure, and especially of motion. Astronomy, for example, is a science about physical things, in which, without an adequate knowledge of mathematics to guide in the framing of hypotheses or judging of them, a thinker is apt to go astray (witness Epicurus and Lucretius); in fact in any subject dealing with things which possess geometrical qualities, the aid of lineal schemes and pictures to the imagination is quite considerable.[30] But more than this, and here Boyle expresses his complete agreement with the mathematical metaphysics of Galileo and Descartes, the whole world seems to be fundamentally mathematical in structure; "nature does play the mechanician" [31]; mathematical and mechanical principles are the "alphabet, in

[29] Boyle, III, 425, ff.
[30] Boyle, III, 429, 431, 441.
[31] Boyle, III, 20, 34, ff.; IV, 76, ff.

which God wrote the world"; which for Boyle is a conclusion justified for the most part by the undeniable fact of the successful explanation of things through the use of these principles. They have proven themselves the right key to the cipher. Had he lived before Galileo, Boyle would undoubtedly have remained in the main an Aristotelian; but the remarkable and experimentally verifiable achievements of the great mathematical physicists had made him (as was the case with other empiricists) a *post factum* convert. Further, inasmuch as God played the mathematician in creating the world, mathematical principles, like the axioms of logic, must be ultimate truths superior to God himself, and independent of revelation[32]; in fact revelation itself must be so interpreted as not to contradict those principles, "for God, being infinitely knowing, and being the author of our reason, cannot be supposed to oblige us to believe contradictions." "I look upon the metaphysical and mathematical principles . . . to be truths of a transcendent kind, that do not properly belong either to philosophy or theology; but are universal foundations and instruments of all the knowledge we mortals can acquire." [33]

This mathematical view of nature involves, of course, a mechanical conception of its operations. "That which I chiefly aim at, is to make it probable to you by experiments, that almost all sorts of qualities, most of which have been by the schools either left unexplicated, or generally referred to I know not what incomprehensible substantial forms, may be produced mechanically; I mean by such corporeal agents, as do not appear either to work otherwise than by virtue of the motion, size, figure, and contrivance of their own parts (which attributes I call the mechanical affections of matter)." [34] These parts are ultimately reducible to atoms, equipped with primary qualities alone, and portrayed by Boyle, in spite of Gassendi's revival of Epicureanism, in essentially Cartesian

[32] Boyle, III, 429.

[33] Boyle, VI, 711, ff.

[34] Boyle, III, 13.

terms.[35] Of such ultimate or primary qualities the most important is motion,[36] for Boyle follows Descartes' conception of the process by which the uniform *res extensa* was originally diversified into its various parts. "I agree with the generality of philosophers so far as to allow, that there is one catholic or universal matter common to all bodies, by which I mean a substance extended, divisible, and impenetrable. But because this matter being in its own nature but one, the diversity we see in bodies must necessarily arise from somewhat else than the matter they consist of, and since we see not how there could be any change in matter, if all its parts were perpetually at rest among themselves, it will follow that to discriminate the catholic matter into variety of bodies, it must have motion in some or all its designable parts; and that motion must have various tendencies, that which is in this part of the matter tending one way, and that which is in that part tending another." [37] In fact it is just this attempt to account for variety and change by reducing them wholly to motion that leads us inevitably to the atomic theory.[38]

[35] Boyle, III, 292. "And there are some . . . qualities, namely size, shape, motion, and rest, that are wont to be reckoned among qualities which may more conveniently be esteemed the primary modes of the parts of matter, since from these simple attributes, or primordial affections, all the qualities are derived."

[36] Following Galileo, Boyle also calls these *absolute* qualities; that is, in no circumstances can they be thought away from bodies. III, 22.

[37] Boyle, III, 15.

[38] Boyle, III, 16: "It will follow, both that matter must be actually divided into parts, that being the genuine effect of variously determined motion, and that each of the primitive fragments, or other distinct and entire masses of matter, must have two attributes; its own magnitude or rather size, and its own figure or shape. And since experience shows us that this division of matter is frequently made into insensible corpuscles or particles, we may conclude, that the minutest fragments, as well as the biggest masses of the universal matter are likewise endowed, each with its own peculiar bulk and shape. . . . Whether these accidents may not conveniently enough be called the moods or primary affections of bodies, to distinguish

Now although the natural world as we see it could not have been produced without that infusion of motion which broke up the primitive matter and forced its parts to combine in the manifold ways which account for present phenomena, yet (for reasons which will appear later) Boyle is eager to insist that matter as such did not need to be set in motion, *i.e.*, motion is not an inherent quality of matter. More's conception of absolute space helped him out at this point. A body is as truly a body when it rests, as when it moves, he points out, hence motion is not of the essence of matter,[39] "which seems principally to consist in extension." [40] Boyle is not quite sure whether impenetrability can be deduced from extension alone[41]; if not it must be included in the essential qualities of matter along with size and figure which are so deducible, but his main point is to insist that matter can in no wise move itself, it is dependent for its motion upon something that is not matter. Boyle criticizes Descartes for appearing to make matter independent of God. According to Cartesian principles God cannot abolish extension or the laws of motion.[42]

Out of matter, then, variously moved in its different parts, both insensibly small and large, all the phenomena of nature without exception are to be explained.[43] Boyle, no more than Descartes or Hobbes, had caught the full vision of Galileo, that motion is to be expressed in exact mathematical terms; his purpose when he descends to the detailed problems of theory is merely to show how, according to the principle of permutations and combinations, a small number of primary differences in bulk, figure, and motion can give rise in their various possible combinations to an almost infinite diversity of

them from those less simple qualities (as colours, tastes, and odours) that belong to bodies upon their account, I shall not now stay to consider." Cf. also 29–35.

[39] Boyle, V, 242.

[40] Boyle, II, 42.

[41] Boyle, IV, 198, ff.

[42] Boyle, IV, 43, ff.

[43] Boyle, IV, 70, ff., especially 77, ff.

phenomena.[44] Boyle illustrates in various ways how the primitive homogeneous matter is broken up under the influence of local motion into pieces of specific bigness and shape, some of which are at rest, others in motion; and that from these considerations it is possible to deduce seven other categories, such as position, order, texture, etc., which furnish us with an adequate alphabet, out of which the book of the universe can be constructed. Lest even this seem insufficient, he points out that local motion itself is a principle of great diversity. "So likewise motion, that seems so simple a principle, especially in simple bodies, may even in them be very much diversified; for it may be more or less swift, and that in an infinite diversity of degrees; it may be simple or compounded, uniform or difform, and the greater celerity may precede or follow. The body may move in a straight line, or in a circular, or in some other curve line . . . the body may also have an undulating motion . . . or may have a rotation about its own middle parts, etc." [45] Boyle was confident, of course, that his own experiments on aerostatics and hydrostatics admirably confirmed this wholly mechanical conception of the origin of forms and qualities.

It is interesting to note that by Boyle's time the new geometrical metaphysics had become so settled in the current of intelligent thinking that rudimentary attempts begin to be made to give new meanings to some of the traditional metaphysical terms, with the intent of better fitting them into the language of the day. He proposes to use the term *form,* for example, to mean (instead of the scholastic essential qualities) "those mechanical affections necessary to constitute a body of

[44] Boyle, III, 297, ff. "The . . . grand difficulty objected against the [corpuscularian] doctrine proposed by me about the origin of qualities . . . is . . . that it is incredible that so great a variety of qualities as we actually find to be in bodies should spring from principles so few in number as two, and so simple as matter and local motion; whereas the latter is but one of the six kinds of motion reckoned up by Aristotle and his followers . . . and the former, being all of one uniform nature, is according to us diversified only by the effects of local motion."

[45] Boyle, III, 299.

that determinate kind." [46] *Nature,* too, he wishes to rescue from the vague and varied uses to which it had been put in ancient and medieval discussions, and define it in terms of the new dualism—it is not a collection of substances nor a mysterious wielder of incalculable forces, but a system of mechanical laws; *i.e.,* it is the world of matter and motion distinct from rational souls and immaterial spirits. [47] Boyle strongly opposes More's doctrine of angels and of a "spirit of nature" or subordinate spiritual being operating toward certain ends, and thereby accounting for such phenomena of attraction as cohesion, suction, gravity and the like. [48] He is thoroughly convinced that these, like other qualitative phenomena, can be explained on a corpuscularian or mechanical basis, though he attempts no solution of the problems involved.

D. Value of Qualitative and Teleological Explanations

But for him the appeal to a mysterious entity is no genuine explanation; to explain a phenomenon is to deduce it from something else in nature more known than the thing to be explained. [49] Substantial forms and other covers for our ignorance, like "nature," are therefore no explanations, they just are as unique as the things to be explained. [50] At the same

[46] Boyle, III, 28.

[47] Boyle, V, 177.—"Of universal nature, the notion I would offer would be some such as this: that nature is the aggregate of the bodies that make up the world, framed as it is, considered as a principle, by virtue of which they act and suffer, according to the laws of motion prescribed by the Author of things . . . I shall express what I call general nature by cosmical mechanism, *i.e.,* a comprisal of all the mechanical affections (figure, size, motion, etc.) that belong to the matter of the great system of the universe."

[48] Boyle, V, 192, ff.

[49] Boyle, III, 46.

[50] Boyle, I, 308, ff.

time some qualitative explanations, where nothing better is available, are not worthless, for Boyle, like More, believes that the new philosophy has gone to unjustifiable extremes in Descartes and Hobbes. The most satisfying explanations, to be sure, are those in terms of bulk, shape, and motion, "yet are not those explications to be despised, wherein particular effects are deduced from the most obvious and familiar qualities or states of bodies, such as heat, cold, weight, fluidity, hardness, fermentation, etc., though these themselves do probably depend on those three universal ones formerly named." Gravity offers a good example. "He, I say, may be allowed to have rendered a reason of a thing proposed, that thus refers the phenomena to that known affection of almost all bodies here below, which we call gravity, though he does not deduce the phenomena from atoms, nor give us the cause of gravity; as indeed scarce any philosopher has yet given us a satisfactory account of it." It was for the same reasons and in the same spirit that Boyle criticized teleological explanations; the validity of final causality, unlike Descartes and Hobbes, he does not at all call in question, but points out that an answer to the ultimate *why* of anything is no substitute for an answer to the immediate *how*. "For to explicate a phenomenon, it is not enough to ascribe it to one general efficient, but we must intelligibly show the particular manner, how that general cause produces the proposed effect. He must be a very dull inquirer who, demanding an account of the phenomena of a watch, shall rest satisfied with being told, that it is an engine made by a watchmaker; though nothing be thereby declared of the structure and coaptation of the spring, wheels, balance, and other parts of the engine, and the manner, how they act on one another, so as to co-operate to make the needle point out the true hour of the day." [51] A total explanation of things is not the object of experimental science; that, indeed, will go far beyond mechanism; there is "the admirable conspiring of the several parts of the universe to the production of particular effects; of all of which it will be difficult to give a satisfactory account without acknowledging an intelligent Author or Dis-

[51] Boyle, V, 245.

poser of things." [52] But, Boyle reiterates in his reply to More's criticisms of his experimental conclusions, ". . . supposing the world to have been at first made, and to be continually preserved by God's power and wisdom; and supposing his general concourse to the maintainance of the laws he has established in it, the phenomena I strive to explicate may be solved mechanically, that is by the mechanical affections of matter, without recourse to nature's abhorrence of a vacuum, to substantial forms, or to other incorporeal creatures. And therefore if I have shown, that the phenomena I have endeavoured to account for, are explicable by the motion, bigness, gravity, shape [note the inclusion of gravity in this list], and other mechanical affections . . . , I have done what I pretended." [53] It was important indeed for the onward march of the new philosophy of science that Boyle's acceptance of teleology as a valid metaphysical principle did not lead him to apply it in physics[54]; here he follows his great predecessors in holding that the immediate and secondary cause of any effect is always a prior motion of some sort. "The world being once constituted by the great Author of things as it now is, I look upon the phenomena of nature to be caused by the local motion of one part of matter hitting against another." [55] "Local motion seems to be indeed the principal amongst second causes, and the grand agent of all that happens in nature; for though bulk,

[52] Boyle, II, 76, ff.

[53] Boyle, III, 608, ff.

[54] Boyle, IV, 459. On space and time, Boyle's ideas are not very clear. His main interest in the latter was to reconcile it with the religious conception of eternity; as for space, he fails to see any relation between it and motion, hence while denying More's notion of absolute space in words he is led to admit it by implication. He appears to follow Descartes' position of the relativity of motion. The universe as a whole is not capable of local motion, for there is no body that it can leave or approach, but yet "if the outermost heavens should be impelled, by the irresistible power of God, this way, or that way, there should ensue a motion without change of place." There appears to be some confusion of thought here, but Boyle nowhere offers us a clearer analysis.

[55] Boyle, III, 42; cf. also IV, 60, 72, ff., 76, ff.

figure, rest, situation, and texture do concur to the phenomena of nature, yet in comparison of motion they seem to be in many cases, effects, and in many others little better than conditions, or requisites, or causes *sine qua non*," [56] but all these remain wholly inefficacious until actual motion occurs. Boyle is eager constantly to affirm, however, in refutation of Hobbes, that this applies only to secondary causes—to assert absolutely that motion is impossible except by a body contiguous and moved, is to involve oneself in an infinite regress and to deny ultimate causality by a spiritual deity.[57]

E. Insistence on Reality of Secondary Qualities—Conception of Man

Boyle's many agreements with Descartes have appeared frequently in the quotations thus far cited; when he comes to treat of man's place in the world and the mechanism of sensation, it is, as we should expect, the Cartesian dualism that furnishes the main background of his thought, but with a significant difference, for which we are prepared by his remarkably moderate treatment of qualitative and teleological explanations. Galileo and Descartes had been eager to banish man from the mathematical world of nature into a secondary and unreal realm—to be sure Descartes had maintained the independence of thinking substance—but the whole effect of his work, like that of Galileo, was to make man's place and importance seem very meagre, secondary, dependent. The real world was the mathematical and mechanical realm of extension and motion, man being but a puny appendage and irrelevant spectator. This view had pervaded the mind of the age; Hobbes' smashing materialism had powerfully aided it; in their absorption in the conquest of nature by mathematical principles, thinkers were forgetting that the being who was gaining this knowledge and victory must by that very achieve-

[56] Boyle, III, 15.

[57] Boyle, IV, 167.

ment be a rather remarkable creature. Confronting this seemingly irresistible tendency to read man out of nature and be-
little his importance, Boyle is eager positively to reassert the
factual place of man in the cosmos and his unique dignity as
the child of God. Hence the primary qualities are not more
real than the secondary; since man with his senses is a part of
the universe, all qualities are equally real. To be sure, "if we
should conceive all the rest of the universe to be annihilated
save one such body, suppose a metal, or a stone, it were hard
to show that there is physically anything more in it than matter, and the accidents we have already named [the primary
qualities] . . . But now we are to consider, that there are *de
facto* in the world certain sensible and rational beings that
we call men; and the body of man having several external
parts, as the eye, the ear, etc., each of a distinct and peculiar
texture, whereby it is capable of receiving impressions from
the bodies about it, and upon that account it is called an organ
of sense; we must consider, I say, that these sensories may be
wrought upon by the figure, shape, motion, and texture of
bodies without them after several ways, some of those external
bodies being fitted to affect the eye, others the ear, others the
nostrils, etc. And to these operations of the objects on the sensories, the mind of man, which upon the account of its union
with the body perceives them, gives distinct names, calling the
one light or colour, the other sound, the other odour, etc." [58]
Easy enough it was for the mind to regard such sensible qualities as really existent in things themselves, "whereas indeed
there is in the body to which these sensible qualities are attributed, nothing of real and physical, but the size, shape, and
motion or rest of its component particles, together with the
texture of the whole, that results from their being so contrived
as they are." At times Boyle is rather muddled about the
matter; in one passage he is disposed to agree with the
Aristotelians that "they [the sensible qualities] have an absolute
being irrelative to us; for snow, for instance, would be white,
and a glowing coal would be hot, though there were no man
or any other animal in the world . . . as the coal will not only

[58] Boyle, III, 22, ff., 35.

heat or burn a man's hand if he touch it, but would likewise heat wax . . . and thaw ice into water, although all the men and sensible beings in the world were annihilated." Of course, this would hardly prove the coal hot, yet his general solution of the problem is fairly conservative; it is that in objects themselves these secondary qualities exist as "a disposition of its constituent corpuscles, that in case it were truly applied to the sensory of an animal, it would produce such a sensible quality which a body of another texture would not, as though if there were no animals there would be no such thing as pain, yet a pin may, upon the account of its figure, be fitted to cause pain in case it were moved against a man's finger . . ." Inasmuch, however, as there are men and animals in the world, such a "disposition" or "fitness" in things is just as real as the qualities it possesses in itself. "To be short, if we fancy any two of the bodies about us, as a stone, a metal, etc., to have nothing at all to do with any other body in the universe, it is not easy to conceive how either one can act upon the other but by local motion . . . or how by motion it can do any thing more than put the parts of the other body into motion too, and thereby produce in them a change of texture and situation, or of some other of its mechanical affections: though this (passive) body being placed among other bodies in a world constituted as ours now is, and being brought to act upon the most curiously contrived sensories of animals, may upon both of these accounts exhibit many differing sensible phenomena, which, however we look upon them as distinct qualities, are consequently but the effects of the often-mentioned catholic affections of matter."

That Boyle should have felt it necessary to point out so emphatically "that there are *de facto* in the world certain sensible and rational beings that we call men," [59] is a highly significant commentary on the scientific mind of his time. In Boyle himself this emphasis is due, not so much to a conviction that the astounding achievements of mechanical science necessarily implied a significant place in the world for its inventor,

[59] Boyle, III, 36.

but rather to his religious interests,[60] the assertion of human worth being uniformly more flavoured with the latter than with the former. "Matter, how vastly extended, and how curiously shaped soever, is but a brute thing that is only capable of local motion, and its effects and consequents on other bodies, or the brain of man, without being capable of any true, or at least any intellectual perception, or true love or hatred; and when I consider the rational soul as an immaterial and immortal being, that bears the image of its divine maker, being endowed with a capacious intellect, and a will, that no creature can force: I am by these considerations disposed to think the soul of man a nobler and more valuable being, than the whole corporeal world." [61] Some touches of the medieval teleological hierarchy are thus reaffirmed in Boyle, against the prevailing current.

Just what is man, however, this curious perceiver of sensible qualities, this being that loves and hates, and has a rational soul? Boyle's views here are strictly Cartesian. Man's body, being body, is mechanical like the rest of nature; men are "engines endowed with wills." [62] Elsewhere the non-corporeal part is characterized as an "immaterial form," [63] or, quite frequently, as above, a "rational soul." More's doctrine of the extension of spirit he entirely rejects; the soul is not only indivisible but also unextended,[64] for which reason, Boyle holds, it must be immaterial and immortal. Furthermore, the prevalent notion of spirit as a thin vapour or breath, he sets definitely aside as a confusion of terms. "When I say that spirit is incorporeal substance . . . if he should answer, that when he hears the words incorporeal substance, he imagines some aerial or other very thin, subtile, transparent body, I shall reply, that this comes from a vicious custom he has brought himself to, of imagining something whenever he will conceive any-

[60] Cf. IV, 171; V, 517.

[61] Boyle, IV, 19, ff.

[62] Boyle, V, 143.

[63] Boyle, III, 40.

[64] Boyle, V, 416.

thing, though of a nature incapable of being truly represented by any image in the fancy. . . . Because the use of imagining, whenever we would conceive things, is so stubborn an impediment to the free actings of the mind, in cases that require pure intellection, it will be very useful, if not necessary, to accustom ourselves not to be startled or frighted with every thing that exceeds or confounds the imagination, but by degrees to train up the mind to consider notions that surpass the imagination and yet are demonstrable by reason." [65]

All this sounds Cartesian enough, and when Boyle comes to describe in detail the process of sensation he is a thoroughly orthodox follower of the ambiguous Cartesian psychology as it has come to be popularly interpreted. Just note with care his portrayal of the facts. The soul is something unextended[66]; at the same time it resides in the conarion, to which the impressions of external bodies on the sensories are carried as motions of nerve fibres, "where these differing motions being perceived by the there residing soul, become sensations, because of the intimate union . . . of the soul with the body." Boyle takes it for granted, too, that our ideas are stored up for future use in a small part of the brain.[67] Hobbes' modification of Descartes has not escaped him. He notes, however, some of the difficulties involved in the union of incorporeal with corporeal substance, being especially interested in the fact that particular sensations are not really explained by the theory. "For I demand why, for instance, when I look upon a bell that is ringing, such a motion or impression in the conarion produces in the mind that peculiar sort of perception, seeing and not hearing; and another motion, though coming from the same bell, at the same time, produces that quite different sort of perception, that we call sound, but not vision; what can be answered but that it was the good pleasure of the author of human nature to have it so." [68] He observes that at such points we are no better off than the scholastics with their occult qualities.

[65] Boyle, VI, 688, ff. Cf. also 796.

[66] Boyle, IV, 44.

[67] Boyle, IV, 454.

[68] Boyle, IV, 43, ff.

F. Pessimistic View of Human Knowledge—Positivism

Here we come upon one of the most interesting and historically significant features of Boyle's philosophy, his epistemology, for Boyle began to see some of the difficulties for a theory of human knowledge involved in this position. Though, to be sure, he appeals to religion to help him over his final difficulties here (thereby following the example set by the other champions of the new science), yet his statement is so closely akin to that of Newton that it deserves careful attention. We might well ask, as we examine the metaphysics of the age—with its prevalent conception of the soul located within the body, where it is affected by the primary motions coming to the various senses and promulgated to its seat in the brain—how any certain knowledge at all is possible of the real corporeal world outside, with which the soul is never in contact? How is it possible for it to build up an orderly system of ideas that shall truly represent a world forever inaccessible to it? How, indeed, do we know that there is any such world? But it took a long time for men to feel this difficulty in all its overwhelming force; even Locke, who in the *Essay* finds himself securely caught in it, fails to see the inevitably sceptical consequence of his position. Galileo and Gilbert had dimly sensed that the new mataphysics meant a rather meagre realm of human knowledge, and the ancients were not unfamiliar with the ultimate difficulties about knowledge that certain doctrines of sensation involved. But now Boyle raises the doubt, still rather naïvely and innocently, on the basis of the new psychology, and it is vital to our purpose to observe that he readily abandons the more consistent form of Descartes' dualism in favour of important elements from Hobbes; he pictures the soul as entirely shut up within the brain. "And if it be a necessary imperfection of human nature that, whilst we remain in this mortal condition, the soul, being confined to the dark prison of the body, is capable . . . but of a dim knowledge; so much the greater value we ought to have for Christian religion, since by its means . . . our faculties will be elevated and enlarged." [69] This dimness and meagre reach of knowledge is what we should expect in a world constituted like ours: "I see no necessity that intelligibility to a human understanding should be necessary to the truth or existence of a thing, any more than that visibility to a human eye should be necessary to the existence of an atom, or of a corpuscle of air, or of effluviums of a loadstone, etc." [70] Viewing such statements in the light of the whole development, how natural they seem! The mind of man had come in touch with a vast realm of being, which seemed to it pre-eminently real, yet in which, in view of the current metaphysical spectacles, its own existence and knowledge seemed incomparably restricted and petty, and to which they were wholly irrelevant. Boyle's further comments in this connexion, however, are rather simple. He observes that we know very little about the celestial globes and the deeply subterranean parts of the earth; our experience and inquiries deal only with the "crust or scurf of the earth," [71] which is but a "small (not to say contemptible) portion." Our knowledge is "confined to but a small share of the superficial part of a physical point."

The moral of all this to Boyle is that we must not reject things because they transcend our intelligence, but consider whether it may not be because our capacities are too limited to grasp them. This applies both to science and religion, especially the latter.

It is largely in this mood that Boyle becomes flavoured in his thinking with that conception of science that we have noted already in Galileo and which has later come to be designated by the name of positivism. Important touches of the positivistic spirit are to be found in Harvey,[72] and Boyle now relates it to the total philosophical situation. Since the reach of human knowledge is so small in comparison with the totality

[69] Boyle, IV, 45. Cf. Locke's *Essay,* II, 11 [17]. Locke was intimately acquainted with both Boyle and Newton.

[70] Boyle, IV, 450; cf. also VI, 694, ff.

[71] Boyle, IV, 50.

[72] Harvey (Everyman edition), p. 16, ff.

of being, it is ridiculous to attempt the projection of great
systems; better to have a little knowledge which is certain because based on experiment, and is growing, though always incomplete and fragmentary, than to construct large speculative
hypotheses of the universe.[73] In much of his work Boyle consciously avoids unyielding theories of phenomena, and contents
himself with gathering facts and offering suggestions which
might prepare the way for some future "sound and comprehensive hypothesis." [74] He severely criticizes the eagerness of
the human mind to know a great deal before it makes sure, by
careful observation and experiment, that its knowledge is
genuine.[75] "It is not, that I at all condemn the practice of
those inquisitive wits, that take upon them to explicate to us
even the abstrusest phenomena of nature. . . . I admire them
when their endeavours succeed, and applaud them even when
they do but fairly attempt . . . but I have hitherto, though
not always, yet not unfrequently found, that what pleased me
for a while, as fairly comporting with the observations, on
which such notions were grounded, was soon after disgraced
by some further or new experiment." [76] Hence while not con-
futing such opinions except where he judged them "impedi-
ments to the advancement of experimental learning," [77] nor
even then unless he believed he "could bring experimental objections against them," Boyle was chiefly anxious to secure the
full recognition on the part of his contemporaries in the new
science of a definitely experimental standard. "For it is none
of my design, to engage myself with, or against any one sect
of naturalists, but barely to invite you to embrace or refuse
opinions, as they are consonant to experiments, or clear reasons
deduced thence, or at least analogous thereunto." Difficult
problems, such as the composition of the continuum, do not
need to be solved before science can proceed further; "because

[73] Boyle, I, 299, ff.

[74] Boyle, I, 695; cf. also I, 662, ff.

[75] Boyle, IV, 460.

[76] Boyle, I, 307; cf. also IV, 235, ff.

[77] Boyle, I, 311, ff.

there is a multitude of considerable things to be discovered or
performed in nature, without so much as dreaming of this
controversy." [78]

Not only is it true that science can proceed to much important assemblage of facts and tentative consideration of hypotheses without holding a firm system of convictions about the
phenomena in question; it is also true that oftentimes alternative hypotheses suggest themselves, either of which may reveal,
in conformity with our general method and criteria (*i.e.,*
atomism, empiricism, etc.), the causes of the facts observed.
In such cases it may be impossible to assert positively that one
of these hypotheses is absolutely true to the exclusion of the
others.[79] Therefore science must often be satisfied with probabilism in its explanations; from the standpoint of human reason, hypotheses differ in *value* and *probability* of truth, but
cannot be judged absolutely. "For the use of an hypothesis
. . . [is] to render an intelligible account of the causes of the
effects, or phenomena proposed, without crossing the laws of
nature, or other phenomena; the more numerous, and the
more various the particles are, whereof some are explicable
by the assigned hypothesis, and some are agreeable to it, or at
least are not dissonant from it, the more valuable is the hypothesis, and the more likely to be true." [80] A third reason for
this tentative attitude is that, for Boyle, the fact of time itself
renders impossible the construction of a complete system of
truth at any given date. More things are constantly happening,
and there is never any guarantee that they will fit into our
present hypotheses, no matter how carefully formed and verified.[81]

Boyle sums up his position on these topics in a paragraph,
which may well be quoted almost *in toto*.[82]

[78] Boyle, IV, 43.

[79] Boyle, II, 45.

[80] Boyle, IV, 234.

[81] Boyle, IV, 796.

[82] Boyle, I, 302, ff.—"And truly . . . if men could be persuaded to mind more the advancement of natural philosophy
than that of their own reputations, it were not, methinks, very

G. Boyle's Philosophy of the Ether

The prevalent notion of the existence of an ethereal medium pervading space Boyle regards from this critical point of view; it is in general a likely hypothesis, but should nevertheless be looked upon as tentative and doubtful, because of lack of adequate experiments on the subject. ". . . That there may be such a substance in the universe, the asserters of it will

uneasy to make them sensible, that one of the considerablest services that they could do mankind, were to set themselves diligently and industriously to make experiments and collect observations, without being overforward to establish principles and axioms, believing it uneasy to erect such theories, as are capable to explicate all the phenomena of nature, before they have been able to take notice of the tenth part of those phenomena, that are to be explicated. Not that I at all disallow the use of reasoning upon experiments, or the endeavouring to discern as early as we can the confederations, and differences, and tendencies of things: for such an absolute suspension of the exercise of reason were exceeding troublesome, if not impossible . . . in physiology it is sometimes conducive to the discovery of truth, to permit the understanding to make an hypothesis, in order to the explication of this or that difficulty, that by examining how far the phenomena are, or are not, capable of being solved by that hypothesis, the understanding may, even by its own errors, be instructed. For it has been truly observed by a great philosopher, that truth does more easily emerge out of error than confusion. That then, that I wish for, as to systems, is this, that men, in the first place, would forbear to establish any theory, till they have consulted with (though not a fully competent number of experiments, such as may afford them all the phenomena to be explicated by that theory, yet) a considerable number of experiments, in proportion to the comprehensiveness of the theory to be erected on them. And, in the next place, I would have such kind of superstructures looked upon only as temporary ones; which though they may be preferred before any others, as being the least imperfect, or, if you please, the best in their kind that we yet have, yet are they not entirely to be acquiesced in, as absolutely perfect, or uncapable of improving alterations."

probably bring for proofs several of the phenomena I am about to relate; but whether there be or be not in the world any matter that exactly answers to the descriptions they make of their first and second elements I shall not here discuss, though divers experiments seem to argue that there is an ethereal substance very subtle and not a little diffused." [83] As to just how he conceives this substance, the following passage is illuminating. "I considered, that the interstellar part of the universe, consisting of air and ether, or fluids analogous to one of them, is diaphanous; and that the ether is as it were, a vast ocean, wherein the luminous globes, that here and there, like fishes, swim by their own motion, or like bodies in whirlpools are carried about by the ambient, are but very thinly dispersed, and consequently that the proportion that the fixed stars and planetary bodies bear to the diaphanous part of the world, is exceeding small, and scarce considerable." [84]

Now it is highly important to observe, in connexion with the theory of the ether, that by Boyle's time an ethereal fluid had become commonly appealed to for the fulfilment of two very diverse functions in the realm of matter. One such function was the communication of motion by successive impact, which became central in the mechanical system outlined by Descartes, and furnished an explanation of all those experiments which told against the existence of a vacuum in nature. This conception of motion as proceeding always by the impact of material bodies was so much in line with the postulates and methods of the new science that it was scarce possible for any thinker of importance to avoid the conviction that something of the sort must be true; consequently the vigour with which philosophers of all groups attacked the notion that there could be any such thing as action at a distance. Even More had to have an extended God in order to show how he could exert his power at any point of space he pleased. According to this conception, the ether was naturally conceived as a homogeneous, phlegmatic fluid, filling all space that was not occupied by other bodies, and possessing no characteristics that could

[83] Boyle, III, 309.

[84] Boyle, III, 706.

not be deduced from extension. Its other function was to account for curious phenomena like magnetism, in which forces were apparently at work of a unique kind, such as could not be reduced to those universal, orderly, mechanical motions, for the propagation of which the ether in its first function was called upon. Thinkers like More, whose main motive was religious, were content with traditional conceptions of a "spirit of nature" at this point, an extended being which possesses powers of vegetation, nourishment, regulation and guidance, without consciousness, reason, or purpose. More scientific minds, too, allowed their imaginations to wander somewhat loosely in these traditional paths, but gradually more hopeful hypotheses were tried. Gilbert's ethereal notions, as we noted, were highly speculative, and followed the ancient system of ideas in large measure; in Boyle the suggestion appears that a more scientific approach to the problem of the ether might be made if we assume in it two kinds of matter, one homogeneous and fitted to perform the first function, the other possessed of such powers as will account for the phenomena of the second. "It may not, therefore, be unseasonable to confess to you that I have had some faint suspicion, that besides those more numerous and uniform sorts of minute particles that are by some of the new philosophers thought to compose the ether I lately discoursed of, there may possibly be some other kind of corpuscles fitted to have considerable operations, when they find congruous bodies to be wrought on by them; but though it is possible, and perhaps probable, that the effects we are considering may be plausibly explicated by the ether, as it is really understood, yet I somewhat suspect that those effects may not be due solely to the causes they are ascribed to, but that there may be, as I was beginning to say, peculiar sorts of corpuscles that have yet no distinct name, which may discover peculiar faculties and ways of working, when they meet with bodies of such a texture as disposes them to admit, or to concur with, the efficacy of these unknown agents. This suspicion of mine will seem the less improbable if you consider, that though in the ether of the ancients there was nothing taken notice of but a diffused and very subtle substance; yet we are at present content to allow that there is always in the air a swarm of steams moving in a determinate course between the north pole and the south." [85]

This distinction between two kinds of ethereal matter, made in order that the ether might furnish an adequate explanation of these two types of phenomena, we shall meet again in Newton, who wrote of its possibilities in a letter to Boyle, some ten years after Boyle had penned this paragraph (1679). In the meantime scientists were quite at sea as to the status of gravity in this connexion. Were the phenomena of gravity explicable mechanically, or were they essentially magnetic or electric in their nature? We have noted how Gilbert championed the latter view—the earth is a huge magnet, and even the relation between the earth and the moon is to be understood magnetically—his view was on the whole dominant among English experimental scientists, while it exercised considerable influence on such continental luminaries as Galileo and Kepler. Descartes was the great champion of the former view; by supposing that the all-pervading ethereal medium fell into a series of vortices of varying sizes, he held it possible to explain the phenomena of gravity entirely mechanically, *i.e.*, without attributing to either the ethereal matter or other bodies any qualities not deducible from extension. As we have observed, the mere fact that the ether assumes and maintains the vortical form implies in it qualities that go far beyond extension, but the weight of Descartes' great name and achievements upheld the conception as an exceedingly alluring one, especially to those who saw in mathematical mechanics the possible key to all the secrets in nature. In terms of the main movement of the times, it seemed like a more *scientific* hypothesis than the other. In the main, Boyle was inclined to side with Descartes on this point, though with a rather loose interpretation of the word "mechanical." Newton, as we shall see, upheld the other view, while he also suggested a possible way of combining the two.

On March 21, 1666, Robert Hooke wrote a letter to Boyle, in which he described various experiments he had made on the subject of gravity, partly to determine whether the force of

[85] Boyle, III, 316.

gravity increased and decreased according to some regular law, and partly to decide whether it was magnetic, electric, or of some other nature.[86] Hooke observed that the results secured were indecisive. A little later in the same year (July 13) Boyle received a letter from John Beale,[87] in which the latter urged Boyle to offer an explanation of gravity, observing that it seemed to have important bearings on both mechanics and magnetism. Early in the seventies Boyle is still unwilling to give any definite hypothesis about gravity, but sees no harm in calling it mechanical in nature, "since many propositions of Archimedes, Stevinus, and those others, that have written of statics, are confessed to be mathematically or mechanically demonstrated, though those authors do not take upon them to assign the true cause of gravity, but take it for granted, as a thing universally acknowledged, that there is such a quality in the bodies they treat of . . . Since such kind of explications have been of late generally called mechanical, in respect of their being generally grounded upon the laws of the mechanics; I, that do not use to contend about names, suffer them quietly to be so." [88] This extract is from Boyle's reply to More's objections to his published assertion that his experiments on the weight and elasticity of the air showed that such phenomena were explicable on mechanical principles; and as long as there was no defined and recognized meaning for the term mechanical, it is difficult to see how such debates could be either avoided or settled. More and Boyle were sufficiently at one, however, in their religious interests not to be in profound disagreement on any subject; in fact ten years later Boyle was careful to speak of gravity in language that would have been entirely pleasing to More.[89]

[86] Boyle, VI, 505, ff.
[87] Boyle, VI, 404, ff.
[88] Boyle, III, 601.
[89] Boyle, V, 204—"It is obvious to them that will observe, that that which makes lumps of earth, or terrestrial matter, fall through the air to the earth is some general agent, whatever that be, which according to the wise disposition of the Author of the universe, determines the motion of those bodies we call heavy, by the shortest ways that are permitted them, towards the central part of the terraquaeous globe."

H. God's Relation to the Mechanical World

Boyle's deeply religious character has been patent enough from many of the quotations already cited. It is time, however, to fix our attention on this side of his philosophy more directly, and to note its ultimate relations, in his own mind, to experimental science. His religious activities were multifarious; among other things he contributed heavily toward the support of missionaries in far corners of the globe, and carried on quite a correspondence with some of them, including John Eliot of New England fame. He founded the famous series of Boyle lectures, in which he hoped that answers would be offered to the new objections and difficulties in the way of accepting the Christian religion, arising from the developments of the time in science and philosophy. Dr. Bentley, an important correspondent of Newton, became the first lecturer on the Boyle foundation. We learn from Birch's *Life of Boyle,* that "he had so profound a veneration for the Deity that the very name of God was never mentioned by him without a pause and a visible stop in his discourse; in which Sir Peter Pett, who knew him for almost forty years, affirms that he was so exact, that he did not remember to have observed him once to fail in it." [90] Experimental science was to Boyle, as to Bacon, itself a religious task. ". . . So much admirable workmanship as God hath displayed in the universe, was never meant for eyes that wilfully close themselves, and affront it with the not judging it worthy the speculating. Beasts inhabit and enjoy the world; man, if he will do more, must study and spiritualize it." [91] He was eager that others might undertake the work of science in the worshipful spirit of religion, praying, for example, in his will that the Royal Society might refer all their attainments to the glory of God.

What, to Boyle, were the fundamental facts of experience

[90] Boyle, I, 138.

[91] Boyle, III, 62.

that clearly point to the existence of God? Two types of fact he offers most profusely in this connexion, the fact of human reason and intelligence, and the fact of order, beauty, and adaptation in the universe at large. "I make great doubt, whether there be not some phenomena in nature, which the atomists cannot satisfactorily explain by any figuration, motion, or connexion of material particles whatsoever: for some faculties and operations of the reasonable soul in man are of so peculiar and transcendent a kind, that as I have not yet found them solidly explicated by corporeal principles, so I expect not to see them in haste made out by such." [92] Just what kind of a God this fact implies, and what his relations with the intelligible world of nature must be in detail, Boyle as we shall see, answers in terms of traditional doctrine rather than by an attempt to secure a fresh insight into the problem. As regards his second, more distinctively teleological argument, compare the following statement, selected from many available: "That the consideration of the vastness, beauty, and regular motions of the heavenly bodies; the excellent structure of animals and plants; besides a multitude of other phenomena of nature, and the subserving of most of these to man; may justly induce him as a rational creature, to conclude, that this vast, beautiful, orderly, and (in a word) many ways admirable system of things, that we call the world, was framed by an Author supremely powerful, wise and good, can scarce be denied by an intelligent and unprejudiced considerer." [93]

Once having established God, Boyle is content to interpret His place in the world and relation to man in accepted Christian fashion. He is the God who has given us direct and special information about himself and our duties to him in the Holy Scriptures, which are an object of study more valuable than any knowledge we can acquire through a study of nature.[94] It is "not grateful, to receive understanding and hope of eternal felicity from God, and not study what we can of His

[92] Boyle, II, 47, ff.
[93] Boyle, V, 515, ff.; cf. 136; IV, 721.
[94] Boyle, IV, 7.

nature and purposes through His revelation . . . [or] to dispute anxiously about the properties of an atom, and be careless about the inquiry into the properties of the great God, who formed all things." [95] Science and theology are thus both parts of a larger whole which far transcends them in reach and worth. "The gospel comprises indeed, and unfolds, the whole mystery of man's redemption, as far forth as it is necessary to be known for our salvation: and the corpuscularian or mechanical philosophy strives to deduce all the phenomena of nature from adiaphorous matter, and local motion. But neither the fundamental doctrine of Christianity, nor that of the powers and effects of matter and motion, seems to be more than an epicycle . . . of the great and universal system of God's contrivances, and makes but a part of the more general theory of things, knowable by the light of nature, improved by the information of the scriptures: so that both these doctrines . . . seem to be but members of the universal hypothesis, whose objects I conceive to be the nature, counsels, and works of God, so far as they are discoverable by us in this life." [96] Boyle pictures the future state as a continuation of our search for knowledge of this vaster realm of the divine activity; the chief difference will be that our present handicap will be removed, as God will then "enlarge our faculties, so as to enable us to gaze, without being dazzled, upon those sublime and radiant truths, whose harmony, as well as splendour, we shall then be qualified to discover, and consequently, with transports, to admire." [97]

This religious faith in the divine origin and control of the universe, coupled with his sense of the meagreness of human knowledge, leads Boyle to a definite rejection of Descartes' assumption that the mechanical laws of motion, discovered and verified in the realm of our experience, must apply without change to the totality of *res extensa*. "Now if we grant, with some modern philosophers, that God has made other worlds besides this of ours, it will be highly probable, that he

[95] Boyle, IV, 26.

[96] Boyle, IV, 19.

[97] Boyle, IV, 32.

has there displayed his manifold wisdom in productions very different from those wherein we here admire it . . . In these other worlds we may suppose, that the original fabric, or that frame, into which the omniscient architect at first contrived the parts of their matter, was very different from the structure of our system; besides this, I say, we may conceive, that there may be a vast difference between the subsequent phenomena and productions observable in one of those systems, from what regularly happens in ours, though we should suppose no more, than that two or three laws of local motion, may be differing in those unknown worlds, from the laws that obtain in ours. . . . God may have created some parts of matter to be of themselves quiescent . . . and yet he may have endowed other parts of matter with a power like that which the atomists ascribe to their principles [second function of the ether] of restlessly moving themselves, without losing that power by the motion they excite in quiescent bodies. And the laws of this propagation of motion among bodies may not be the same with those that are established in our world." [98]

As we should expect from these arguments for God's existence and power, the first and foremost function of the Deity in the economy of the universe was to set it in motion, in such ways that the orderly and harmonious system now revealed in it should result.[99]

[98] Boyle, V, 139.

[99] Boyle, V, 413, ff.—"The most wise and powerful Author of nature, whose piercing sight is able to penetrate the whole universe and survey all parts of it at once, did, at the beginning of things, frame things corporeal into such a system, and settled among them such laws of motion, as he judged suitable to the ends he proposed to himself in making the world; and as by virtue of his vast and boundless intellect, that he at first employed, he was able, not only to see the present state of things he had made, but to foresee all the effects, that particular bodies so and so qualified, and acting according to the laws of motion by him established, could in such and such circumstances have on one another; so, by the same omniscient power, he was able to contrive the whole fabric, and all the parts of it, in such manner, that whilst his general concourse maintained the order of nature, each part of this great engine, the world, should, without either intention or knowledge, as

The frequent use of the phrase "general concourse," which had already occurred in Descartes, indicates in the next place the sense on Boyle's part that God was somehow needed constantly to keep the universe from going to pieces; to this his religious interest mainly impelled him, though he was also to some extent moved by the same considerations that influenced More. Boyle feels, too, that a mechanical universe would inevitably fly apart—those forces which hold its different parts together in an orderly whole, are essentially spiritual in their nature. "This most potent Author, and Opificer of the world, hath not abandoned a masterpiece so worthy of him, but does still maintain and preserve it, so regulating the stupendously swift motions of the great globes, and other vast màsses of the mundane matter, that they do not, by any notable irregularity, disorder the grand system of the universe, and reduce it to a kind of chaos, or confused state of shuffled and depraved things." [100] Just how much is meant in this conception of God's "general concourse" maintaining the system of the world, is exceedingly difficult to make out in harmony with the rest of Boyle's philosophy, especially when we note his insistence that secondary or physical causes operate quite mechanically, once regular motion has been established.[101]

The key to this difficulty in Boyle, such as it is, seems to be found in his answer to the deists, who denied the necessity of any such general concourse, holding that "after the first formation of the universe, all things are brought to pass by the settled laws of nature. For though this be confidently, and not without colour pretended; yet . . . I look upon a law as being indeed but a notional thing, according to which an intelligent

regularly and constantly act towards the attainment of the respective ends which he designed them for, as if themselves really understood and industriously prosecuted, those ends."

[100] Boyle, V, 519, cf. also 198, ff.

[101] Boyle, IV, 68, ff.;—"The laws of motion being settled, and all upheld by his incessant concourse and general providence, the phenomena of the world thus constituted are physically produced by the mechanical affections of the parts of matter, and what they operate upon one another according to mechanical laws."

and free agent is bound to regulate his actions. But inanimate bodies are utterly incapable of understanding what a law is . . . and therefore the actions of inanimate bodies, which cannot incite or moderate their own actions, are produced by real power, not by laws." [102] This thought, that inasmuch as the world cannot know what it is doing, its orderly and law-abiding behaviour must be accounted for by real, constant, intelligent power, occurs in other passages[103] in Boyle. Nowhere is there any clear attempt to reconcile this with the position that the laws of motion and the phenomena of gravity represent quite self-sufficient mechanical operations.

God is thus conceived, not only as the first cause of things, but also as an active, intelligent being in the present, ever watchful to maintain the harmonious system of the world and to realise desirable ends in it.[104] His "knowledge reaches at once, to all that he can know; his penetrating eyes pierce quite through the whole creation at one look. . . . God beholds at once all, that any one of his creatures in the vast universe, either does or thinks. Next the knowledge of God is not a progressive, or discursive thing, like that acquired by our ratiocinations, but an intuitive knowledge . . . God . . . needs not know any one thing by the help of another, but knows everything in itself (as being the Author of it) and all things being equally known to him, he can, by looking if I may so speak, into himself, see there, as in a most divine and universal looking-glass, everything that is knowable most distinctly, and yet all at once." [105] This encomium of the divine intelligence reminds us of Galileo and Descartes; it even savours somewhat of More's extended Deity, which Boyle had previously denied. In one interesting passage, in fact, Boyle quite forgets his antagonism to this doctrine of the Cambridge divine. Things happen "as if there were *diffused through* the universe an intelligent being, watchful over the public good of it, and careful to administer all things wisely for the good

102 Boyle, V, 520.

103 Boyle, cf. II, 38, 40, ff.

104 Boyle, V, 140.

105 Boyle, V, 150.

of the particular parts of it, but so far forth as is consistent with the good of the whole, and the preservation of the primitive and catholic laws established by the supreme cause." [106]

Now in such a passage as this Boyle is obviously going beyond even the conception of God as needed to maintain the system of the world by his "general concourse"; he is adding the doctrine of a particular providence and attempting to reconcile it with the rule of universal law in the Stoic fashion. Particular individuals, or parts of the universe, are "only so far provided for, as their welfare is consistent with the general laws settled by God in the universe, and to such of those ends as he proposed to himself in framing it, as are more considerable than the welfare of those particular creatures." [107] At the same time consistency with the general laws just mentioned must not be pressed, for "this doctrine [is not] inconsistent with the belief of any true miracle, for it supposes the ordinary and settled course of nature to be maintained, without at all denying, that the most free and powerful Author of nature is able, whenever He thinks fit, to suspend, alter, or contradict those laws of motion, which he alone at first established and which need his perpetual concourse to be upheld." [108] God might thus at any time, "by withholding his concourse, or changing these laws of motion, that depend entirely upon his will . . . invalidate most, if not all, the axioms of natural philosophy." [109]

Hence, although God ordinarily confines the motions of matter to the regular laws originally established in it, yet he has by no means surrendered his right to change its operations in the interest of some new or special purpose. What types of event does Boyle intend to include under the head of miracles in this sense? First, of course, the miracles recorded in revelation. It will not follow from the existence of regular laws in nature, "that the fire must necessarily burn Daniel's three com-

[106] Boyle, II, 39. Italics ours.

[107] Boyle, V, 251, ff.

[108] Boyle, V, 414.

[109] Boyle, IV, 161, ff.

panions or their clothes, that were cast . . . into the midst of a burning fiery furnace, when the author of nature was pleased to withdraw his concourse to the operation of the flames, or supernaturally to defend against them the bodies that were exposed to them." [110] Secondly, Boyle counts a miracle the union of a rational, immortal soul with a physical body at birth;[111] thirdly, prayer for special help in times of sickness he does not think it becomes a Christian philosopher to pronounce hopeless;[112] and fourthly, he is disposed to think that there are many more irregularities in the cosmos at large than we are tempted to admit. "When I consider the nature of brute matter, and the vastness of the bodies that make up the world, the strange variety of those bodies that the earth does comprise, and others of them may not absurdly be presumed to contain; and when I likewise consider the fluidity of that vast interstellar part of the world wherein these globes swim; I cannot but suspect that there may be less of accurateness, and of constant regularity, than we have been taught to believe in the structure of the universe." [113] As examples he cites the spots on the sun, which he interprets as an irregular vomiting of quantities of opaque matter; and the comets, which were a great matter of wonder and mystery to all scientists of the day. Boyle holds it more satisfactory to attribute these types of event to the immediate interposition of the divine author of things, than to call in some third entity or subordinate being, such as nature. God doubtless has ends far transcending those which are revealed in the harmonious system discovered by science.

It is noticeable, however, that Boyle is eager not to overstress the importance of miracles; the main argument for God and providence is the exquisite structure and symmetry of the world—regularity, not irregularity—and at moments when his scientific passion is uppermost, he almost denies everything he has claimed for the present direct interposition of the deity.

[110] Boyle, IV, 162.
[111] Boyle, III, 48, ff.
[112] Boyle, V, 216, ff.
[113] Boyle, III, 322.

If God "but continue his ordinary and general concourse, there will be no necessity of extraordinary interpositions, which may reduce him to seem, as it were, to play after games; all those exigencies, upon whose account philosophers and physicians seem to have devised what they call nature, being foreseen and provided for in the first fabric of the world; so that mere matter so ordered, shall . . . do all . . . according to the catholic laws of motion." [114] The universe is distinctly not a puppet, whose strings have to be pulled now and again, but "it is like a rare clock, such as may be that at Strasburg, where all things are so skilfully contrived, that the engine being once set a-moving, all things proceed according to the artificer's first design, and the motions . . . do not require the peculiar interposing of the artificer, or any intelligent agent employed by him, but perform their functions upon particular occasions, by virtue of the general and primitive contrivance of the whole engine."

This reinterpretation of theism, which we meet with in Boyle, to the end of relating it definitely to the new scientific conception of the world, we shall find repeated almost point for point in Newton, save for being shorn of its most extreme ambiguities. The only other influences at all comparable in this aspect of Newton's philosophy were those of More and of the theosophist, Jacob Boehme. The former was Newton's colleague at Cambridge, and the latter, whom he read copiously, must have strengthened his conviction that the universe as a whole is not mechanically but only religiously explicable.

We are now equipped to consider, in somewhat fuller detail than has been devoted to any thinker thus far, the metaphysics of the man whose epoch-making conquests for science enabled him to turn the bulk of the convictions so far reached from still dubitable assumptions into almost hallowed axioms for the subsequent course of modern thought. Before we do so, however, let us summarize the central steps in the remarkable movement we have been tracing.

[114] Boyle, V, 163.

I. Summary of the Pre-Newtonian Development

Copernicus dared to attribute to the earth a diurnal motion on its axis and an annual motion around the sun, because of the greater mathematical simplicity of the astronomical system thus attained, a venture whose metaphysical implications he could accept because of the widespread revival in his day of the Platonic-Pythagorean conception of the universe, and which was suggested to his mind by the preceding developments in the science of mathematics. Kepler, moved by the beauty and harmony of this orderly system of the universe and by the satisfaction it accorded his adolescent deification of the sun, devoted himself to the search for additional geometrical harmonies among the exact data compiled by Tycho Brahe, conceiving the harmonious relations thus laid bare as the cause of the visible phenomena and likewise as the ultimately real and primary characteristics of things. Galileo was led by the thought of the motion of the earth and its mathematical treatment in astronomy to see if the motions of small parts of its crust might not be mathematically reducible, an attempt whose successful issue crowned him as the founder of a new science and led him in his efforts to see the fuller bearings of what he had accomplished to further metaphysical inferences. The scholastic substances and causes, in terms of which the fact of motion and its ultimate *why* had been accounted for teleologically, were swept away in favour of the notion that bodies are composed of indestructible atoms, equipped with none but mathematical qualities, and move in an infinite homogeneous space and time in terms of which the actual process of motion could be formulated mathematically. Intoxicated by his success and supported by the onrushing Pythagorean tide, Galileo conceived the whole physical universe as a world of extension, figure, motion, and weight; all other qualities which we suppose to exist *in rerum natura* really have no place there but are due to the confusion and deceitfulness of our senses. The real world is mathematical, and an appropriate positive conception of causality is presented; all immediate causality is lodged in quantitatively reducible motions of its atomic elements, hence only by mathematics can we arrive at true knowledge of that world. In so far, in fact, as we cannot attain mathematical knowledge it is better to confess our ignorance and proceed by tentative steps towards a fuller future science than to propound hasty speculations for grounded truths. In Descartes the early conviction that mathematics is the key to unlock the secrets of nature was powerfully strengthened by a mystic experience and directed by his pristine invention, that of analytical geometry. Could not the whole of nature be reduced to an exclusively geometrical system? On this hypothesis Descartes constructed the first modern mechanical cosmology. But what about the non-geometrical qualities? Some, those with which Galileo had been struggling, Descartes hid in the vagueness of the ether; others, encouraged by Galileo's example and led by his metaphysical propensities, he banished out of the realm of space and made into modes of thought, another substance totally different from extension and existing independently of it. "When any one tells us that he sees colour in a body or feels pain in one of his limbs, this is exactly the same as if he said that he there saw or felt something, of the nature of which he was entirely ignorant, or that he did not know what he saw or felt." But these totally different substances are in obvious and important relations. How is this to be accounted for? Descartes found himself quite unable to answer this overwhelming difficulty without speaking of the *res cogitans* as though it were after all confined to an exceedingly meagre location within the body. This pitiful position was definitely accorded the mind in Hobbes, who had already begun an attempt to reduce everything, thought included, to bodies and motions, and to develop a plausible account of secondary qualities which should reduce them to phantasmic unrealities and show why they appear without us when really caused by the clash of motions within. Further, Hobbes' union of this attempt with a thoroughgoing nominalism made him bold to proclaim frankly for the first time in the new movement the doctrine that causality is always to be found in particular motions, and that valid explanations in any field whatever must be explanations in terms of elementary parts whose temporal relations are to be conceived after the fashion of efficient causality solely. More, painfully following the developments of the new scientific philosophy, was willing to assent to everything asserted so far (except the Hobbesian reduction of the mind to vital motions), if it be granted that God is infinitely extended throughout space and time and has at his disposal a subordinate spiritual being, the spirit of nature, by which he can hold together in an orderly and purposive system a world which if left to mechanical forces alone would inevitably fly apart. This conception, More maintained, would have the additional advantage of properly disposing of space—our scientific methods imply its absolute and real existence, and it reveals an exalted set of attributes—it is therefore to be regarded as the omnipresence of God, as distinguished from his other faculties. Barrow presents a similar treatment of time, but with a significant difference. Apart from the religious reference, neither space nor time is aught but potentiality, yet language about them appropriate only to that reference is freely used in purely scientific connexions, furthering among those more interested in science than religion the conception of space and time as infinite, homogeneous, absolute entities, quite independent of bodies, motions, and human knowledge.

In the meantime a more empirical scientific movement was under way, led in England by such investigators as Gilbert and Harvey, and proceeding by the method of specific hypothesis and experiment rather than that of geometrical reduction. This method was applied to the solution of certain hitherto refractory physical problems and to the revolutionizing of chemistry by Robert Boyle, who had also been powerfully stimulated by Gassendi's revival of Epicurean atomism. It was highly significant, however, that Boyle, though not an important mathematician himself, took over *in toto* the view of nature and of man's relation to it proffered by Galileo and Descartes, with the exception that chiefly for religious reasons he reaffirmed man's teleological importance in the cosmic scheme and consequently maintained the equal reality of secondary qualities with the primary. We observe at the same time that for Boyle the popularly accepted position of the mind inside the brain being further reflected upon, human knowledge is an essentially incomplete and meagre affair, and hence his tentative, positivistic emphasis is strong. Likewise in his day the notion of an all-pervading ether appears to have been used to fulfil two distinct and definite functions—to account for the propagation of motion across a distance, and to explain such phenomena as cohesion, magnetism, etc., which had hitherto escaped exact mathematical reduction. Finally, his consuming religious zeal led him to attempt, not without inconsistency, to combine the notion of a present divine providence with the conception of the world as a vast clock-like machine, set in motion in the beginning by the Creator and thence running merely by the operation of its own secondary causes.

Were we attempting a complete picture of the philosophy of science in the sixteenth and seventeenth centuries, many more significant figures would have to be added to our treatment, such as, to take only the most outstanding names, Huyghens, Malebranche, Leibniz, Pascal, and Spinoza. But it cannot be shown that the philosophy of these men influenced Newton, or otherwise entered significantly into the doctrine of man's relation to nature which, further developed and supported by his work, became a part of the general intellectual background of subsequent thinkers. In fact, from this point of view, Leibniz appears rather as the first great protestant against the new metaphysical orthodoxy.

Section 1. Newton's Method

It has been often remarked that history is made rapidly
when the great man and his opportunity appear simultaneously.
In the case of Newton there is no question about the reality
and importance of precisely such a coincidence. That the subsequent history for nearly a hundred years of mathematics,
mechanics, and astronomy (in considerable part, too, of
optics) presented itself primarily as a period of the fuller appreciation and further application of Newton's achievements,
and this a century studded with stars of the first magnitude in
each of these fields, can hardly be accounted for otherwise
than by supposing that the field had been ripe for a mighty
genius and the genius at hand to reap the harvest. Newton
himself on one occasion remarked, "If I have seen farther
[than other men], it is because I have stood upon the shoulders
of giants." It is indeed true that his forerunners, especially
men like Galileo, Descartes, and Boyle, were giants—they had
prepared the way for the most stupendous single achievement
of the human mind—but that Newton saw farther was, of
course, not merely due to his place in the line. For him to
invent the needed tool and by its aid to reduce the major
phenomena of the whole universe of matter to a single mathematical law, involved his endowment with a degree of all
the qualities essential to the scientific mind—pre-eminently the
quality of mathematical imagination—that has probably never
been equalled. Newton enjoys the remarkable distinction of
having become an authority paralleled only by Aristotle to an
age characterized through and through by rebellion against
authority. However, we must not pause over these encomiums;
Newton's supremacy in modern science, the most successful
movement of thought that history so far records, stands unquestioned.

Would that in the pages of such a man we might find a clear statement of the method used by his powerful mind in the accomplishment of his dazzling performances, with perhaps specific and illuminating directions for those less gifted; or an exact and consistent logical analysis of the ultimate bearings of the unprecedented intellectual revolution which he carried to such a decisive issue! But what a disappointment as we turn the leaves of his works! Only a handful of general and often vague statements about his method, which have to be laboriously interpreted and supplemented by a painstaking study of his scientific biography—though, to be sure, he hardly suffers in this respect by comparison with even the best of his forerunners, such as Descartes and Barrow—one of the most curious and exasperating features of this whole magnificent movement is that none of its great representatives appears to have known with satisfying clarity just what he was doing or how he was doing it. And as for the ultimate philosophy of the universe implied by the scientific conquests, Newton did little more than take over the ideas on such matters which had been shaped for him by his intellectual ancestry, merely bringing them occasionally up to date where his personal discoveries obviously made a difference, or remoulding them slightly into a form more palatable to certain of his extra-scientific interests. In scientific discovery and formulation Newton was a marvellous genius; as a philosopher he was uncritical, sketchy, inconsistent, even second-rate.

His paragraphs on method are, however, superior to his other metaphysical pronouncements, a fact which is natural enough in view of the more immediate scientific bearing of the former and Newton's possession of a valuable heritage in the discussion and practice of his great predecessors. Let us see how he describes his method, so far as is necessary for an appreciation of his metaphysical influence.

Newton observes in his preface to the *Principia* that "all the difficulty of philosophy seems to consist in this—from the phenomena of motions to investigate the forces of nature, and then from these forces to demonstrate the other phenomena." This statement is highly interesting in that it reveals at once the precise field to which Newton confined his work. It is the phenomena of *motions* that is to be the object of our study, and that study is to proceed by the discovery of forces (defined, of course, as the cause of all changes in motion), from which in turn demonstrations are to be drawn, applying to, and confirmed by, other motions. In fact Newton never rose, in his conception of method, to any higher degree of generality than that revealed in his own practice—it is always *his* method that he is talking about. This is, perhaps, to be expected, though it is somewhat disappointing philosophically.

A. The Mathematical Aspect

The phrase "to demonstrate the other phenomena" at once suggests the fundamental place of mathematics in Newton's method, which he himself insists upon in elucidating the meaning of his chosen title—*Mathematical Principles of Natural Philosophy*—which, by the way, aptly expresses in brief form the fundamental assumption of the new movement. "We offer this work as mathematical principles of philosophy. . . . By the propositions mathematically demonstrated in the first book, we then derive from the celestial phenomena the forces of gravity with which bodies tend to the sun and the several planets. Then, from these forces, by other propositions which are also mathematical, we deduce the motions of the planets, the comets, the moon, and the sea. I wish we could derive the rest of the phenomena of nature by the same kind of reasoning from mechanical principles; for I am induced by many reasons to suspect that they may all depend upon certain forces by which the particles of bodies, by some causes hitherto unknown, are either mutually impelled towards each other, and cohere in regular figures, or are repelled and recede from each other; which forces being unknown, philosophers have hitherto attempted the search of nature in vain; but I hope the principles here laid down will afford some light either to that or some truer method of philosophy." [1]

[1] *Preface,* Motte translation.

This passage plunges us at once into the central rôle which Newton conceives mathematics to play in natural philosophy and his constant hope that all natural phenomena might in the end prove explicable in terms of mathematical mechanics. Judging from his remarks thus far quoted, the procedure of science is twofold, the deduction of forces from certain motions, and the demonstration of other motions from the forces thus known.

We might expect to find a strong statement of the place of mathematics in philosophical method in his *Universal Arithmetic,* which contains the substance of his lectures at Cambridge in the years 1673–83. In this we are disappointed, his directions on translating problems into the mathematical language being applied only to questions which already obviously involved quantitative relationships.[2] The most interesting feature philosophically in the book is the setting up of arithmetic and algebra as the basic mathematical sciences,[3] in opposition to the "universal geometry" of Descartes, Hobbes, and Barrow. Either is to be used, however, where it furnishes the easiest and simplest method of demonstration.[4] Newton was led to this shift mainly by methodological considerations, his invention of the fluxional calculus furnishing him with a tool whose operations could not be fully represented geometrically. At the same time some of his remarks on method in these lectures are suggestive. Inasmuch as we are to treat mechanics and optics algebraically, we must introduce symbols to represent all of their properties with which we are concerned (such as the direction of motion and of force, and the position, brightness, and distinctness of optical images) in their mathematical reduction.[5] This thought is not further elaborated, and when Newton comes to detailed directions he does not tell us how to pick out such qualities, but takes it for granted that they have already been clearly analysed out of the phenomena. "Having therefore any problem proposed, compare the quan-

[2] Ralphson and Cunn translation, London, 1769, pp. 174, 177.
[3] *Arithmetic,* pp. 1, ff. 9.
[4] *Arithmetic,* p. 465, ff. Cf. p. 357.
[5] *Arithmetic,* p. 10.

tities which it involves, and making no difference between the given and sought ones, consider how they depend one upon another, that you may know what quantities, if they are assumed, will, by proceeding synthetically, give the rest." [6] "For you may assume any quantities by the help whereof it is possible to come to equations; only taking this care, that you obtain as many equations from them as you assume quantities really unknown." [7]

If, however, we turn to the *Opticks*, published first in 1704 but representing for the most part work done thirty to forty years earlier, we find brief indications of a somewhat more general conception of mathematical method, which we wish Newton might have developed at greater length. "And these theorems being admitted into optics [respecting the refraction and composition of light], there would be scope enough of handling that science voluminously after a new manner; not only by teaching those things that tend to the perfection of vision, but also by determining mathematically all kinds of phenomena of colours which could be produced by refractions. For to do this, there is nothing else requisite than to find out the separations of heterogeneous rays, and their various mixtures and proportions in every mixture. By this way of arguing I invented almost all the phenomena described in these books, beside some others less necessary to the argument; and by the successes I met with in the trials, I dare promise, that to him who shall argue truly, and then try all things with good glasses and sufficient circumspection, the expected event will not be wanting. But he is first to know what colours will arise from any others mixed in any assigned proportion." [8] Newton here evidently conceives himself to have extended the bounds of mathematical optics by applying the mathematical method to the phenomena of colours, having done so by finding out the "separations of heterogeneous rays and their various mixtures and proportions in every mixture." At the end of the first

[6] *Arithmetic,* p. 202.

[7] *Arithmetic,* p. 209.

[8] *Opticks,* 3rd edition, London, 1721, p. 114, ff. In these quotations the spelling is modernized.

book he sums up his conclusions on this point by asserting that as a result of his precise experimental determination of the qualities of refrangibility and reflexibility, "the science of colours becomes a speculation as truly mathematical as any other part of optics." [9] Newton's eagerness thus to reduce another group of phenomena to mathematical formulæ illustrates again the fundamental place of mathematics in his work, but as regards the method by which he accomplished that reduction his statements are too brief to be of much aid. Let us turn to the other and equally prominent aspect of his method, the experimental.

B. The Empirical Aspect

It is obvious to the most cursory student of Newton that he was as thoroughgoing an empiricist as he was a consummate mathematician. Not only does he hold, with Kepler, Galileo, and Hobbes, that "our business is with the causes of sensible effects," [10] and insist, in every statement of his method, that it is the observed phenomena of nature that we are endeavouring to explain; but experimental guidance and verification must accompany every step of the explanatory process.[11] For Newton there was absolutely no *a priori* certainty, such as Kepler, Galileo, and pre-eminently Descartes believed in, that the world is through and through mathematical, still less that its secrets can be fully unlocked by the mathematical methods already perfected. The world is what it is; so far as exact mathematical laws can be discovered in it, well and good; so far as not, we must seek to expand our mathematics or resign ourselves to some other less certain method. This is obviously

[9] *Opticks,* p. 218.

[10] *System of the World,* 3rd Vol. of Motte's translation of Newton's *Mathematical Principles of Natural Philosophy,* London, 1803, p. 10.

[11] *Opticks,* pp. 351, 377; *Principles,* Preface, I, 174; II, 162, 314.

the spirit of the paragraph from the preface of the *Principia* already quoted: "I wish we could derive the rest of the phenomena of nature by the same kind of reasoning from mechanical principles. . . . but I hope the principles here laid down will afford some light either to that or some truer method of philosophy." The tentative mood of empiricism is frankly present here, and hence it is that for Newton, in marked contrast with Galileo and Descartes, there is a distinct difference between mathematical truths and physical truths. "That the resistance of bodies is in the ratio of the velocity, is more a mathematical hypothesis than a physical one," [12] and a similar passage occurs in connexion with his investigation of fluids.[13] Problems like these, of course, even Galileo and Descartes would not have presumed to settle *a priori,* but simply because it is impossible to deduce answers to them from the fundamental mathematical principles accepted as the structure of nature; it is just when deductions from such principles lead to alternative possibilities that experiment need be called in to decide. For Newton, however, mathematics must be continually modelled on experience; and wherever he permitted himself lengthy deductions from principles he zealously insisted on the purely abstract character of the results till they became physically verified.

Newton was thus the common heir of the two important and fruitful movements in the preceding development of science, the empirical and experimental as well as the deductive and mathematical. He was the follower of Bacon, Gilbert, Harvey, and Boyle, just as truly as the successor of

[12] *Principles,* II, 9.

[13] *Principles,* II, 62—"If in this manner particles repel others of their own kind that lie next them, but do not exert their virtue on the more remote, particles of this kind will compose such fluids as are treated of in this proposition. If the virtue of any particle diffuse itself every way *in infinitum,* there will be required a greater force to produce an equal condensation of a greater quantity of the fluid. But whether elastic fluids do really consist of particles so repelling each other is a physical question. We have here demonstrated mathematically the property of fluids consisting of particles of this kind that hence philosophers may take occasion to discuss that question."

Copernicus, Kepler, Galileo, and Descartes; and if it were possible wholly to separate the two aspects of his method, it would have to be said that Newton's ultimate criterion was more empirical than mathematical. Despite the title of his great work, he had far less confidence in deductive reasoning as applied to physical problems than the average modern scientist. Continually he called in experimental verification, even for the solution of questions whose answers would seem to be involved in the very meanings of his terms, such as the proportionality of resistance to density.[14] Having defined mass in terms of density and also in terms of resistance, such proportionality would seem to be involved in the very meaning of the words. In the *Universal Arithmetic*, he even intimates that some problems cannot properly be translated into the mathematical language at all, a hideous heresy to Galileo or Descartes. It is not too much to say that for Newton mathematics was solely a method for the solution of problems posed by sensible experience. He was little interested in mathematical reasonings which were not destined for application to physical problems; they were essentially a helpful tool in the reduction of physical phenomena. This is clearly proclaimed in the preface to the *Principia*: "Since the ancients . . . made great account of the science of mechanics in the investigation of natural things; and the moderns, laying aside substantial forms and occult qualities, have endeavoured to subject the phenomena of nature to the laws of mathematics, I have in this treatise cultivated mathematics so far as it regards philosophy. The ancients considered mechanics in a twofold respect; as rational, which proceeds accurately by demonstration; and practical." Newton observes that that which is perfectly accurate came to be called geometrical; what is less so, mechanical: but this distinction must not lead us to forget that the two appeared originally as a single science of mechanical practice.[15] For example, "to describe right lines and circles are problems, but not geometrical problems. The solution of these problems is required from mechanics; and by geometry

[14] *Opticks*, p. 340, ff.

[15] The whole preface should be read in this connexion.

the use of them, when so solved, is shown; and it is the glory of geometry that from those few principles, *fetched from without,* it is able to do so many things. *Therefore geometry is founded in mechanical practice, and is nothing but that part of universal mechanics which accurately proposes and demonstrates the art of measuring.* But since the manual arts are chiefly conversant in the moving of bodies, it comes to pass that geometry is commonly referred to their magnitudes, and mechanics to their motion. In this sense rational mechanics will be the science of motions resulting from any forces whatsoever, and of the forces required to produce any motion, accurately proposed and demonstrated." The empirical and practical stress here is central; geometry is a part of universal mechanics; it and the other branches of mechanics together make up a single science of the motions of bodies, and that science developed originally in response to practical needs.

c. Attack on "Hypotheses"

We should expect then in Newton a strong insistence on the necessity of experiment and small patience with ideas about the world which were not deductions, through experiment, from sensible phenomena, or exactly verifiable in experience. His works are filled with a constant polemic against "hypotheses", by which he usually meant ideas of this character. In the days of his early optical experiments this polemic takes the mild form of declaring for the postponement of hypotheses till accurate experimental laws are established by a study of the available facts.[16] As a matter of fact, after properties and

[16] *Isaaci Newtoni Opera quae exstant Omnia,* ed. Samuel Horsley, 5 Vols., London, 1779, ff., Vol. IV, p. 314, ff.—"If any one offers conjectures about the truth of things from the mere possibility of hypotheses, I do not see how anything certain can be determined in any science . . . wherefore I judged that one should abstain from considering hypotheses, as from a fallacious argument." "For the best and safest method of philosophizing seems to be, first diligently to investigate the properties of things and establish them by experiments, and

laws are thus established experimentally, all the proffered hypotheses that cannot be reconciled with them are at once rejected, and often several different hypotheses will be found reconcilable if properly interpreted.[17] But Newton's absorbing interest lay in the properties and experimental laws immediately demonstrable from the facts, and these he insisted on absolutely distinguishing from hypotheses. Nothing angered him more than to have his doctrine of the refrangibility of light called an hypothesis; in answer to the charge he affirms with emphasis that his theory "seemed to contain nothing else than certain properties of light, which I have discovered and regard it not difficult to prove; and if I had not perceived them to be true I would have preferred to reject them as futile and inane speculation, rather than to acknowledge them as my hypothesis." [18] This affirmation he follows up with other vigorous assertions of the superiority of the way of experiments to the method of deduction from *a priori* assumptions. "In the meanwhile give me leave to insinuate, Sir, that I cannot think it effectual for determining truth, to examine the several ways by which phenomena may be explained, unless where there can be a perfect enumeration of all those ways. You know, the proper method for inquiring after the properties of things, is to deduce them from experiments. . . . And therefore I could wish all objections were suspended, taken from hypotheses, or any other heads than these two: of showing the insufficiency of experiments to determine these queries, or prove any other parts of my theory, by assigning the flaws and defects in my conclusions drawn from them; or of producing other experiments, which directly contradict me, if any such may seem to occur." [19] Newton by no means refrained entirely from hypothetical speculations on the nature of light,

then later seek hypotheses to explain them." "For hypotheses ought to be fitted merely to explain the properties of things and not attempt to predetermine them except so far as they can be an aid to experiments."

[17] *Opera,* IV, 318, ff.

[18] *Opera,* IV, 310. Cf. also p. 318, ff.

[19] *Opera,* IV, 320.

but he attempted to keep clear the distinction between such suggestions and his exact experimental results. He was especially provoked by Hooke's abuse, as he regarded it, of his suggestion that the rays of light are corporeal. "This, it seems, Mr. Hooke takes for my hypothesis. It is true, that from my theory I argue the corporeity of light, but I do it without any absolute positiveness, as the word *perhaps* intimates, and make at most but a very plausible consequence of the doctrine, and not a fundamental supposition . . . Had I intended any such hypothesis, I should somewhere have explained it. But I knew that the properties, which I declared of light, were in some measure capable of being explicated not only by that, but by many other mechanical hypotheses; and therefore I chose to decline them all, and speak of light in general terms, considering it abstractedly as something or other propagated every way in straight lines from luminous bodies, without determining what that thing is." [20] This position he clarifies by further statements. "I do not think it needful to explicate my doctrine by any hypothesis at all." [21] "You see, therefore, how much it is beside the business in hand, to dispute about hypothesis." [22] "But if there be yet any doubting [my conclusions], it is better to put the event on further circumstances of the experiment, than to acquiesce in the possibility of any hypothetical explanation." [23]

It is proved a forlorn hope, however, that his scientific contemporaries would come to appreciate the fundamental distinction between hypothesis and experimental law—Newton was involved in squabble after squabble about the nature and validity of his doctrines—with the result, that as the years passed, he felt himself forced to the conviction that the only safe method was to ban hypotheses entirely from experimental philosophy, confining himself rigorously to the discovered and exactly verifiable properties and laws alone. This position is decisively taken in the *Principia* and in all subsequent works;

[20] *Opera,* IV, 324, ff.

[21] *Opera,* IV, 328.

[22] *Opera,* IV, 329.

[23] *Opera,* IV, 335.

in the *Opticks,* to be sure, he could not avoid some lengthy speculations, but conscientiously excluded them from the main body of the work, proposing them merely as queries to guide further experimental inquiry. The classic pronouncement on the rejection of hypothesis occurs at the end of the *Principia.* "Whatever is not deduced from the phenomena is to be called an hypothesis; and hypotheses, whether metaphysical or physical, whether of occult qualities or mechanical, have no place in experimental philosophy. In this philosophy particular propositions are inferred from the phenomena, and afterwards rendered general by induction. Thus it was that the impenetrability, the mobility, and the impulsive force of bodies, and the laws of motion and of gravitation, were discovered." [24]

With these illuminating assertions in mind we must press as exceedingly important the fourth *Rule of Reasoning in Philosophy,* which, if read aright, absolves Newton from the charge of having accepted in his philosophy certain *a priori* principles, apparently assumed in the other three rules; although, to be sure, his guarded language, especially in the third rule, ought to dissuade us from any such complaint. The first rule is the principle of simplicity: "We are to admit no more causes of natural things than such as are both true and sufficient to explain their appearances. To this purpose, the philosophers say, that nature does nothing in vain, and more is in vain when less will serve; for nature is pleased with simplicity, and affects not the pomp of superfluous causes." [25] The second rule is, that "to the same natural effects we must, as far as possible, assign the same causes." The later more mathematical expression of this principle is that where different events are expressed by the same equations, they must be regarded as produced by the same forces. The third rule appears even more definitely than these to go beyond strict empirical principles. "The qualities of bodies, which admit neither intension nor remission of degrees, and which are found to belong to all bodies within the reach of our experiments, are to be esteemed the universal qualities of all bodies

[24] *Principles,* II, 314. Cf. also *Opticks,* p. 380.

[25] *Principles,* II, 160, ff.

whatsoever." Is not this a highly speculative assumption of the Cartesian sort, that it is legitimate to generalize *ad infinitum* the qualities discovered in the small realm of our experience; or is it perhaps a purely methodological postulate? Newton goes on to explain that he regards this rule as nothing more than a combination of the experimental method with the first principle of the uniformity of nature. "For since the qualities of bodies are only known to us by experiments, we are to hold for universal all such as universally agree with experiments; and such as are not liable to diminution can never be quite taken away. We are certainly not to relinquish the evidence of experiments for the sake of dreams and vain fictions of our own devising; nor are we to recede from the analogy of nature, which uses to be simple, and always consonant to itself." We are thus brought back to the first two principles, that of the simplicity and uniformity of nature and the identity of causes where effects are the same. Are these apriorisms speculative assumptions about the structure of the universe, which make it always possible to reduce its phenomena to laws, especially mathematical laws; or were they to Newton a matter of method merely, to be used tentatively as a principle of further inquiry? It is perhaps impossible to answer this question with absolute confidence. At those times when the theological basis of Newton's science was uppermost in his mind, it is probable that he would have answered substantially as Galileo and Descartes did. But in his strictly scientific paragraphs the emphasis is overwhelmingly in favour of their tentative, positivistic character, hence the fourth rule of reasoning in philosophy, which we are now to quote, must be regarded as imposing definite limits on all of the other three.

"In experimental philosophy we are to look upon propositions collected by general induction from phenomena as accurately or very nearly true, notwithstanding any contrary hypotheses that may be imagined, till such time as other phenomena occur, by which they may either be made more accurate, or liable to exceptions. This rule we must follow, that the argument of induction may not be evaded by hypotheses." In other words, we have no metaphysical guarantee whatever against there appearing exceptions to even our most confidently adopted principles; empiricism is the ultimate test. That this applies to the basic principle of the simplicity and uniformity of nature itself appears from an interesting passage in the *Opticks*. That it should be so is very reasonable [*i.e.*, that the theorem of the uniform proportion of the sines applies to all the rays of light], nature being ever conformable to herself; but an experimental proof is desired." [26] No deduction from an accepted principle, no matter how general or clearly derived from past phenomena, can therefore pass for absolute or physically certain, without careful and continued experimental verification.

D. Newton's Union of Mathematics and Experiment

How, now, did Newton propose to unite the mathematical and experimental methods? A full statement of his position on this point can only be given after a careful examination of his practice, for his words are disappointingly inadequate. The best passage is in his letter to Oldenburg in response to Hooke's attack, from which we have already quoted. "In the last place, I should take notice of a casual expression, which intimates a greater certainty in these things, than I ever promised, *viz. the certainty of mathematical demonstrations*. I said indeed, that the science of colours was mathematical, and as certain as any other part of optics; but who knows not that optics, and many other mathematical sciences, depend as well on physical sciences, as on mathematical demonstrations? And the absolute certainty of a science cannot exceed the certainty of its principles. Now the evidence, by which I asserted the propositions of colours, is in the next words expressed to be from experiments, and so but physical: whence the propositions themselves can be esteemed no more than physical principles of a science. And if those principles be such, that on them a mathematician may determine all the phenomena

[26] P. 66.

of colours, that can be caused by refractions, and that by disputing or demonstrating after what manner, and how much, those refractions do separate or mingle the rays, in which several colours are originally inherent; I suppose the science of colours will be granted mathematical, and as certain as any part of optics. And that this may be done, I have good reason to believe, because ever since I became first acquainted with these principles, I have, with constant success in the events, made use of them for this purpose." [27] Here again, Newton's failure to rise to any higher degree of generality than that characteristic of his own practice is disappointingly evident; at the same time he is saying some important and instructive things. Certain propositions about colours are derived from experiments, which propositions become the principles of the science, and are of such a sort that mathematical demonstrations can be made from them of all the phenomena of colour-refraction. This somewhat clearer form of Newton's own conception of his *modus operandi* a painstaking study of his scientific biography will generalize and greatly illumine in detail.

Newton's whole experimental-mathematical method would seem to be analysable, in the light of such a supplementary study, into three main steps. First, the simplification of phenomena by experiments, so that those characteristics of them that vary quantitatively, together with the mode of their variation, may be seized and precisely defined. This step has been practically neglected by later logicians, but it is clearly the way in which such fundamental concepts as refrangibility in optics and mass in physics were accurately fixed by Newton, and the simpler propositions about refraction, motion, and force discovered. Second, the mathematical elaboration of such propositions, usually by the aid of the calculus, in such a way as will express mathematically the operation of these principles in whatever quantities or relations they might be found. Third, further exact experiments must be made (1) to verify the applicability of these deductions in any new field

[27] *Opera,* IV, 342. Oldenburg was Secretary of the Royal Society.

and to reduce them to their most general form; (2) in the case of more complex phenomena, to detect the presence and determine the value of any additional causes (in mechanics, forces) which can then themselves be subjected to quantitative treatment; and (3) to suggest, in cases where the nature of such additional causes remains obscure, an expansion of our present mathematical apparatus so as to handle them more effectively. Thus, for Newton, careful experimentation must occur at the beginning and end of every important scientific step, because it is always the sensible facts that we are seeking to comprehend;[28] but the comprehension, so far as it is exact, must be expressed in the mathematical language. Hence by experiments we must discover those characteristics which can be handled in that language, and by experiments our conclusions must be verified. "Our purpose is only to trace out the quantity and properties of this force [attraction] from the phenomena and to apply what we discover in some simple cases, as principles, by which, in a mathematical way, we may estimate the effects thereof in more involved cases. For it would be endless and impossible to bring every particular to direct and immediate observation. We said, *in a mathematical way,* to avoid all questions about the nature or quality of this force (attraction), which we would not be understood to determine by any hypothesis." [29] We are now prepared to consider Newton's somewhat more general statement of his method in the last pages of the *Opticks,* where the positivistic consequence of his experimentalism and rejection of hypothesis is especially stressed.

These principles (mass, gravity, cohesion, etc.) I consider not as occult qualities, supposed to result from the specific forms of things, but as general laws of nature, by which the things themselves are formed; their truth appearing to us by phenomena, though their causes be not yet discovered. For these are manifest qualities, and their causes only are occult. And the *Aristotelians* gave the name

[28] Cf. *Opticks,* pp. 351, 364, ff.

[29] *System of the World* (*Principles,* Vol. III), p. 3.

of occult qualities not to manifest qualities, but to such qualities only as they supposed to lie hid in bodies, and to be the unknown causes of manifest effects; such as would be the causes of gravity, and of magnetic and electric attractions, and of fermentations, if we should suppose that these forces or actions arose from qualities unknown to us and incapable of being discovered and made manifest. Such occult qualities put a stop to the improvement of natural philosophy and therefore of late years have been rejected. To tell us that every species of things is endowed with an occult specific quality by which it acts and produces manifest effects, is to tell us nothing: *But to derive two or three general principles of motion from phenomena, and afterwards to tell us how the properties and actions of all corporeal things follow from those manifest principles, would be a very great step in philosophy, though the causes of those principles were not yet discovered:* and therefore I scruple not, to propose the principles of motion abovementioned, they being of very general extent, and leave their causes to be found out.[30]

We shall return later to this fundamental contrast which Newton conceived to exist between his own method and that of the preceding Aristotelian and Cartesian systems, with the resulting confidence which it gave him. An interesting question remains however to be asked about his method. Do not the very initial experiments and observations, as a result of which the mathematical behaviour of phenomena is defined, presuppose something which we can only speak of as an hypothesis, to direct those experiments to a successful issue? In the days of his early optical labours Newton would not have entirely refused assent; there are sometimes hypotheses which definitely "can be an aid to experiments."[31] But in his classic writings even such guiding ideas seem to be denied place and function. Apparently we need an hypothesis only in this very general sense, namely the expectation that inasmuch as na-

[30] *Opticks,* p. 377. Italics ours.

[31] Cf. p. 211, footnote.

ture has hitherto revealed herself as being to a large extent, a simple and uniform mathematical order, there are exact quantitative aspects and laws in any group of phenomena which simplifying experiments will enable us to detect, and enlarged experiments reduce to their most general form. Thus Newton feels it possible to speak of his method as *deducing* principles of motion *from phenomena*,[32] because these principles are exact and complete statements of the phenomena as far as their motion is concerned. And when induction is applied to these principles, their exactitude and completeness as a reduction of the phenomena are not at all lost; Newton simply means by it that they are expressed in their most general form as perceived to apply over a wider field. Thus there is no place for hypothesis in natural philosophy at all according to Newton's final view; we analyse phenomena to deduce their mathematical laws, of which those that are of wide applicability are rendered general by induction. The word induction does not derogate from the mathematical certainty of the results, and it must not mislead us when stressed in Newton's concluding statement of his method in the *Opticks*. It emphasizes his ultimate empiricism merely.

As in mathematics, so in natural philosophy, the investigation of difficult things by the method of analysis, ought ever to precede the method of composition. This analysis consists in making experiments and observations, and in drawing general conclusions from them by induction, and admitting of no objections against the conclusions, but such as are taken from experiments or other certain truths. For hypotheses are not to be regarded in experimental philosophy. And although the arguing from experiments and observations by induction be no demonstration of general conclusions: yet it is the best way of arguing which the nature of things admits of, and may be looked upon as so much the stronger, by how much the induction is more general. And if no exception occur from phenomena, the conclusion may be pronounced generally. But if at any time afterwards any exception shall occur from experiments, it

[32] *Principles,* II, 314.

may then begin to be pronounced with such exceptions as occur. By this way of analysis we may proceed from compounds to ingredients, and from motions to the forces producing them; and in general, from effects to their causes, and from particular causes to more general ones, till the argument end in the most general. This is the method of analysis: and the synthesis consists in assuming the causes discovered, and established as principles, and by them explaining the phenomena proceeding from them, and proving the explanations. In the first two books of these Optics, I proceeded by this analysis to discover and prove the original differences of the rays of light in respect of refrangibility, reflexibility, and colour, and their alternative fits of easy reflection and easy transmission, and the properties of bodies, both opaque and pellucid, on which their reflections and colours depend. And these discoveries being proved, may be assumed in the method of composition for explaining the phenomena arising from them: an instance of which method I gave in the end of the first book.[33]

It is abundantly clear from these earnest statements that Newton conceived himself to have made a most remarkable methodological discovery, despite the fact that he was unable to state his method in its full generality. Galileo had set aside explanation in terms of the ultimate *why* of physical events in favour of explanation in terms of their immediate *how, i.e.,* a mathematical formula expressing their processes and motions. But Galileo still carried over many metaphysical prejudices from his ancestry, while for the rest he erected his mathematical method into a metaphysics, and was able (excepting a few passages) to follow no clear distinction in his works between the scientific study of perceived motions and these more ultimate ideas. In Descartes the metaphysic of mathematics was still more central and controlling; the passion for a complete system of the universe still less surrendered. Boyle, for his part, was quite confident that ultimately the world is to be interpreted religiously, but as far as experi-

[33] *Opticks,* p. 380, ff. Compare with a statement of method in Kepler, VII, 212.

mental science is concerned he was ready to stress the meagreness of human knowledge and its tentative and gradual progress. Inasmuch, however, as Boyle was not a mathematician,
he saw no way to win certainty in science. Science is composed
of hypotheses, which have, to be sure, been tested and verified
as far as possible by experiments, but inasmuch as at any time
a contrary experiment may appear, we must be satisfied with
probabilism merely. Newton, as we have seen, was willing to
grant the possibility of exceptions, but he was in no wise willing
to grant that science was composed of hypotheses. Anything
that is not immediately deduced from the phenomena is to be
called an hypothesis and has no place in science, especially
attempts to explain the nature of the forces and causes revealed in the phenomena of motion. Such explanations by
their very nature are insusceptible of experimental verification.
We know, for example, that certain motions take place in
nature which we have been able to reduce to mathematical
law, and regarding these motions as the effects of a certain
kind of force, we call that force gravity. "But hitherto I have
been unable to discover the cause of those properties of
gravity from phenomena, and I frame no hypotheses." [34] The
ultimate nature of gravity is unknown; it is not necessary for
science that it be known, for science seeks to understand how
it acts, not what it is. *For Newton, then, science was composed
of laws stating the mathematical behaviour of nature solely—
laws clearly deducible from phenomena and exactly verifiable
in phenomena—everything further is to be swept out of science,
which thus becomes a body of absolutely certain truth about
the doings of the physical world.* By his intimate union of the
mathematical and experimental methods, Newton believed
himself to have indissolubly allied the ideal exactitude of the
one with the constant empirical reference of the other. *Science
is the exact mathematical formulation of the processes of the
natural world.* Speculation is at a discount, but motion has
unconditionally surrendered to the conquering mind of man.

[34] *Principles*, II, 314.

Section 2. The Doctrine of Positivism

Now, someone will ask, if this be a correct portrayal of Newton's method, is there not a flagrant contradiction in such a phrase as "the metaphysics of Newton"? Was not this rejection of hypothesis his most distinctive attainment, and did he not measurably succeed, at least in the main body of his works, in banning ideas about the nature of the universe at large? Is there not full justification for his claim to have discovered and used a method by which a realm of certain truth might be opened up and gradually widened quite independently of assumed solutions of ultimate problems? Newton, we are told, was the first great positivist.[35] Following Galileo and Boyle, but more consistently, he turned his back on metaphysics in favour of a small but growing body of exact knowledge. With his work the era of great speculative systems ended and a new day of exactitude and promise for man's intellectual conquest of nature dawned. How, then, speak of him as a metaphysician?

The main outlines of the answer to this criticism must be apparent from the whole course of our discussion. To answer it somewhat in detail, however, will furnish a helpful introduction and outline to our analysis of Newton's metaphysics.

To begin with, there is no escape from metaphysics, that is, from the final implications of any proposition or set of propositions. The only way to avoid becoming a metaphysician is to say nothing. This can be illustrated by analysing any statement you please; suppose we take the central position of positivism itself as an example. This can perhaps be fairly stated in some such form as the following: It is possible to acquire truths about things without presupposing any theory of their ultimate nature; or, more simply, it is possible to have a correct knowledge of the part without knowing the nature of

[35] Brewster, *Memoirs of the Life, Writings, and Discoveries of Sir Isaac Newton*, Edinburgh, 1855, Vol. II, p. 532.

the whole. Let us look at this position closely. That it is in some sense correct would seem to be vouched for by the actual successes of science, particularly mathematical science; we can discover regular relations among certain pieces of matter without knowing anything further about them. The question is not about its truth or falsity, but whether there is metaphysics in it. Well, subject it to a searching analysis, and does it not swarm with metaphysical assumptions? In the first place it bristles with phrases which lack precise definition, such as "ultimate nature", "correct knowledge", "nature of the whole", and assumptions of moment are always lurking in phrases which are thus carelessly used. In the second place, defining these phrases as you will, does not the statement reveal highly interesting and exceedingly important implications about the universe? Taking it in any meaning which would be generally accepted, does it not imply, for example, that the universe is essentially pluralistic (except, of course, for thought and language), that is, that some things happen without any genuine dependence on other happenings; and can therefore be described in universal terms without reference to anything else? Scientific positivists testify in various ways to this pluralistic metaphysic; as when they insist that there are isolable systems in nature, whose behaviour, at least in all prominent respects, can be reduced to law without any fear that the investigation of other happenings will do more than place that knowledge in a larger setting. Doubtless, strictly speaking, we could not say that we knew what would happen to our solar system if the fixed stars were of a sudden to vanish, but we do know that it is possible to reduce the major phenomena of our solar system to mathematical law on principles that do not depend on the presence of the fixed stars, and hence with no reason to suppose that their disappearance would upset our formulations in the least. Now this is certainly an important presumption about the nature of the universe, suggesting many further considerations. Let us forbear, however, to press our reasoning further at this point; the lesson is that even the attempt to escape metaphysics is no sooner put in the form of a proposition than it is seen to involve highly significant metaphysical postulates.

For this reason there is an exceedingly subtle and insidious danger in positivism. If you cannot avoid metaphysics, what kind of metaphysics are you likely to cherish when you sturdily suppose yourself to be free from the abomination? Of course it goes without saying that in this case your metaphysics will be held uncritically because it is unconscious; moreover, it will be passed on to others far more readily than your other notions inasmuch as it will be propagated by insinuation rather than by direct argument. That a serious student of Newton fails to see that his master had a most important metaphysic, is an exceedingly interesting testimony to the pervading influence, throughout modern thought, of the Newtonian first philosophy.

Now the history of mind reveals pretty clearly that the thinker who decries metaphysics will actually hold metaphysical notions of three main types. For one thing, he will share the ideas of his age on ultimate questions, so far as such ideas do not run counter to his interests or awaken his criticism. No one has yet appeared in human history, not even the most profoundly critical intellect, in whom no important *idola theatri* can be detected, but the metaphysician will at least be superior to his opponent in this respect, in that he will be constantly on his guard against the surreptitious entrance and unquestioned influence of such notions. In the second place, if he be a man engaged in any important inquiry, he must have a method, and he will be under a strong and constant temptation to make a metaphysics out of his method, that is, to suppose the universe ultimately of such a sort that his method must be appropriate and successful. Some of the consequences of succumbing to such a temptation have been abundantly evident in our discussion of the work of Kepler, Galileo, and Descartes. Finally since human nature demands metaphysics for its full intellectual satisfaction, no great mind can wholly avoid playing with ultimate questions, especially where they are powerfully thrust upon it by considerations arising from its positivistic investigations, or by certain vigorous extra-scientific interests, such as religion. But inasmuch as the positivist mind has failed to school itself in careful metaphysical thinking, its ventures at such points will be apt to appear pitiful, inadequate, or even fantastic. Each of these three types is exemplified in Newton. His general conception of the physical world and of man's relation to it, including the revolutionary doctrine of causality and the Cartesian dualism in its final ambiguous outcome (which were the two central features of the new ontology) with their somewhat less central corollaries about the nature and process of sensation, primary and secondary qualities, the imprisoned seat and petty powers of the human soul, was taken over without examination as an assured result of the victorious movement whose greatest champion he was destined to become. His views on space and time belong in part to the same category, but were in part given a most interesting turn by convictions of the third sort. To the second type belongs his treatment of mass, that is, it gains its metaphysical importance from a tendency to extend the implications of his method. Of the third type, mainly, are his ideas of the nature and function of the ether, and of God's existence and relation to the world uncovered by science. We can hardly do better than allow this analysis of the three types to furnish us with an outline of the succeeding sections.

The theology of Newton received in the generation after him a severe battering at the hands of Hume and the French radicals; somewhat later by the keen analysis of Kant. Also his scientific reasons offered for the existence of God appeared no longer cogent after the brilliant discoveries of subsequent investigators like Laplace. The rest of the new metaphysics, however, as further developed at his hands, passed with his scientific exploits into the general current of intelligent opinion in Europe, was taken for granted because insinuated without defensive argument, and borrowing an unquestioned certainty from the clear demonstrability of the mechanical or optical theorems to which it was attached, it became the settled background for all important further developments in science and philosophy. Magnificent, irrefutable achievements gave Newton authority over the modern world, which, feeling itself to have become free from metaphysics through Newton the positivist, has become shackled and controlled by a very definite metaphysics through Newton the metaphysician. What are the essential elements of that metaphysics?

Section 3. Newton's General Conception of the World, and of Man's Relation to It

We may begin by summarizing briefly the points which Newton merely adopted from his forebears, indicating simply the precise form in which he passed them on to the modern world at large. Just as Boyle, though not a skilled mathematician himself, had accepted without serious question the main structure of the universe as portrayed in Galileo, Descartes, and Hobbes, so Newton, although his mathematics was ultimately a tool for the service of experimental philosophy, took over without criticism the general view of the physical world and of man's place in it which had developed at the hands of his illustrious predecessors. For Newton too the world of matter was a world possessing mathematical characteristics fundamentally. It was composed ultimately of absolutely hard, indestructible particles, equipped with the same characteristics which had now become familiar under the head of primary qualities, with the exception that Newton's discovery and exact definition of a new exact-mathematical quality of bodies, the *vis inertiæ*, induced him to join it to the list. All changes in nature are to be regarded as separations, associations, and motions of these permanent atoms.[36]

At the same time it must be acknowledged that Newton's strong empiricism tended continually to tame and qualify his mathematical interpretation of the atomic theory. The atoms are predominantly mathematical, but they are also nothing but smaller elements of sensibly experienced objects. This is evident from his most systematic statement in the *Principia*.

> We no other way know the extension of bodies than by our senses, nor do these reach it in all bodies; but because we perceive extension in all bodies that are sensible, therefore we ascribe it universally to all others also. That abundance of bodies are hard, we learn by experience; and

[36] *Opticks*, p. 376.

because the hardness of the whole arises from the hardness of the parts, we therefore justly infer the hardness of the undivided particles not only of the bodies we feel but of all others. That all bodies are impenetrable, we gather not from reason, but from sensation. The bodies which we handle we find impenetrable, and thence conclude impenetrability to be a universal property of all bodies whatsoever. That all bodies are movable, and endowed with certain powers (which we call the *vires inertiae*) of persevering in their motion, or in their rest, we only infer from the like properties observed in the bodies which we have seen. The extension, hardness, impenetrability, mobility, and *vis inertiæ* of the whole, result from the extension, hardness, impenetrability, mobility, and *vires inertiae* of the parts, and thence we conclude the least particles of all bodies to be also all extended, and hard, and impenetrable, and movable, and endowed with their proper *vires inertiae*.[37]

Newton even suggests that with the invention of more powerful microscopes we might be able to see the largest of these particles.[38] In this statement the ultimacy of empiricism and the experimental reference are surely just as evident as the fact that just those qualities are seized upon as fundamental in nature which it had been found possible by Newton's time to handle by the exact-mathematical method. The world of physics is the sensible world, but it is uniquely characterized by the qualities which its reduction to mathematical law necessarily emphasized. "All these things being considered, it seems probable to me, that God in the beginning formed matter in solid, massy, hard, impenetrable, movable particles, of such sizes and figures, and with such other properties, in such proportion to space, as most conduced to the end for which he formed them; and that these primitive particles, being solids, are incomparably harder than any porous bodies compounded of them; even so very hard, as never to wear or break in pieces: no ordinary power being able to divide what God

[37] *Principles*, II, 161.

[38] *Opticks*, p. 236, ff.

himself made one in the first creation." [39] "Yet, had we proof of but one experiment that any undivided particle, in breaking a hard and solid body, suffered a division, we might by virtue of this rule conclude that the undivided as well as the divided particles may be divided and actually separated to infinity." [40] "While the particles continue entire, they may compose bodies of one and the same nature and texture in all ages: but should they wear away or break in pieces, the nature of things depending on them would be changed . . . And therefore that Nature may be lasting, the changes of corporeal things are to be placed only in the various separations and new associations and motions of these permanent particles; compound bodies being apt to break, not in the midst of solid particles, but where those particles are laid together, and only touch in a few points." [41]

Such being the basic structure of the physical world, how does Newton conceive of man and his relation to it? Here, too, the British genius accepted without question the main features of the physiology and metaphysics of Galileo and Descartes, and in this case his ordinarily careful empirical testing of ideas failed to exert itself. In the passage from the *Principia,* cited above, and elsewhere when his empiricism is not forgotten, Newton speaks of man as being in immediate perceptual and knowing contact with physical things themselves—it is they that we see, hear, smell, and touch.[42] When, however, especially in the *Opticks,* he treats more directly of man's relation to nature, we discover our mistake. Full assent is given to the now orthodox view. Man's soul (as with Boyle, identical with his mind) is locked up within his body and has no immediate contact whatsoever with the outside world; it is present in a particular part of the brain, called for that reason the *sensorium,* to which motions are conveyed from external objects by the nerves, and from which motions are transmitted to the muscles by the animal spirits. In connexion with sight,

[39] *Opticks,* p. 375, ff. Cf. also p. 364, ff.

[40] *Principles,* II, 161.

[41] *Opticks,* p. 376.

[42] *Principles,* II, 312.

physiological investigation had by Newton's time combined
with the Democritean-Cartesian-Hobbesian metaphysics to
suggest an especially complicated set of barriers between the
experience of vision and the object we suppose ourselves to
see; not only is the soul confined to the brain, to which motions
must be conveyed from the inaccessible thing outside, but even
the motions as finally transmitted come not from the external
object, but from its image on the retina. "When a man views
any object, the light which comes from the several points of
the object is so defracted by the transparent skins and humours
of the eye . . . as to converge and meet again at so many
points in the bottom of the eye, and there to paint the picture
of the object upon that skin (called the *Tunica Retina*) with
which the bottom of the eye is covered . . . And these pictures propagated by motion along the fibres of the optic nerves
into the brain, are the cause of vision." [43] God only can see
objects themselves[44]; in the case of men "the images only
carried through the organs of sense into our little sensoriums,
are there seen and beheld by that which in us perceives and
thinks." Thus again, speaking in the twenty-third and twenty-
fourth queries of the *Opticks* about the functions of his
hypothesized ethereal medium, he asks: "Is not vision performed chiefly by the vibrations of this medium, excited in the
bottom of the eye by the rays of light, and propagated through
the solid, pellucid, and uniform capillamenta of the optic
nerves into the place of sensation? And is not hearing performed by the vibrations either of this or of some other medium, excited in the auditory nerves by the tremors of the air,
and propagated through the solid, pellucid, and uniform capillamenta of those nerves into the place of sensation? And so
of the other senses. Is not animal motion performed by the
vibrations of this medium, excited in the brain by the power
of the will, and propagated from thence through the solid,
pellucid, and uniform capillamenta of the nerves into the muscles, for contracting and dilating them?" [45]

[43] *Opticks*, p. 12.

[44] *Opticks*, p. 345. Cf. p. 379.

[45] *Opticks*, p. 328. Cf. p. 319, ff.

When we come from these quotations to Newton's clearest statements on the doctrine of primary and secondary qualities, we are prepared for no appreciable divergence from the doctrine as it had been handed on to him by his metaphysical forerunners. Because of his own labours in the field of optics, such statements, as we might expect, relate especially to colours.

Newton conceived his experiments on refraction and reflection to have definitely overthrown the theory that colours are qualities of objects. "These things being so, it can be no longer disputed whether there be colours in the dark, or whether they be the qualities of the objects we see; no, nor perhaps whether light be a body. For, since colours are the qualities of light, having its rays for their entire and immediate subject, how can we think those rays qualities also, unless one quality may be the subject of, and sustain another? which is, in effect, to call it substance . . . Besides, who ever thought any quality to be a heterogeneous aggregate, such as light is discovered to be? But to determine more absolutely what light is, after what manner refracted, and by what modes or actions it produceth in our minds the phantasms of colours, is not so easy, and I shall not mingle conjectures with certainties." [46] Apparently Newton's first alternative to the rejected theory of colours as qualities of objects, is that they are qualities of light, having its rays for their subject. We discover at the end of the quotation, however, that this must have been a slip of language. Newton there absolves himself from any intention of mingling conjectures with certainties. This remark implies that the preceding assumption is no conjecture, namely, that colours have no existence even in light, but are phantasms produced in our minds by the modes or actions of light; the only conjectural matter being the process by which this takes place. In the *Opticks* this position is asserted at somewhat greater length. "If at any time I speak of light and rays as coloured or endued with colours, I would be understood to speak not philosophically and properly, but grossly, and according to such conceptions as vulgar people in seeing all these experiments

[46] *Opera,* IV, 305. Note the scholastic terms and assumptions.

would be apt to frame. For the rays to speak properly are not coloured. In them there is nothing else than a certain power and disposition to stir up a sensation of this or that colour. For as sound in a bell or musical string or other sounding body, is nothing but a trembling motion, and in the air nothing but that motion propagated from the object, and in the sensorium 'tis a sense of that motion under the form of sound; so colours in the object are nothing but a disposition to reflect this or that sort of rays more copiously than the rest; in the rays they are nothing but their dispositions to propagate this or that motion into the sensorium, and in the sensorium they are sensations of those motions under the forms of colours." [47]

Here the current doctrine of secondary qualities is clearly proclaimed. They have no real existence outside of human brains, save as a disposition of the bodies or the rays to reflect or propagate certain motions. Outside, nothing but the particles of matter, equipped with the qualities which have become mathematically handled, moving in certain ways. How do these motions excite the various sensations of colour? Newton at first (cf. above) professed himself to offer no answer to this problem. In view, however, of his experiments on refraction and his acceptance of the atomic theory, he could hardly avoid suggesting a general explanation in his *Opticks*. "Do not several sorts of rays make vibrations of several bignesses, which according to their bignesses excite sensations of several colours much after the manner that the vibrations of the air, according to their several bignesses, excite sensations of several sounds? And particularly do not the most refrangible rays excite the shortest vibrations for making a sensation of deep violet, the least refrangible the largest for making a sensation of deep red, and the several intermediate sorts of rays, vibrations of several intermediate bignesses to make sensations of the several intermediate colours? May not the harmony and discord of colours arise from the proportions of the vibrations propagated through the fibres of the optic nerves into the brain, as the harmony and discord of sounds arise from the proportions of the vibrations of the air? For some colours,

[47] *Opticks,* p. 108, ff.

if they be viewed together, are agreeable to one another, as those of gold and indigo, and others disagree." [48] This mathematical theory of colour harmony is an interesting reminder of Kepler's attempt to reduce the music of the spheres to our form of musical notation. Newton follows it with the hypothesis that the images of an object seen with both eyes unite where the optic nerves meet before they come into the brain "in such a manner that their fibres make but one entire species, or picture, half of which on the right side of the sensorium comes from the right side of both eyes through the right side of both optic nerves to the place where the nerves meet, and from thence on the right side of the head into the brain, and the other half on the left side of the sensorium comes in like manner from the left side of both eyes." This remarkable notion was forced upon Newton and his contemporaries in their attempt to explain why it is that we see an object single instead of double. Believing, as they did, that we do not see objects themselves, but that it is their images on the two retinæ that are carried to the sensorium, this was a real difficulty that had to be somehow met.

Newton never states his conviction on the fundamental issue between More and Descartes, that of the extension of spirit, but the mere fact that he did not champion Descartes' attempt to assign a different ultimate status to spirit was sufficient to throw his whole weight, to his contemporaries and followers, on the side of the popular interpretation of the great French thinker. Largely justified, as we have seen, by the latter's own ambiguities, vigorously furthered by the writings of Hobbes and Boyle, the conviction was spreading among zealots of the new era that the human mind is a unique but small substance imprisoned in the brain. Now, too, the significant passages in Newton with which we have been occupied naturally seemed to them to imply exactly this status. More had secured no following among intelligent people for his attempt to assign a possible extension of the soul somewhat beyond the limits of the human body—this was quite irreconcilable with the mood of science and offered no compensations in the way of a

[48] *Opticks,* p. 320, ff.

solution of ultimate problems, epistemological or otherwise—
hence it is safe to say that at Newton's time for practically all
educated people, especially those to whom ideas meant images,
the soul was conceived as occupying a seat, or a small portion
of extension, within the brain, which place had come to be
known as the sensorium. There was nothing in Newton to
upset this notion and everything to support it. Furthermore,
had Newton expressed himself definitely on this point, it is
highly probable that he would have approved precisely this
current view. He agreed with More on the extension of God,
as we shall see later, and he certainly believed in extended
ethereal spirits. Why would he not, then, have believed in the
spatiality of the human soul, though it is obvious from the
above citations that More's speculative spiritualism is not
present—the soul's place is entirely enclosed by the brain?

Hence in spite of Newton's earnest attempt to be empirical
through and through, in spite of his eagerness never to let his
mathematical method run away with him, the general picture
of the universe and of man's place in it which went forth under
his name was essentially that which had already been constructed and powerfully worked out by the great mathematical metaphysicians who had preceded him, and that in its most
ambiguous and least construable form. The tremendous problems thrust upon us by that picture he, no more than they,
appreciated, for in the main he also adopted their way, especially More's, of evading those problems by the appeal to God.
But it was of the greatest consequence for succeeding thought
that now the great Newton's authority was squarely behind
that view of the cosmos which saw in man a puny, irrelevant
spectator (so far as a being wholly imprisoned in a dark room
can be called such) of the vast mathematical system whose
regular motions according to mechanical principles constituted
the world of nature. The gloriously romantic universe of Dante
and Milton, that set no bounds to the imagination of man as
it played over space and time, had now been swept away.
Space was identified with the realm of geometry, time with
the continuity of number. The world that people had thought
themselves living in—a world rich with colour and sound, red-
olent with fragrance, filled with gladness, love and beauty,

speaking everywhere of purposive harmony and creative ideals —was crowded now into minute corners in the brains of scattered organic beings. The really important world outside was a world hard, cold, colourless, silent, and dead; a world of quantity, a world of mathematically computable motions in mechanical regularity. The world of qualities as immediately perceived by man became just a curious and quite minor effect of that infinite machine beyond. In Newton the Cartesian metaphysics, ambiguously interpreted and stripped of its distinctive claim for serious philosophical consideration, finally overthrew Aristotelianism and became the predominant world-view of modern times.

Section 4. Space, Time, and Mass

But Newton did more than accept and support the prevailing picture of man and his world that had developed among his predecessors. He himself made the most remarkable discoveries about that world that redound to the credit of modern science, and it is natural that in connexion with those discoveries he should have had occasion to state, in more explicit and propagable form than they, just how that world of nature beyond man is to be conceived. Since Newton nature came to be thought of by the modern mind as essentially a realm of masses, moving according to mathematical laws in space and time, under the influence of definite and dependable forces. How in detail did Newton portray these entities, especially space and time; and how did he come to sum up the irreducible characteristics of bodies under the term "mass"? It is to be observed that in this aspect of his work, Newton reveals to some extent each of the types of metaphysical beliefs noted in Section 2; in part he adopts ultimate views that were ready to his hand; in part he extends the implications of his mathematical method; in part he is resting upon the validity of certain quite extra-scientific convictions. The important thing to note is that here too his experimentalism quite fails him; he propounds, and that in the main body of his classic work, conceptions that were quite beyond the reach of sensible, experimental verification.

A. Mass

This apriorism, however, is not strongly pronounced in the case of mass. The definition of physical bodies as masses was the signal achievement needed in modern mechanics after the nature of space had been discovered by Galileo and Descartes and that of time formulated by Barrow. For Galileo, as for Newton's great contemporary Huyghens, mass was equivalent to weight; and for Descartes, motion being conceived as a mathematical concept in general, the possibility of reducing all varieties of motion to exact formulæ was not seriously considered. The fundamental fact of physical nature that made the Cartesian mechanics inadequate was the fact that two bodies geometrically equivalent may move differently when placed in identical relations with the same other bodies. Descartes, of course, was aware of this fact, but instead of trying to reduce it mathematically he chose to hide it under the speculative glamour of the theory of vortices.

Newton perceived this fact, and in the case of the most prominent differences of motion of this sort, the phenomena of gravity, succeeded in achieving the mathematical reduction. Moreover, he supplied the definitions of all the fundamental concepts necessary for the complete submission of motion to mathematical law. In the case of certain important phenomena which he had been unable himself to include within the scope of his principles, the advance was later made by the further application of his concepts, as in the inclusion of magnetism within Newtonian mechanics by Gauss. In Newton's case the discovery was intimately related to the famous first law of motion, already reached by Galileo and expressed in a fairly satisfactory fashion by Descartes and Hobbes. Every body tends to remain in its state of rest or of uniform motion in a straight line, but its tendency to do so varies in degree. Now this variation, Newton saw, was susceptible of exact quantitative formulation. Under the application of the same force (and here the second and third laws of motion are implied) different bodies depart from that state of rest or of uniform motion, *i.e.*, are accelerated, differently. Inasmuch as those differences are, and can be, solely differences of acceleration, they can be exactly compared in mathematical terms. Thus we can regard all bodies as possessing a *vis inertiæ*, or inertia, which is an exact-mathematical characteristic inasmuch as it is measurable by the acceleration imparted to them by a given external force. When we speak of bodies as masses, we mean that, in addition to geometrical characteristics, they possess this mechanical quality of *vis inertiæ*. It is obvious from the above that force and mass are entirely correlative terms, but once the discovery of mass was made it became easier to define force in terms of mass rather than *vice versa,* inasmuch as force is invisible, while a standard mass is a physical object that can be perceived and used. The same may be said of the concepts density and pressure, which were now given a more helpful place in mechanics when defined in terms of mass and bulk. It is probable that Newton's discovery of mass was influenced to some extent by Boyle's experiments on compressing gases. Boyle had found that the product of pressure by volume in the case of any gas was always a constant, and it is that constant which now, in proportionate relation to the *vis inertiæ* of other substances, becomes the mass of the gas. This relation to Boyle is suggested by the fact that Newton's definition of mass in the first paragraph of the *Principia* is in terms of density and volume; indeed, having chosen to define it in terms then more familiar rather than present it as an ultimate quality of bodies, he could hardly have done better.

The discovery that the same mass has a different weight at different distances from the centre of the earth, together with the mathematical elaboration of Kepler's laws of motion, led gradually, through the work of Borelli, Huyghens, Wren, Halley, and Hooke, to Newton's magnificent formulation of the law of gravitation, which united astronomy and mechanics in one mathematical science of matter in motion. The departure of the celestial masses from uniform motion in a straight line can be expressed by the same equation as the fall of terrestrial bodies to the earth. Every body in our world-system tends toward every other body directly in proportion to the product of their masses, and inversely in proportion to the square of the distance between their centres. Indeed, with the concepts of mass, force, and acceleration as Newton left them, especially with his calculus as a tool for the rapid and effective handling of problems regarding motion, it is difficult to conceive of any changes in motion whatsoever that are not mathematically reducible in his terms, though, of course, only such accelerations as are caused by fairly regular and constant forces is it worth the investigator's time and energy to attempt to reduce. Where changes of motion are irregular or unique, the problem usually remains unsolved, not because the tools are not at hand for their complete disposition, but because it is worth no one's while to effect the reduction.

What about the metaphysical bearings of the Newtonian concept of mass? Did Newton conceive of physical bodies as merely masses, that is, possessing none but geometrical qualities and *vis inertiæ*? Probably not. And yet the effect of his work was decidedly to encourage others so to conceive them. Here is a paradox demanding some explanation.

It is clear from Newton's writings, especially the *Principia* and the *Opticks,* that the major trend of his own thinking was decidedly against divesting bodies of all qualities but those which his own mathematical methodology would require him to leave. This was in great part a corollary of his vigorous empiricism. It will be remembered from the previous chapter that those characteristics which Newton listed as the primary qualities of elementary particles of bodies were ultimately justified empirically. To be sure, Newton does not equip them with all sensible qualities, due to his acceptance of the main features of the mathematical metaphysic of his scientific ancestry, especially the doctrine of primary and secondary qualities; yet he was thoroughly opposed to any attempt rigidly to sift them down to the fewest required for his scientific method. Had his thinking moved in such paths he would surely have deduced mobility from *vis inertiæ* and impenetrability from extension. Even this would have left hardness unreduced to the two qualities which constitute a body a mass; doubtless

Newton included it in part because of its necessity in his atomic theory of fluids and gases,[49] but in the main there is no reason to doubt that it rests on the experimental basis by which it was defended. We have no sensible experience of any bodies without some degree of hardness (*solidity* was the more popular term at the time); hence by generalization we ascribe it to all bodies.

In view of this strong empirical stress creeping into his atomism itself, how was it that Newton historically came to pose as the champion of the more rigid mechanical view of the physical realm? The main outlines of the answer have been indicated in the preceding chapter. But let us press the question more specifically. Of course it is understandable enough that the bulk of his scientific followers, not being in sympathy with Newton's extreme empiricism and not sharing much of his theological restraint, were ever ready to do for him what Galileo and Descartes had done for themselves, *i.e.*, transform a method into a metaphysics. But how could they blindly ignore the master's own words? The fact was, however, Newton had supplied them with more than the opportunity they needed. Just as Descartes had worked out an elaborate theory of an ethereal medium to explain everything about the motions of bodies which did not seem to be deducible from extension, so Newton played with an ethereal hypothesis which might serve to mechanize all motions which could not be deduced from the notion of mass. We shall consider this hypothesis in detail in the next chapter. Moreover, in his *magnum opus* there is a definite subordination of the hypothetical causes of these refractory phenomena to the *vis inertiæ* of bodies.[50] Gravity, for example, must not be ascribed to bodies universally, because it permits of remission by degrees (cf. third rule), and we have no assurance of its existence beyond our solar system. That it is a mass, however, is an essential quality of any body as such, and the principles of motion which result from, or rather explain, the notion of mass, are to be regarded as axioms of natural philosophy universally and necessarily

[49] *Opticks,* p. 364, ff.

[50] *Principles,* II, 162, ff.

true.[51] Supported by the ethereal speculations and by these suggestions in Newton that extension and *vis inertiæ* are more ultimate than other characteristics of body, it was easy for his followers to forget his sweeping empiricism; with his superb and staggering reduction of the motions of matter to exact mathematical formulæ in terms of mass to excite their constant amazement; with, too, the early discovery that all the basic units of mechanics could be defined in units of mass, space and time, it was a simple enough metaphysical advance of the kind with which we are now surely familiar enough, from the statement that *bodies are masses,* to the assumption that *bodies are nothing but masses,* and that all residual phenomena can be explained by factors external to the bodies themselves. Thus Newton, quite in opposition to certain presumptions fundamental in his own thinking, appeared to succeeding generations in the light of a hearty upholder of the full mechanical conception of physical nature. The idea of mass had been incorporated into the Cartesian geometrical machine; and its substitution for the fanciful vortices only made the world-system seem all the more rigidly mechanical.

B. Space and Time

When we come to Newton's remarks on space and time, however, he takes personal leave of his empiricism, and a position partly adopted from others, partly felt to be demanded by his mathematical method, and partly resting on a theological basis, is presented, and that in the main body of his chief work. Newton himself asserts that in "philosophical disquisitions", which apparently means here when offering ultimate characterizations of space, time, and motion, "we ought to abstract from our senses, and consider things themselves, distinct from what are only sensible measures of them." [52] This is surely a peculiar observation from a philosopher of sensible

[51] *Principles,* I, 1, ff., 14, ff.

[52] *Principles,* I, 9.

experience; it will be our business in the balance of this chapter to understand Newton's position and account for this deviation from his experimental principles.

Newton introduces his comments on these matters with the remark that his main purpose is to remove certain vulgar empirical prejudices. "Hitherto I have laid down the definitions of such words as are less known, and explained the sense in which I would have them to be understood in the following discourse. I do not define time, space, place, and motion, as being well known to all. Only I must observe that the vulgar conceive those quantities under no other notions but from the relation they bear to sensible objects. And thence arise certain prejudices, for the removing of which, it will be convenient to distinguish them into absolute and relative, true and apparent, mathematical and common." [53] After this introductory polemic against the relativists of his day, Newton proceeds to define his distinctions.

I. Absolute, true, and mathematical time, of itself, and from its own nature, flows equably without regard to anything external, and by another name is called duration: relative, apparent, and common time, is some sensible and external (whether accurate or unequable) measure of duration by the means of motion, which is commonly used instead of true time; such as an hour, a day, a month, a year.

II. Absolute space, in its own nature, without regard to anything external, remains always similar and immovable. Relative space is some movable dimension or measure of the absolute spaces; which our senses determine by its position to bodies, and which is vulgarly taken for immovable space; such is the dimension of a subterraneous, an aerial, or celestial space, determined by its position in respect of the earth. Absolute and relative space are the same in figure and magnitude; but they do not remain always numerically the same. For if the earth, for instance, moves, a space of our air, which relatively and in respect of the earth always remains the same, will at one time be one part of the absolute space into which the air passes; at another time it will

[53] *Principles*, I, 6, ff.

be another part of the same, and so, absolutely understood, it will be perpetually mutable.

III. Place is a part of space which a body takes up, and is according to the space, either absolute or relative. . . .

IV. Absolute motion, is the translation of a body from one absolute place into another; and relative motion, the translation from one relative place into another. Thus in a ship under sail, the relative place of a body is that part of the ship which the body possesses; or that part of its cavity which the body fills, and which therefore moves together with the ship: and relative rest, is the continuance of the body in the same part of the ship, or its cavity. But real, absolute rest, is the continuance of the body in the same part of that immovable space in which the ship itself, its cavity and all that it contains, is moved. Wherefore, if the earth is really at rest, the body which relatively rests in the ship, will really and absolutely move with the same velocity which the ship has on the earth. But if the earth also moves, the true and absolute motion of the body will arise, partly from the true motion of the earth in immovable space; partly from the relative motion of the ship on the earth: and if the body moves also relatively in the ship; its true motion will arise, partly from the true motion of the earth, in immovable space, and partly from the relative motions as well of the ship on the earth as of the body in the ship; and from these relative motions will arise the relative motion of the body on the earth. . . .

Absolute time, in astronomy, is distinguished from relative, by the equation or correction of the vulgar time. For the natural days are truly unequal, though they are commonly considered as equal, and used for a measure of time: astronomers correct this inequality for their more accurate deducing of the celestial motions. It may be, that there is no such thing as an equable motion, whereby time may be accurately measured. All motions may be accelerated and retarded, but the true, or equable progress of absolute time is liable to no change. The duration or perseverance of the existence of things remains the same; whether the motions are swift or slow, or none at all: and therefore it ought to be distinguished from what are only sensible measures thereof; and out of which we collect it, by means of the astronomical equation. The necessity of which equation, for determining the times of a phenomenon, is evinced as well from the experiments of the pendulum clock, as by eclipses of the satellites of Jupiter.

As the order of the parts of time is immutable, so also is the order of the parts of space. Suppose those parts to be moved out of their places, and they will be moved (if the expression may be allowed) out of themselves. For times and spaces are, as it were, the places as well of themselves as of all other things. All things are placed in time as to order of succession; and in space as to order of situation. It is from their essence or nature that they are places; and that the primary places of things should be movable, is absurd. These are, therefore, the absolute places, and translations out of those places, are the only absolute motions.

But because the parts of space cannot be seen, or distinguished from one another by our senses, therefore in their stead we use sensible measures of them. For from the positions and distances of things from any body considered as immovable, we define all places: and then with respect to such places, we estimate all motions, considering bodies as transferred from some of those places into others. And so instead of absolute places and motions we use relative ones; and that without any inconvenience in common affairs: but in philosophical disquisitions, we ought to abstract from our senses and consider things themselves, distinct from what are only sensible measures of them. For it may be that there is no body really at rest, to which the places and motions of others may be referred.

Before we proceed further with Newton's argument, let us pause for a brief analysis of the position so far stated. Space and time are vulgarly regarded as entirely relative, that is, as distances between sensible objects or events. In reality, there is in addition to such relative spaces and times absolute, true, and mathematical space and time. These are infinite, homogeneous, continous entities, entirely independent of any sensible object or motion by which we try to measure them; time flowing equably from eternity to eternity; space existing all at once in infinite immovability. Absolute motion is the transfer of a body from one part of absolute space to another; relative motion a change in its distance from any other sensible body; absolute rest the continuance of a body in the same part of absolute space; relative rest its continuance in the same distance from some other body. Absolute motion is to be computed, in the case of any body, by mathematically combining its relative motions on the earth plus the motion of the earth in absolute space. Thus, in the case of a body moving on a ship, its absolute motion will be determined by a mathematical combination of its motion on the ship, that of the latter on the earth, and that of the earth in absolute space. Absolute time we can approximate by equating or correcting our vulgar time through a more accurate study of the celestial motions. It may be, however, that we can nowhere find a genuinely equable motion, whereby time may be accurately measured. All motions, even those which, to the best of our observations, appear quite uniform, may really be somewhat accelerated or retarded, while the true or equable progress of absolute time is liable to no change. Similarly, space is immovable by its own essence or nature, that is, the order of its parts cannot be changed. If they could be changed they would be moved out of themselves; thus to regard the primary places of things, or the parts of absolute space, as movable, is absurd. However, the parts of absolute space are not visible or sensibly distinguishable; hence, in order to measure or define distances, we have to consider some body as immovable, and then estimate the motions and measure the distances of other bodies in relation to it. Thus instead of absolute space and motion we use relative ones, which is suitable enough in practice, but considering the matter philosophically, we must admit that there may be no body really at rest in absolute space, our adopted centre of reference being possibly itself in motion. Hence, by observation and experiment, we can do no more than approximate either of these two absolute, true, and mathematical entities; they are ultimately inaccessible to us. "It is possible, that in the remote regions of the fixed stars, or perhaps far beyond them, there may be some body absolutely at rest; but impossible to know, from the position of bodies to one another in our regions, whether any of these do keep the same position to that remote body; it follows that absolute rest cannot be determined from the position of bodies in our regions." [54]

The question forcibly arises in our minds at this point: how, then, do we know that there are such things as absolute space, time, and motion? In view of their admitted inaccessibility to observation and experiment, in view of the complete relativity to sensible bodies of all our measurements and formulæ, of what possible standing and use are they in mechanics, and how does Newton, the experimentalist and rejector of hypotheses, dare to introduce them with his definitions of mass and force and his axioms of motion? How, even, we might add, would he be able to tell whether this hypothetical celestial body were really at rest in absolute space, even though it fell under our observations, inasmuch as space by its own nature is infinite and homogeneous, its parts indistinguishable from each other?

Newton's answer in effect is, that we can know absolute motion by certain of its properties, and absolute motion implies absolute space and time.

But we may distinguish rest and motion, absolute and relative, one from the other by their properties, causes, and effects. It is a property of rest, that bodies really at rest [*i.e.,* in absolute space] do rest in respect of one another.

It is a property of motion that the parts, which retain given positions to their wholes, do partake of the motions of those wholes. For all the parts of revolving bodies endeavour to recede from the axis of motion; and the impetus of bodies moving forwards, arises from the joint impetus of all the parts. Therefore, if surrounding bodies are moved, those that are relatively at rest within them, will partake of their motion. Upon which account, the true and absolute motion of a body cannot be determined by the translation of it from those which only seem at rest; for the external

[54] *Principles,* I, 9.

bodies ought not only to appear at rest, but to be really at rest. . . .

A property near akin to the preceding, is this, that if a place is moved, whatever is placed therein, moves along with it. . . . Wherefore entire and absolute motions can be no otherwise determined than by immovable places; and for that reason I did before refer those absolute motions to immovable places, but relative ones to movable places. Now no other places are immovable but those that, from infinity to infinity, do all retain the same given positions one to another; and upon this account must ever remain unmoved; and do thereby constitute, what I call, immovable space.[55]

This section commences with great promise, but so far our difficulties are hardly explained. We are to distinguish absolute from relative rest and motion by their properties, causes and effects. It is a property of motion, that parts, retaining given positions in a system, partake of whatever motion or rest is true of the system, therefore absolute motion, either of the part or of the rest of the system, cannot be determined by their relations to each other, but only by reference to immovable space. But immovable space is quite inaccessible to observation or experiment: our difficulty persists, how can we tell whether any given body is at rest or moving in it? However, Newton next proceeds to discuss the causes and effects of motion. Here we shall perhaps find a more helpful clue.

The causes by which true and relative motions are distinguished, one from the other, are the forces impressed on the bodies to generate motion. True motion is neither generated nor altered, but by some force impressed upon the body moved: but relative motion may be generated or altered without any force impressed upon the body. For it is sufficient only to impress some force on other bodies with which the former is compared, that by their giving way, that relation may be changed, in which the relative rest or motion of this other body did consist. Again, true motion suffers always some change from any force impressed upon

[55] *Principles,* I, 9, ff.

the moving body; but relative motion does not necessarily undergo any change by such forces. For if the same forces are likewise impressed on those other bodies, with which the comparison is made, that the relative position may be preserved, then that condition will be preserved in which the relative motion consists. And, therefore, any relative motion may be changed when the true motion remains unaltered, and the relative may be preserved when the true suffers some change. Upon which accounts, true motion does by no means consist in such relations.

The effects which distinguish absolute from relative motion are, the forces of receding from the axis of circular motion. For there are no such forces in a circular motion purely relative, but in a true and absolute circular motion, they are greater or less, according to the quantity of the motion. If a vessel, hung by a long cord, is so often turned about that the cord is strongly twisted, then filled with water, and held at rest together with the water; after, by the sudden action of another force, it is whirled about the contrary way, and while the cord is untwisting itself, the vessel continues for some time in this motion; the surface of the water will at first be plain, as before the vessel began to move; but the vessel, by gradually communicating its motion to the water, will make it begin sensibly to revolve, and recede by little and little from the middle, and ascend to the sides of the vessel, forming itself into a concave figure (as I have experienced), and the swifter the motion becomes, the higher will the water rise, till at last, performing its revolutions in the same times with the vessel, it becomes relatively at rest in it. This ascent of the water shows its endeavour to recede from the axis of its motion; and the true and absolute circular motion of the water, which is here directly contrary to the relative, discovers itself, and may be measured by this endeavour. At first, when the relative motion of the water in the vessel was greatest, it produced no endeavour to recede from the axis: the water showed no tendency to the circumference, nor any ascent towards the sides of the vessel, but remained of a plain surface, and therefore its true circular motion had not yet begun. But afterwards when the relative motion of the water had decreased, the ascent thereof towards the sides of the vessel proved its endeavour to recede from the axis; and this endeavour showed the real circular motion of the water perpetually increasing, till it had acquired its greatest quantity when the water rested relatively in its vessel. . . .

It is indeed a matter of great difficulty to discover, and effectually to distinguish, the true motions of particular bodies from the apparent: because the parts of that immovable space in which those motions are performed, do by no means come under the observation of our senses. Yet the thing is not altogether desperate; for we have some arguments to guide us, partly from the apparent motions, which are the differences of the true motions; partly from the forces, which are the causes and effects of the true motions. For instance, if two globes, kept at a given distance one from the other by means of a cord that connects them, were revolved about their common centre of gravity, we might, from the tension of the cord, discover the endeavour of the globes to recede from the axis of their motion, and from thence we might compute the quantity of their circular motions. . . . And thus we might find both the quantity and the determination of this circular motion, even in an immense vacuum, where there was nothing external or sensible with which the globes could be compared. But now, if in that space some remote bodies were placed that kept always a given position one to another, as the fixed stars do in our regions, we could not indeed determine from the relative translation of the globes among those bodies, whether the motion did belong to the globes or to the bodies. But if we observed the cord, and found that its tension was that very tension which the motions of the globes required, we might conclude the motion to be in the globes, and the bodies to be at rest; and then, lastly, from the translation of the globes among the bodies, we should find the determination of their motions.[56]

Again let us subject this argument to careful analysis. As

[56] *Principles,* I, 10, ff.

Newton himself sums up the matter, there are two ways by which absolute motions (and hence absolute space and time) may be demonstrated and measured: "partly from the apparent motions, which are the differences of the true motions: partly from the forces, which are the causes and effects of the true motions." Let us examine the latter of these first.

Relative motion may take place, in the case of any body, without the application to it of any force, other bodies with which it is compared being impelled to change their relations with it. True motion cannot take place, however, without the application of force, and *vice versa,* wherever force is applied, absolute motion must occur. Hence wherever force is operative, there we must conclude absolute motion to exist.

In the light of the scientific advance since Newton, it is difficult to see any cogency in this part of the argument. For we can discover the presence of force only by changes in motion—indeed for most modern scientists force has no meaning beyond that of the unknown cause of mass-accelerations—hence while accelerations always imply forces, it is not allowable to proceed in the reverse direction and assert that the operation of force always means absolute motion. We can argue from effect to cause but not from cause to effect; the cause is entirely unknown and hypothetical until the effect appears. It is remarkable how very gradually modern science succeeded in divesting its conception of power or force of animistic trappings; indeed the purification may only be said to have been definitely begun when it was discovered that our immediate feeling of effort, which was undoubtedly the basis of the earlier animism in the scientific notion of force, may be present without, due to some pathological condition, the occurrence of the appropriate limb-movements. When such a fact comes home to a man he is prepared to see in force only a name for the unknown cause of changes in motion. But, of course, Newton lived before this purging had gone very far; because he shared the crude psychology of the time, he believed it possible to know the existence of force quite apart from, and antecedent to, its effected motions. Hence wherever there is force operating, there must be acceleration of the affected mass, *i.e.,* absolute motion. But for us the argument in this direction is illegitimate, and the difficulty still remains.

Newton is on sounder ground, however, when he passes from force as the cause of motion to force as its effect. The examples of the vessel of water and the two globes really prove something important. Expressing the situation in common parlance, the whirling vessel gradually communicates its motion to the contained water, whose motion results in a centrifugal force, measurable by the degree of concavity assumed by the water, or in the case of the globes by the tension of the cord. Here we have certain motions as the cause of certain forces, the latter expressing themselves in measurable additional phenomena. These phenomena are not present when the antecedent motions are relative (*i.e.*, when the water was at rest within the whirling vessel, each moving most rapidly relatively to the other), hence when they are present we must be dealing not with relative motions but with motions that may appropriately be called absolute. The reason is a simple one. Consider again the water revolving rapidly with reference to the surrounding earth and the fixed stars, the centrifugal forces revealed in the degree of concavity of its surface. May we, if we like, take the water to be at rest and attribute motion to the fixed stars? Let us quickly check the vessel and whirl it in the opposite direction. The water will soon slow down relatively to the fixed stars, assume a plane surface, and then gradually move in the present direction of the vessel, appearing in concavity once more. What would become of our laws of motion and our concepts of force, mass, and causality, if we believed that by a simple turn of the hand we could check a rapid angular revolution of the whole universe, except a pot of water, and throw it into an equally rapid revolution in the opposite direction? Obviously we could work out no consistent account of the major data of physics in such a fashion—our most fundamental and the trustworthy generalizations would have gone by the board. In other words, we *cannot but* assume the fixed stars to be at rest and attribute motion to the water. The freedom of choice implied by the relativist turns out to be wholly illusory; in the interest of clear thinking about the most obvious facts of the physical world we simply have to do just what we do. Wherever, in any change of spatial relationships, forces measurable by other phenomena are generated in one of the bodies and not in the other, we attribute the motion to the former—in the language of early mechanics, we say that its motion is absolute, the motion of the other, relative. Else our world would appear a chaos instead of an ordered system. It is only when we consider a given motion entirely by itself that we are at all free to choose. Indeed, that in some fundamental sense the phenomena of revolution about an axis are independent of the earth and the fixed stars, is evident from the fact which Newton notes, that were there no other body in the universe the distinction between the plane and the concave surface of the water would be just as real and determinate, though in that case the terms rest and motion would have no meaning.

Furthermore, Newton holds, although this thought is not developed as thoroughly as the other, wherever there are relative or apparent motions, there must at least be as much absolute motion as is the difference of the relative motions. Thus in the case of the vessel, the water, and the surrounding universe; when, as in the first part of the experiment, the two latter are at rest with respect to each other, there must be absolute circular motion of a certain angular velocity, whether it be the vessel or the water and surrounding environment in motion. Similarly in the case of two equal masses which are changing position relatively to each other at a certain velocity. Whichever we take as our point of reference, there is motion at that velocity present, and if both be at the same time moving away from a third body the amount of absolute motion is increased. This applies to any system of bodies; it is impossible to take any point of reference without discovering at least as much motion in the system as amounts to the differences of their relative motions. Hence there must be at least so much absolute motion. Notice that in Newton's statements here the doctrine of absolute motion is not opposed to the conception of motion as relative; it simply asserts that bodies *do change their spatial relations in such and such precise ways, and that our system of reference is not arbitrary.*

c. Criticism of Newton's Philosophy of Space and Time

Now the existence of absolute motion in this sense, that is, the fact that bodies change their distance-relations, and that in any direction and with any velocity, implies that there is *infinite room* in which they can move; and the exact measurability of that motion implies that *this room is a perfect geometrical system and a pure mathematical time—in other words, absolute motion implies absolute duration and absolute space*. Thus far Newton's mathematical method as applied in the *Principia* adopts and perfects the notions of space and time which had begun to undergo philosophical handling, and by somewhat analogous considerations, in the work of More and Barrow. Did absolute space and time, as Newton proclaimed them, mean merely and precisely this, the conceptions would be logically unimpeachable and would deserve inclusion among the definitions and axioms which furnish the foundation of his mechanics, in spite of the fact that they are quite inaccessible experimentally. That motion is experimentally discoverable and measurable presupposes them. To this extent Newton has justification for these concepts, and the fact, so often observed by himself, that space and time "do not come under the observation of our senses", need not distress him as an intelligent empiricist.

But thus far alone can we go with Newton; no farther. For note: absolute space and time as thus understood, by their own nature negate the possibility that sensible bodies can move *with reference* to them—such bodies can only move *in* them, *with reference to other bodies*. Why is this so? Simply because they are infinite and homogeneous entities; one part of them is quite indistinguishable from any other equal part; any position in them is identical with any position; for wherever that part or position may be it is surrounded by an infinite stretch of similar room in all directions. Taking any body or system of bodies by itself, therefore, it is impossible to say intelligibly that it is either moving or at rest in absolute space or absolute time; such a statement only becomes meaningful when another phrase is added—*with reference to such and such another body*. Things move *in* absolute space and time, but *with reference to* other things. A sensible centre of reference must always be definitely or tacitly implied.

Now it is clear that Newton did not feel this implication of the meaning of space and time or observe the distinction. For he speaks about the possibility of combining the motion of an object on a ship and that of the ship on the earth *with the motion of the earth in absolute space*; furthermore in many passages, both in the *Principia* and in the briefer *System of the World,* he discusses the question whether the centre of gravity of the solar system be at rest or in uniform motion in absolute space.[57] Since in his day there was no way of getting a definite point of reference among the fixed stars, such a question is obviously unintelligible—the very nature of absolute space negates the possibility of its having any assignable significance. How, then, did Newton allow himself to fall into the error, and include such statements in the main body of his classic work?

The answer to this question is to be found in Newton's theology. To him, as to More and Barrow, space and time were not merely entities implied by the mathematico-experimental method and the phenomena it handles; they had an ultimately religious significance which was for him fully as important; they meant the omnipresence and continued existence from everlasting to everlasting of Almighty God. The precise functions of God in Newton's metaphysics will be treated in a later chapter; here we shall simply observe how the concept of the Deity furnishes the key to Newton's present inconsistency.

Some pious folk were greatly disturbed by the fact that in the first edition of the *Principia,* in conformity with Newton's positivism and his chosen policy of banning from the main body of his scientific works all hypotheses and ultimate ex-

[57] *Principles,* I, 27, ff.; II, 182; *System of the World,* (Vol. III), 27. Compare the present discussion of Newton's doctrine of space and time with those of Mach, *Science of Mechanics;* Broad, *Scientific Thought;* and Cassirer, *Substanz-und Funktionsbegriff.*

planations, infinite, absolute space and time, were portrayed as vast, independent entities in which masses mechanically moved. The world outside of man appeared nothing but a huge machine—God appeared to be swept out of existence and there was nothing to take his place but these boundless mathematical beings. The religious fears excited are expressed in such a work as Berkeley's *Principles of Human Knowledge* (1710), in which absolute space was attacked as an atheistic conception. That this was not at all Newton's intention is evident from his early letters, especially those to Dr. Bentley[58] in 1692. His close acquaintance and sympathy with Barrow's views we have already noted, and we must expect that he had kept in touch with his colleague More's philosophy ever since in his boyhood days at Grantham school he had lived under the same roof with one of the great Platonist's intense admirers.[59] For the similarities between the two men are too striking to be accidental.

Hence when the second edition of the *Principia* appeared in 1713, Newton added his famous *General Scholium*, in which he expresses himself with no reserve.

From his true dominion it follows that the true God is a living, intelligent, and powerful Being; and from his other perfections, that he is supreme, or most perfect. He is eternal and infinite, omnipotent and omniscient; that is, his duration reaches from eternity to eternity; his presence from infinity to infinity; he governs all things, and knows all things that are or can be done. He is not eternity or infinity, but eternal and infinite; he is not duration or space, but he endures and is present. He endures for ever, and is everywhere present; and *by existing always and everywhere, he constitutes duration and space*. . . . He is omnipresent, not *virtually* only, but also *substantially*, for virtue cannot subsist without substance. In him are all things contained and moved; yet neither affects the other: God suffers nothing from the motion of bodies; bodies find no resistance from the

[58] Cf. Section 6, p. 285, ff.

[59] *Collections for the History of the Town and Soke of Grantham*, London, 1806, p. 176.

omnipresence of God. It is allowed by all that the Supreme God exists necessarily; and by the same necessity he exists *always* and *everywhere*. Whence also he is all similar, all eye, all ear, all brain, all arm, all power to perceive, to understand, and to act; but in a manner not at all human, in a manner not at all corporeal, in a manner utterly unknown to us.[60]

Elsewhere Newton speaks of God as "containing in himself all things as their principle and place" [61]; we read in a creed among his manuscripts that "the Father is immovable, no place being capable of becoming emptier or fuller of him than it is by the eternal necessity of nature. All other beings are movable from place to place." [62]

In the light of these pronouncements it is clearly evident that when Newton spoke of bodies or of the centre of gravity of the solar system moving in absolute space his mind was not confined to the mathematical and mechanical bearings superficially apparent—he meant also that they were moving *in God*—in the eternal and omniscient presence of the Creator of all things. Let us specifically relate this thought to the problem as we finally stated it, that of Newton's failure to see that absolute space and time as described in the main body of the *Principia* negate the possibility that things can be intelligibly said to move *with reference* to them, but only *in* them with reference to other things. Recall the arguments of More on space, and the curious passage in Boyle in which he speaks of God as impelling by his will the whole material universe in some direction, with resulting motion but no change of place. Newton, of course, conceived of God mainly as More did, combining among his attributes those which had reference to the mathematical order and harmony of the world with the traditional ones of his absolute dominion and wilful control of events. All this enriches our background for two still more specific statements in the *Queries* to Newton's *Opticks,* in which space is described as the *divine sensorium*—it is that in

[60] *Principles,* II, 311, ff. Italics ours.
[61] Brewster, *Memoirs,* II, 154.
[62] Brewster, II, 349.

which the intellect and will of God comprehend and guide the doings of the physical world. Absolute space for Newton is not only the omnipresence of God; it is also the infinite scene of the divine knowledge and control.

Whereas the main business of natural philosophy is to argue from phenomena without feigning hypotheses, and to deduce causes from effects, till we come to the very first cause, which certainly is not mechanical; and not only to unfold the mechanism of the world, but chiefly to resolve these and such like questions. . . . Is not the sensory of animals that place to which the sensitive substance is present, and into which the sensible species of things are carried through the nerves and brain, that there they may be perceived by their immediate presence to that substance? And these things being rightly dispatched, does it not appear from phenomena that there is a Being incorporeal, living, intelligent, omnipresent, who in *infinite space, as it were in his sensory,* sees the things themselves intimately, and thoroughly perceives them, and comprehends them wholly by their immediate presence to himself; of which things the images only [*i.e.,* on the retina] carried through the organs of sense into our little sensoriums, are there seen and beheld by that which in us perceives and thinks. And though every true step made in this philosophy brings us not immediately to the knowledge of the first cause, yet it brings us nearer to it, and on that account is to be highly valued.[63]

In the second passage Newton specifically insists on the active divine control of the world in addition to the enjoyment of perfect knowledge. God, "being in all places, is more able *by his will to move the bodies within his boundless uniform sensorium,* and thereby to form and reform the parts of the universe, than we are by our will to move the parts of our own bodies. And yet we are not to consider the world as the body of God, or the several parts thereof, as the parts of God. He is a uniform being, void of organs, members, or parts, and they are his creatures subordinate to him, and subservient to

[63] *Opticks,* p. 344, ff. Italics ours.

his will; and he is no more the soul of them, than the soul of a man is the soul of the species of things carried through the organs of sense into the place of its sensation, where it perceives them by means of its immediate presence, without the intervention of any third thing. The organs of sense are not for enabling the soul to perceive the species of things in its sensorium, but only for conveying them thither; and God has no need of such organs, he being everywhere present to the things themselves." [64]

Do we not here have exactly the explanation of which we are in search? Absolute space is the divine sensorium. Everything that happens in it, being present to the divine knowledge, must be immediately perceived and intimately understood. Certainly, at least, God must know whether any given motion is absolute or relative. *The divine consciousness furnishes the ultimate centre of reference for absolute motion.* Moreover, the animism in Newton's conception of force perhaps plays a part in the premises of the position. God is not only infinite knowledge, but also Almighty Will. He is the ultimate originator of motion and is able at any time now to add motion to bodies within his boundless sensorium. Thus all real or absolute motion in the last analysis is the resultant of an expenditure of the divine energy, and whenever the divine intelligence is cognizant of such an expenditure, the motion so added to the system of the world must be absolute. Logically, of course, it is difficult to find cogency in this reasoning. The reference to God's creative energy involves the same passage from force to motion which earlier in the chapter appeared invalid. And even the ascription of perfect knowledge to God becomes baffling if the accurate distinction between absolute and relative motion is included. For, we might object, how could he tell the difference between them? Inasmuch as he is supposed to be everywhere equally present, there is no focus of the divine attention at any given point to which motions could be referred. Being present with every motion, all would be at rest; being confined to none, every motion would be absolute. But, of course, explanations in terms of pious reverence are

[64] *Opticks,* p. 377, ff. Italics ours.

not critically examined. The omniscience of God and his transcendence of human knowledge were traditionally accepted and reflectively untested postulates with Newton.[65] In a universe conceived as existing in the sensorium of God, would it not be easy enough to assume without logical sifting that it was possible to speak intelligibly of bodies moving with reference to absolute space and time? An important notion crept into Newton's mathematical science at this point which was in the last analysis the product of his theological convictions.

In any case when, in the eighteenth century, Newton's conception of the world was gradually shorn of its religious relations, the ultimate justification for absolute space and time as he had portrayed them disappeared, and the entities were left empty, but still absolute according to his only partially justified description; as to the rest, divested of both logical and theological excuse, but yet unquestioningly assumed as an infinite theatre in which, and an unchangeable entity against which, the world-machine continued its clock-like movements. From accidents of God they became sheer, fixed, geometrical measure for the motions of masses. And this loss of their divinity completed the de-spiritualization of nature. With God expanded throughout all space and time there was still something spiritual left in the world outside of man—pious souls who would otherwise have viewed with alarm the final form of the Cartesian dualism and the current doctrine of primary and secondary qualities were reconciled—with God, however, banished from existence, all the spirituality left in the world was locked up in the sensoriums of scattered human beings. The vast realm outside was a mathematical machine merely; it was a system of masses moving in absolute space and time. For it was necessary to postulate nothing further. In terms of these three entities all its manifold changes seemed capable of exact and final formulation.

As regards space, the metaphysical difficulties involved in this conclusion were touched upon in the chapter on Descartes. In Newton's presentation, however, the anomalies in the conception of time in modern science are overlaid with an in-

[65] *Principles,* II, 312, ff.

genious use of language. Newton speaks of absolute time as "flowing equably without regard to anything external". But in what sense can we speak of time as *flowing?* Things flow *in time,* rather. Why, then, does Newton describe time by such a phrase? The fact is, the idea of time thrust upon the world by modern science is a mixture of two peculiar conceptions. On the one hand, time is conceived as a homogeneous mathematical continuum, extending from the infinite past to the infinite future. Being one and entire, its whole extent is somehow present at once; it is necessarily bound together and all subject to knowledge. The laws of motion, together with the doctrine of the constancy of energy, inevitably result in this picture of the whole sweep of time as a realm mathematically determinate in terms of an adequate present knowledge. But carry this conception to the limit, and does not time quite disappear as anything ultimately different from space? Once the Platonic year is discovered, everything that can happen is a *present* event. Accordingly there is another element in the conception of time, which accords more congenially with the nominalistic predilections of some of the later medievalists and most of the early British scientists. Time is a succession of discrete parts, or moments, no two of which are present simultaneously, and hence nothing exists or is present except the moment *now.* But the moment now is constantly passing into the past, and a future moment is becoming now. Hence from this point of view time simmers down till it is contracted into a mathematical limit between the past and the future. Obviously, this limit can be described as flowing equably in time, but it is hardly time itself. Motion is inexplicable in terms of such a conception; any given motion will occupy more time than a sheer limit between what has gone by and what is yet to come. How combine these two elements into a single, mathematically usable idea, that shall, moreover, find some justification in actual experience? Newton does so by ingeniously applying to time as an infinite continuum language that properly applies only to this moving limit; hence the "equable flow", in which description he hardly does more than follow his predecessor Barrow. The basic difficulty here, as pointed out in the chapter on Galileo, is that the scientific notion of time has almost entirely lost touch with duration as immediately experienced. Until a closer relation is regained, it is probable that science will never reach a very satisfactory description of time. Newton the empiricist might have supplied us such a description had his mathematical training and metaphysical assumptions not led him to rest satisfied with an ambiguous formula. Attempts by contemporary philosophers of science to solve this problem would be more apt to become fruitful, did they devote themselves to a more thorough study of the history of the concept.

Section 5. *Newton's Conception of the Ether*

The presence of theological assumptions in Newton's doctrine of time and space suggests that there was a strongly conservative aspect of his philosophy; in this and the succeeding chapter it will be our business to present those views in which his conservatism affected his metaphysical position still more definitely. The tendency toward radicalism in cosmology which is so noticeable in Galileo, Descartes, and especially Hobbes, is not to be found in Newton's thinking. Rather, on every important point in respect to which they were challenged by zealous religionists like More and Boyle, Newton took his stand with the latter. He did so in such a way, however, as we shall see, that these elements in his metaphysics rapidly lost their influence and did not suffice to save most of those whose thinking was affected by his exploits from the embarrassments involved in the more revolutionary doctrines.

It was observed in the last chapter that Newton attempted to account for all the qualities of experienced bodies that could not be gathered up under the conception of them as masses by following Descartes' example and postulating an ethereal medium which pervades all space and by its pressure or other operations on bodies causes such residual phenomena, but he was more consistent than Descartes in recognizing certain clear distinctions between the ether and sensible bodies. It is readily apparent that to Newton's mind the world was not fully explained by the ultimate categories already invoked. The *res cogitans* scattered about in human brains furnished a haven for many otherwise inexplicable odds and ends; the notions of space, time, and mass construed the external world so far as it was mathematically reducible; but there were additional features not as yet metaphysically provided for; two more categories, the ether and God, are needed adequately to explain them.

As for the idea of the ether, we have noted certain salient facts about its history, and have observed how Gilbert, More, Boyle, and others turned to it when in metaphysical predicament due to the continuance in their minds of certain assumptions from earlier thought or to the recognition of facts recalcitrant to the extreme mechanical view. It was difficult for thinkers really to carry through Descartes' bold suggestion that everything in the world that is not mathematical is to be shoved into human minds as a mode of thought, for there were many problems that could hardly be handled in such terms alone. Indeed, Descartes himself had appealed in such circumstances to an ethereal matter, though claiming in words that it, no more than the visible bodies, possessed qualities undeducible from extension. Newton followed in the general current here; attempts at a further speculative solution of the universe by the aid of the ether appear in almost all of his early writings, and in the queries attached to the *Opticks* his final fancies about it are lengthily offered. What are the facts which might demand such an explanation?

A. The Function of the Ether

Here we find in Newton a further and more explicit development of the position already taken in Boyle. As we saw, by Boyle's time the notion of an ethereal medium had come to supply two distinct functions; it propagated motion across distances, and it possessed qualities which accounted for extramechanical phenomena like electricity, magnetism, and cohesion. Newton began where Boyle left off. For him, too, in his early work at least, action at a distance was inconceivable. Especially did his studies on optics lead him to think such a medium necessary in order to explain the propagation of light. In all his quarrels with Hooke, Pardies, and others about the nature of light and the validity of his experimental conclusions concerning certain of its properties, accompanied by his violent denunciation of hypotheses and serious attempt to rid his own pronouncements of any imaginative savour, it never occurred to him to doubt the existence of a medium which at least performed the function of transmitting light. Amid all their disagreements Newton agreed with Hooke to this extent, that there existed an ether, and that it was a medium susceptible of vibrations.[66] Having taken over the notion from the current of the times, and feeling it to be thus well grounded, it was easy for Newton to extend its use to other phenomena which involved action at a distance and which others were accounting for in the same fashion, such as gravity, magnetism, electric attraction, and the like. An interesting passage, which combines this conviction that action at a distance is impossible with other reminders of More's philosophy, occurs in Newton's third letter to Bentley: "It is inconceivable, that inanimate brute matter should, without the mediation of something else, which is not material, operate upon, and affect other matter without mutual contact; as it must do, if gravitation, in the sense of Epicurus, be essential and inherent in it. And this is one reason, why I desired you would not ascribe innate gravity to me. That gravity should be innate, inherent, and essential to matter, so that one body may act upon another, at a distance through a vacuum, without the mediation of anything else, by and through which their action and force may be conveyed from one to another, is to me so great an absurdity, that I believe no man who has in philosophical matters a competent faculty of thinking, can ever fall into it. Gravity must be caused by an agent acting constantly according to certain laws; but whether this agent be material or immaterial, I have left to the consideration of my readers." [67]

[66] *Opera*, IV, 380.

[67] *Opera*, IV, 438.

In the second place, Newton lived before the day when scientists believed it possible to postulate the conservation of energy without calling in other than accepted mechanical principles to maintain its constancy. When two bodies collide in space, and by reason of imperfect elasticity, friction, and what not, fail to move away from each other with the same velocity at which they approached, the contemporary scientist is able to locate the apparently lost energy in other forms, such as increased molecular motion within the bodies, expressed in heat. In Newton's time such a doctrine was already being championed by Leibniz, but it had no influence on Newton and may even have been unknown to him. Hence to his mind the world of matter appeared a very imperfect machine; motion was everywhere on the decay.

And thus nature will be very conformable to herself and very simple, performing all the great motions of the heavenly bodies by the attraction of gravity which intercedes those bodies, and almost all the small ones of their particles by some other attractive and repelling powers which intercede the particles. The *vis inertiæ* is a passive principle by which bodies persist in their motion or rest, receive motion in proportion to the force impressing it, and resist as much as they are resisted. By this principle alone there never could have been any motion in the world. Some other principle was necessary for putting bodies into motion; and now they are in motion, some other principle is necessary for conserving motion. For from the various composition of two motions, 'tis very certain that there is not always the same quantity of motion in the world. For if two globes joined by a slender rod, revolve about their common centre of gravity with a uniform motion, while that centre moves on uniformly in a right line drawn in the plane of their circular motion; the sum of the motions of the two globes, as often as the globes are in the right line described by their common centre of gravity, will be bigger than the sum of their motions, when they are in a line perpendicular to that right line. By this instance it appears that motion may be got or lost. But by reason of the tenacity of fluids, and attrition of their parts, and the weakness of elasticity in solids, motion is much more apt to be lost than got, and is always upon the decay. For bodies which are either absolutely hard, or so soft as to be void of elasticity, will not rebound from one another. Impenetrability makes them only stop. If two equal bodies meet directly in vacuo they will by the laws of motion stop where they meet, and lose all their motion, and remain in rest, unless they be elastic, and receive new motion from their spring. If they have so much elasticity as suffices to make them rebound with a quarter, or half, or three quarters of the force with which they come together, they will lose three quarters, or half, or a quarter of their motion.[68]

After illustrating by a few further examples Newton continues:

Seeing therefore the variety of motion which we find in the world is always decreasing, there is a necessity of conserving and recruiting it by active principles, such as are the cause of gravity, by which planets and comets keep their motions in their orbs, and bodies acquire great motion in falling; and the cause of fermentation, by which the heart and blood of animals are kept in perpetual motion and heat; the inward parts of the earth are constantly warmed, and in some places grow very hot; bodies burn and shine, mountains take fire, the caverns of the earth are blown up, and the sun continues violently hot and lucid, and warms all things by his light. For we meet with very little motion in the world, besides what is owing to these active principles. And if it were not for these principles the bodies of the earth, planets, comets, sun, and all things in them would grow cold and freeze, and become inactive masses; and all putrefaction, generation, vegetation, and life would cease, and the planets and comets would not remain in their orbs.

These two needs Newton proposes to supply by the adoption and more explicit formulation of Boyle's two-fold conception of the ether, in connexion with which he advances

[68] *Opticks*, p. 372, ff.

various suggestive or fantastic speculations. His own thought on the subject appears to have been closely stimulated by Boyle, with whom he was in intimate converse on just such matters, as his letter to the famous chemist in 1678 proves.[69] None of the presentations of his view is, however, satisfactorily definite or final; his opinions of the ether fluctuated, and he himself recognized them as a metaphysical hypothesis merely, without the standing of an experimental law. At the time they had first begun to take important shape in his mind, he had already been involved in discouraging wrangles about the implications of his optical discoveries, and had made the clear distinction between hypothesis and experimental law, banning the former from the positive pronouncements of science.

B. Newton's Early Speculations

It is important to observe that from the beginning Newton appears to have totally rejected the Cartesian conception of the ethereal medium as a dense, compact fluid, such as alone could swing the planets around their orbits by its vortex motion—the prevalent conception of his time both among English and continental scientists—and developed from Boyle's premises a more original speculation.[70] In his argument against

[69] Quoted extensively below, p. 273, ff.

[70] *Opticks,* 336, ff.—"Are not all hypotheses erroneous, in which light is supposed to consist of impression or motion, propagated through a fluid medium? For in all these hypotheses, the phenomena of light have been hitherto explained by supposing that they arise from new modifications of the rays; which is an erroneous supposition." Newton proceeds to cite certain facts observed or experimentally discovered which tend against such hypotheses, whence continuing: "And it is difficult to explain by these hypotheses, how rays can be alternately in fits of easy reflection and easy transmission; unless perhaps one might suppose that there are in all space two ethereal vibrating mediums, and that the vibrations of one of them constitute light, and the vibrations of the other are swifter, and as often as they overtake the vibrations of the first, put them into those fits. But how two ethers can be diffused

through all space, one of which acts upon the other, and by consequence is reacted upon, without retarding, shattering, dispersing, and confounding one another's motions, is inconceivable. And against filling the heavens with fluid mediums, unless they be exceeding rare, a great objection arises from the regular and very lasting motions of the planets and comets in all manner of courses through the heavens. For thence it is manifest, that the heavens are void of all sensible resistance and by consequence of all sensible matter.

"For the resisting power of fluid mediums arises partly from the attrition of the parts of the medium, and partly from the *vis inertiæ* of the matter. . . .

"Now that part of the resisting power of any medium which arises from the tenacity, friction, or attrition of the parts of the medium, may be diminished by dividing the matter into smaller parts, and making the parts more smooth and slippery: but that part of the resistance which arises from the *vis inertiæ,* is proportional to the density of the matter, and cannot be diminished by dividing the matter into smaller parts, nor by any other means than by decreasing the density of the medium. And for these reasons the density of fluid mediums is very nearly proportional to their resistance . . . and by consequence, if the heavens were as dense as water, they would not have much less resistance than water; if as dense as quicksilver, they would not have much less resistance than quicksilver; if absolutely dense, or full of matter without any vacuum, let the matter be never so subtle and fluid, they would have a greater resistance than quicksilver. A solid globe in such a medium would lose above half its motion in moving three times the length of its diameter, and a globe not solid (such as are the planets) would be retarded sooner. And therefore to make way for the regular and lasting motions of the planets and comets, it's necessary to empty the heavens of all matter, except perhaps some very thin vapours, steams, or effluvia, arising from the atmospheres of the earth, planets, and comets, and from such an exceedingly rare ethereal medium as we described above. A dense fluid can be of no use for explaining the phenomena of nature, the motions of the planets and comets being better explained without it. It serves only to disturb and retard the motions of those great bodies, and make the frame of nature languish: and in the pores of bodies, it serves only to stop the vibrating motions of their parts, wherein their heat and activity consists. And as it is of no use, and hinders the operations of nature, and makes her languish, so there is no evidence for its existence, and therefore it ought to be rejected. And if it be rejected, the hypotheses that light consists in pression or motion propagated through such a medium, are rejected with it.

such a conception of the ether Newton presupposes his refutation of the whole vortex theory of planetary motion in the *Principia*. Obviously, if the dense ethereal fluid be at rest rather than in a series of vortical whirlings, its resistance will make the regular and continued celestial motions impossible. Just what, now, did Newton propose to substitute for this fluid, in the hope of fulfilling by it the two functions needed? His first and rather elaborate presentation of the ether occurs in a letter to Oldenburg late in 1675, introduced by an illuminating statement of his conception at that time of the place and function of hypothesis.[71] It should be noted, the conviction of the ether's existence and general nature is not a part of what is here presented as hypothesis; so much is assumed unqualifiedly by Newton. "Were I to assume an hypothesis, it should be this, if propounded more generally so as not to determine what light is, further than that it is something or other capable of exciting vibrations in the ether; for thus it will become general and comprehensive of other hypotheses so as to leave little room for new ones to be invented; and, therefore, because I have observed the heads of some great virtuosos to run much upon hypotheses, as if my discourse wanted an hypothesis to explain them by, and found that some, when I could not make them take my meaning when I spake of the nature of light and colours abstractedly, have readily apprehended it when I illustrated my discourse by an hypothesis; for this reason I have here thought fit to send you a description of the circumstances of this hypothesis, as much tending to the illustration of the papers I herewith send you." Newton adds that he does not assume as true either this or any other hypothesis, though for convenience' sake writing as if he assumed it, and therefore people must not measure the certainty of his other writings by this or hold him obliged to an-

"And for rejecting such a medium, we have the authority of those the oldest and most celebrated philosophers of Greece and Phœnicia, who made a vacuum and atoms, and the gravity of atoms, the first principles of their philosophy; tacitly attributing gravity to some other cause than dense matter."

[71] Brewster, I, 390, ff. Oldenburg was Secretary of the Royal Society.

swer objections to it; "for I desire to decline being involved in such troublesome, insignificant disputes." It is evident, however, that at the time Newton clearly thought the following suppositions about the ether very probable.

But to proceed to the hypothesis:—I. It is to be supposed therein, that there is an ethereal medium, much of the same constitution with air, but far rarer, subtler, and more strongly elastic. Of the existence of this medium, the motion of a pendulum in a glass exhausted of air almost as quickly as in the open air is no inconsiderable argument. But it is not to be supposed that this medium is one uniform matter, but composed partly of the main phlegmatic body of ether, partly of other various ethereal spirits, much after the manner that air is compounded of the phlegmatic body of air intermixed with various vapours and exhalations. For the electric and magnetic effluvia, and the gravitating principle, seem to argue such variety. Perhaps the whole frame of nature may be nothing but various contextures of some certain ethereal spirits or vapours, condensed as it were by precipitation, much after the manner that vapours are condensed into water, or exhalations into grosser substances, though not so easily condensable; and after condensation wrought into various forms, at first by the immediate hand of the Creator, and ever since by the power of nature, which, by virtue of the command, increase and multiply, became a complete imitator of the copy set her by the Protoplast. Thus perhaps may all things be originated from ether.

In connexion with this interesting speculation, the question might be raised whether by the "main phlegmatic body of ether" Newton is not thinking of the Cartesian fluid, only rejecting the latter at a later date. This possibility is negated, however, by the similarity between the descriptive language used here and in his later attack on the Cartesians—his medium is described in both places as very rare, subtle, elastic, and the like. Now besides the "main phlegmatic body of the ether", which is doubtless by the method of difference regarded merely as a medium of transmission, there are diffused through it "various ethereal spirits" which furnish the explanation for such phenomena as involve other principles than the propagation of motion,[72] including electricity, magnetism, and gravity; with the added fancy that the whole frame of material nature may be composed of such spirits in a very condensed form. Newton proceeds to explain in detail how various types of phenomena may be accounted for by the help of this hypothesis; electricity, gravity, cohesion, animal sensation and motion, the refraction, reflection, and colours of light furnishing the most prominent subjects for discussion. As illustrative of the trend of his thought at this time we shall select for compact presentation his ethereal explanation of gravity.

After suggesting that electrical attraction and repulsion may be accounted for in terms of condensation and refraction of one of the hypothesized ethereal spirits, Newton goes on:

So may the gravitating attraction of the earth be caused by the continual condensation of some other such like ethereal spirit, not of the main body of phlegmatic ether, but of something very thinly and subtlely diffused through it, perhaps of an unctuous, or gummy, tenacious and springy nature; and bearing much the same relation to ether which the vital aerial spirit requisite for the conservation of flame and vital motions does to air. For if such an ethereal spirit may be condensed in fermenting or burning bodies, or otherwise coagulated in the pores of the earth and water into some kind of humid active matter for the continual uses of nature (adhering to the sides of those pores after the manner that vapours condense on the sides of the vessel), the vast body of the earth, which may be everywhere to the very centre in perpetual working, may continually condense so much of this spirit as to cause it from above to descend with great celerity for a supply; in which descent it may bear down with it the bodies it pervades with force proportional to the superficies of all their parts it acts upon, nature making a circulation by the slow ascent of as much matter out of the bowels of the earth in an aerial form, which for a time constitutes the atmosphere, but being continually buoyed up by the new air, exhalations, and vapours

[72] Note p. 400 also.

274

rising underneath, at length (some part of the vapours which return in rain excepted) vanishes again into the ethereal spaces, and there perhaps in time relents and is attenuated into its first principle. For nature is a perpetual circulatory worker, generating fluids out of solids, and solids out of fluids, fixed things out of volatile, and volatile out of fixed, subtle out of gross, and gross out of subtle, some things to ascend and make the upper terrestrial juices, rivers, and the atmosphere, and by consequence others to descend for a requital to the former. And as the earth, so perhaps may the sun imbibe this spirit copiously, to conserve his shining, and keep the planets from receding farther from him: and they that will may also suppose that this spirit affords or carries with it thither the solary fuel and material principle of light, and that the vast ethereal spaces between us and the stars are for a sufficient repository for the food of the sun and planets.[73]

This explanation of gravity in terms of a continual circulation of ethereal spirit under the condensation of the earth, sun, and other attracting bodies, appealed to Newton in part because its mathematical conditions agreed with his deductions from Kepler's planetary laws. He notes this agreement in the correspondence between himself and Halley just before the *Principia* was published, when he still appears to look with considerable favour on the notion.[74]

[73] P. 393, ff.

[74] W.W.R. Ball, *An Essay on Newton's Principia*, London, 1893, p. 166, ff.—"I there suppose [*i.e.*, in the above hypothesis] that the descending spirit acts upon bodies here on the superficies of the earth with force proportional to the superficies of their parts; which cannot be, unless the diminution of its velocity in acting upon the first parts of any body it meets with, be recompensed by the increase of its density arising from that retardation. Whether this be true is not material. It suffices, that 'twas the hypothesis. Now if this spirit descend from above with uniform velocity, its density, and consequently, its force, will be reciprocally proportional to the square of its distance from the centre. But if it descend with accelerated motion, its density will everywhere diminish as much as its velocity increases; and so its force (according to

A little more than three years later, Newton wrote a letter to Boyle in which many of the same subjects are treated. It is strongly noticeable, however, that in this letter the extravagance of his former speculations has been considerably toned down, and toward the end of the letter he falls upon a new explanation of gravity which, though still in ethereal terms, is at once a more simple and less fanciful mechanical account of the facts. The distinction between the main body of the phlegmatic ether and the various ethereal spirits diffused through it and performing individual functions seems to have almost disappeared in favour of a uniform medium save as graduated in degrees of density and grossness. It is obvious that Newton's thought is striving to rid itself of all the magical and fantastic elements possible. The introduction to the letter is included, as an indication of Newton's intimate relations with Boyle at this time.

Honoured Sir:—I have so long deferred to send you my thoughts about the physical qualities we speak of, that did I not esteem myself obliged by promise, I think I should be ashamed to send them at all. The truth is, my notions about things of this kind are so indigested, that I am not well satisfied myself in them; and what I am not satisfied in, I can scarce esteem fit to be communicated to others; especially in natural philosophy, where there is no end of fancying. But because I am indebted to you, and yesterday met with a friend, Mr. Maulyverer, who told me he was going to London, and intended to give you the trouble of a visit, I could not forbear to take the opportunity of conveying this to you by him.

It being only an explication of qualities which you desire of me, I shall set down my apprehensions in the form of suppositions as follows. And first, I suppose that there is diffused through all places an ethereal substance, capable of contraction and dilation, strongly elastic, and, in a word, much like air in all respects, but far more subtle.

the hypothesis) will be the same as before, that is, still reciprocally as the square of its distance from the centre." Cf. also pp. 158, 161.

2. I suppose this ether pervades all gross bodies, but yet so as to stand rarer in their pores than in free spaces, and so much the rarer, as their pores are less; and this I suppose (with others) to be the cause why light incident on those bodies is refracted towards the perpendicular; why two well-polished metals cohere in a receiver exhausted of air; why ☿ stands sometimes up to the top of a glass pipe, though much higher than thirty inches; and one of the main causes why the parts of all bodies cohere; also the cause of filtration, and of the rising of water in small glass pipes above the surface of the stagnating water they are dipped into; for I suspect the ether may stand rarer, not only in the insensible pores of bodies, but even in the very sensible cavities of those pipes; and the same principle may cause menstruums to prevade with violence the pores of the bodies they dissolve, the surrounding ether, as well as the atmosphere, pressing them together.

3. I suppose the rarer ether within bodies, and the denser without them, not to be terminated in a mathematical superficies, but to grow gradually into one another; the external ether beginning to grow rarer, and the internal to grow denser, at some little distance from the superficies of the body, and running through all intermediate degrees of density in the intermediate spaces.[75]

Newton then propounds in terms of this conception of the ether an elaborate explanation of the refraction of light, cohesion, and the action of acids upon various substances. As he nears the end of the letter, the notion of the ether as being graduated in density according to its distance from the central pores of solid bodies has evidently suggested to his mind the simple explanation of gravity referred to.

I shall set down one conjecture more, which came into my mind now as I was writing this letter; it is about the cause of gravity. For this end I will suppose ether to consist of parts differing from one another in *subtilty* by indefinite degrees; that in the pores of bodies there is less of

[75] Brewster, I, 409, ff.

the grosser ether, in proportion to the finer, than in the regions of the air; and that yet the grosser ether in the air affects the upper regions of the earth, and the finer ether in the earth the lower regions of the air, in such a manner, that from the top of the air to the surface of the earth, and again from the surface of the earth to the centre thereof, the ether is insensibly finer and finer. Imagine now any body suspended in the air, or lying on the earth, and the ether being by the hypothesis grosser in the pores, which are in the upper parts of the body, than in those which are in its lower parts, and that grosser ether being less apt to be lodged in those pores than the finer ether below, it will endeavour to get out and give way to the finer ether below, which cannot be, without the bodies descending to make room above for it to go out into.

From this supposed gradual subtilty of the parts of ether some things above might be further illustrated and made more intelligible; but by what has been said, you will easily discern whether in these conjectures there be any degree of probability, which is all I aim at. For my own part, I have so little fancy to things of this nature, that had not your encouragement moved me to it, I should never, I think, have thus far set pen to paper about them.[76]

This rather crude hypothesis of gravity was much pondered over by Newton, and assumed a more mature form in query twenty-one of his *Opticks,* from which we shall quote below. These citations from Newton's early correspondence clearly indicate that while his opinions fluctuated as to the detailed method of applying the theory of the ether to such phenomena and hence because of his avowed experimentalism always presented such opinions tentatively and with some diffidence; yet as to the existence of such a medium and the legitimacy of the appeal to it for a solution of certain difficulties he had no doubt whatsoever. For More, the world would fly to pieces without the ethereal spirit; for Newton it would run down and become motionless if it were not for the continual recruiting of motion in these various ways by active principles lodged

[76] P. 418, ff.

in the ether. And he never gave up hope that experimental evidence might eventually be secured which would establish or definitely overthrow some of these specific conjectures.[77] It was in this spirit and to this purpose that he proposed many of the thirty-one queries attached to the *Opticks*.

This judgment of Newton's ethereal hypothesis is interestingly confirmed by the last paragraph of the *Principia*.

And now we might add something concerning a certain most subtle spirit which pervades and lies hid in all gross bodies; by the force and action of which spirit the particles of bodies mutually attract one another at near distances, and cohere if contiguous; and electric bodies operate to greater distances, as well repelling as attracting the neighbouring corpuscles; and light is emitted, reflected, refracted, inflected, and heats bodies; and all sensation is excited, and the members of animal bodies move at the command of the will, namely by the vibrations of this spirit, mutually propagated along the solid filaments of the nerves, from the outward organs of sense to the brain, and from the brain into the muscles. But these are things that cannot be explained in few words, nor are we furnished with that sufficiency of experiments which is required to an accurate determination and demonstration of the laws by which this electric and elastic spirit operates.[78]

In other words, the existence of this spirit and its causal relation to such phenomena is assumed to be indubitable; the only uncertainty, and hence the reason why these matters cannot be properly treated in the *Principia*, is that we have so far been unable to obtain accurate experimental laws expressing the operations of this pervasive medium. It is worthy of note that here also there is no hint of the manifold distinctions about the ether made in his letter of 1675; it appears to be conceived as a single medium.

[77] *Opticks*, p. 369.

[78] *Principles*, II, 314.

c. Development of a More Settled Theory

It is in the *Opticks,* and especially in one of those queries which were last appended to the work, that Newton's final statements on the nature and functions of the ether are proffered. Here we find his earlier suppositions clarified and developed in greater detail; here also the explanation of gravity hit upon in the course of his letter to Boyle is presented in a refined and simplified form.

The passage opens with the statement of an interesting fact for explanation: [79] A thermometer enclosed in a vacuum and carried from a cold place into a warm one "will grow warm as much and almost as soon as the thermometer which is not *in vacuo.* . . . Is not the heat of the warm room conveyed through *the vacuum* by the vibrations of a much subtiler medium than air, which after the air was drawn out remained in the *vacuum?* . . . . And is not this medium exceedingly more rare and subtle than the air, and exceedingly more elastic and active? And doth it not readily pervade all bodies? And is it not (by its elastic force) expanded through all the heavens?

"Is not this medium much rarer within the dense bodies of the sun, stars, and planets and comets, than in the empty celestial space between them? And in passing from them to great distances, doth it not grow denser and denser perpetually, and thereby cause the gravity of those great bodies towards one another, and of their parts towards the bodies; every body endeavouring to go from the denser parts of the medium towards the rarer? For if this medium be rarer within the sun's body than at its surface, and rarer there than at the hundredth part of an inch from its body, and rarer there than at the fiftieth part of an inch from its body, and rarer there than at the orbit of *Saturn*; I see no reason why the increase of density should stop anywhere, and not rather be continued through all

[79] *Opticks,* p. 323, ff.

distances from the sun to *Saturn,* and beyond. And though this increase of density may at great distances be exceeding slow, yet if the elastic force of this medium be exceeding great, it may suffice to impel bodies from the denser parts of the medium towards the rarer, with all that power which we call gravity. And that the elastic force of this medium is exceeding great, may be gathered from the swiftness of its vibrations". Newton here cites the velocity of sound and of light by way of illustration, and enters upon a disquisition in which he repeats some of his earlier speculations on the possibility of explaining refraction, sensation, animal motion, magnetism, and the like by the aid of the ether. He then launches on a further description of the medium. "And if any one should suppose that ether (like our air) may contain particles that endeavour to recede from one another (for I do not know what this ether is), and that its particles are exceedingly smaller than those of air, or even than those of light: the exceeding smallness of its particles may contribute to the greatness of the force by which those particles may recede from one another, and thereby make that medium exceedingly more rare and elastic than air, and by consequence exceedingly less able to resist the motions of projectiles, and exceedingly more able to press upon gross bodies, by endeavouring to expand itself.

"May not planets and comets, and all gross bodies, perform their motions more freely, and with less resistance, in this ethereal medium than in any fluid which fills all space adequately without leaving any pores, and by consequence is much denser than quicksilver or gold? And may not its resistance be so small, as to be inconsiderable? For instance: if this ether (for so I will call it) should be supposed 700,000 times more elastic than our air, and above 700,000 times more rare; its resistance would be above 600,000,000 times less than that of water. And so small a resistance would scarce make any sensible alteration in the motions of the planets in ten thousand years."

Newton's ether as finally portrayed is thus a medium of essentially the same nature as air, only much rarer. Its particles are very small and are present in greater quantity according as they are more distant from the inner pores of solid bodies. They are elastic, *i.e.*, they possess mutually repulsive powers, being constantly in the endeavour to recede one from another, which endeavour is the cause of the phenomena of gravitation. Other phenomena of the types above noted are attributed to additional active powers possessed by the ether, or are occasionally spoken of as following likewise from the operation of these repulsive forces. But the active powers apparently cannot be dispensed with, inasmuch as the universal machine is on the decline and the ether is burdened with the responsibility of constantly replenishing the vigour and motion of the cosmos through the exercise of these active principles. It is interesting biographically to observe that in Newton's later writings the number of inexplicable elements or qualities that are invoked to account for the variety of extra-mechanical phenomena is greatly reduced as compared with the early attempts. In fact, in one instructive section of the *Opticks* he repeats in the form of a vast cosmic hypothesis his suggestion in the preface of the *Principia* that all the phenomena of nature may be soluble in terms of atomism and determinate attractive and repulsive forces. For this his earlier speculation on the possibility of deriving solid bodies ultimately from ethereal substances and his constantly expressed faith in all kinds of transmutations in nature had paved the way. The hypothesis, in brief, is that the whole of the physical world may consist of particles which attract each other in proportion to their size, the attraction passing through a zero point into repulsion as we get down to the very minute particles that compose what we call the ether.[80] Thus at one stroke the formation of solid bodies out of the mutual attractions of the larger particles, and the all-pervading ethereal medium with its repulsive endeavours and its variations of density are made quite plausible. It is regrettable that Newton did not allow his disciplined imagination to pursue such suggestions till he had evolved the simplest possible definite theory of the physical universe as a whole.

Did Newton think of the ether as a material or immaterial

[80] *Opticks,* p. 363, ff.

substance? Was the influence of More over him, already observed at so many points, sufficient to make him follow the great Platonist and his predecessor Gilbert in conceiving the ethereal medium as something spiritual rather than material? The reader has noticed that in the quotations so far drawn Newton uses the term "spirit" almost as frequently as "medium," except when referring to the "main body of the phlegmatic ether," and in the third letter to Bentley. Likewise in the *Principia*[81] the question is raised and left ostensibly open whether the interplanetary medium be a corporeal or incorporeal one. Does Newton use these terms in the same sense that his English predecessors applied to them?

Thus put, the question is impossible to answer. In fact, if we focussed our attention on the cosmic theory just considered, we should have to deny any difference in substance between the ether and solid bodies, which would make the former necessarily corporeal; and yet in his early letter it was suggested that solid bodies arise by concretions of various ethereal spirits, which would seem to make the bodies ultimately spiritual. The fact is, Newton's positivism was powerful enough to prevent his carrying his speculations very far in this direction. The ultimate nature of anything he rather consistently denied knowledge of, and our curiosity must therefore remain unsatisfied on this point. Bodies existed, displayed certain qualities, and acted in certain mathematical ways; the ether, he was convinced, likewise existed, and provided for the propagation and increase where needed of the decaying motion in the world; he called it a spirit, and believed thoroughly in the possibility of universal transmutations in nature; but questions as to their inner substance or final relations he considered so far beyond the scope of profitable science as not to deserve careful attention. Furthermore, the spirituality of the cosmos to him was amply guaranteed by the fact that all things and their forces were originally given existence and direction by a spiritual Creator. Religiously as well, then, such a question as we have proposed was unimportant. To Newton's theism and its relation to his science we now turn.

[81] Vol. I, 174.

Section 6. God—Creator and Preserver of the Order of the World

Thus far the metaphysical ideas of Newton which we have been investigating exemplify in the main the first and second of the three types distinguished in Section 2 of the present chapter. They are either appropriated uncritically from the scientific tide of the day or rest upon some feature of his method for their final justification. His treatment of space and time, however, has led us by anticipation into the importance of his ultimately theistic interpretation of the universe, and now as we face the latter more directly it will be helpful first to note that his theological views represent predominantly a metaphysical element of the third type. Religion was a fundamental interest to Newton. It dealt with a realm for the most part different from the object of science; its method was quite disparate, for its conclusions, in the main, were insusceptible of proof or disproof by scientific standards. To be sure, Newton was confident, as we shall see, that certain empirical facts open to anybody's observation, implied unqualifiedly the existence of a God of a certain definite nature and function. God was not detached from the world that science seeks to know; indeed, every true step in natural philosophy brings us nearer to a knowledge of the first cause,[82] and is for this reason to be highly valued—it will enlarge the bounds of moral philosophy also, inasmuch as "so far as we can know by natural philosophy what is the first cause, what power he has over us, and what benefits we receive from him, so far our duty towards him, as well as that towards one another, will appear to us by the light of nature." [83] So, although religion and science are fundamentally different interpretations of the universe, each valid in its own way, yet for Newton in the last analysis, the realm of science was dependent on the God of religion,

[82] *Opticks*, p. 345.

[83] *Opticks*, p. 381.

and led the reverent mind to a fuller assurance of his reality and a readier obedience to his commands. Thus in spite of their incommensurable character and his considerable success in banning religious prejudices from his positive scientific theorems, the fact that God's existence and control was never questioned by the man who wrote almost as many theological dissertations as scientific classics had its strong and significant reactions on positions which he would have called purely scientific.

A. Newton as Theologian

Newton's place in the religious unsettlement of his era would be an interesting topic for studious application. He was accused by the ultra-orthodox of being an Arian, apparently on ample grounds. Among other heretical suggestions, he wrote a brief essay on *Two Notable Corruptions of Scripture*,[84] in each case the effect of his thesis being to cast doubt on the traditional assumption that the doctrine of the Trinity was taught in the New Testament. A strongly Arian flavour pervades most of his theological efforts, from which we shall take a quotation or two for another purpose, namely to show that religion was something quite basic to him and in no sense a mere appendage to his science or an accidental addition to his metaphysics. Newton believed that scientific fact involved theism, but he would have been a theist had his scientific powers remained forever dormant. Newton evidently cherished a kind of religious experience, nourished largely, of course, by tradition, that was in the main detachable from the theism postulated as a corollary to science. This fact has its relevant bearings on his clear and continued conviction that the world of science is by no means the whole world.

> We are, therefore, to acknowledge one God, infinite, eternal, omnipresent, omniscient, omnipotent, the creator of all things, most wise, most just, most good, most holy.

[84] *Opera,* Vol. V.

We must love him, fear him, honour him, trust in him, pray to him, give him thanks, praise him, hallow his name, obey his commandments, and set times apart for his service, as we are directed in the third and fourth Commandments, for this is the love of God, that we keep his commandments, and his commandments are not grievous. I John v. 3. And these things we must do not to any mediators between him and us, but to him alone, that he may give his angels charge over us, who, being our fellow-servants, are pleased with the worship we give to their God. And this is the first and the principal part of religion. This always was, and always will be the religion of God's people, from the beginning to the end of the world.[85]

Newton's longer theological treaties, such as the *Observations on the Prophecies*,[86] but confirm these indications that he was a pious, believing Christian in all that the term then implied, as well as a master scientist.[87] His Arianism was

[85] Brewster, II, 348, ff.

[86] *Opera*, Vol. V.

[87] From a manuscript entitled, *On our Religion to God, to Christ, and the Church,* Brewster, II, 349, ff., the following excerpts are illustrative:
"There is one God, the Father, ever living, omnipresent, omniscient, almighty, the maker of heaven and earth, and one Mediator between God and man, the man Christ Jesus. . . .
"The Father is omniscient, and hath all knowledge originally in his own breast, and communicates knowledge of future things to Jesus Christ; and none in heaven or earth, or under the earth, is worthy to receive knowledge of future things immediately from the Father but the Lamb. And therefore the testimony of Jesus is the spirit of prophecy, and Jesus is the Word or Prophet of God. . . .
"We are to return thanks to the Father alone for creating us, and giving us food and raiment and other blessings of this life, and whatsoever we are to thank him for, or desire that he would do for us, we ask of him immediately in the name of Christ. . . .
"To us there is but one God, the Father, of whom are all things, and one Lord Jesus Christ, by whom are all things, and we by him. That is, we are to worship the Father alone as God Almighty, and Jesus alone as the Lord, the Messiah, the

radical for the age, but it did not prevent his approaching the world of science under the necessity of seeing it cloaked by a divine glory and suffused with the religious significance that followed from the conviction that it had been created and ordered by the hands of the God who had been worshipped from his youth as Father of the Christian Saviour and infallible Author of the Christian Scriptures.

Great King, the Lamb of God who was slain, and hath redeemed us with his blood, and made us kings and priests."

In a very interesting tract on church union, Brewster, II, 526, ff., Newton adds to his propaganda as a pioneer in that field some propositions on church government:

"It is therefore the duty of bishops and presbyters to govern the people according to the laws of God and the laws of the king, and in their councils to punish offenders according to those laws, and to teach those who do not know the laws of God; but not to make new laws in the name of either God or the king.

"The Church is constituted and her extent and bounds of communion are defined by the laws of God, and these laws are unchangeable.

"The laws of the king extend only to things that are left indifferent and undetermined by the laws of God, and particularly to the revenues and tranquillity of the church, to her courts of justice, and to decency and order in her worship; and all laws about things left indifferent by the laws of God ought to be referred to the civil government. . . .

"To impose any article of communion not imposed from the beginning is a crime of the same nature with that of those Christians of the circumcision who endeavoured to impose circumcision and the observation of the law upon the converted Gentiles. For the law was good if a man could keep it, but we were to be saved not by the works of the law, but by faith in Jesus Christ, and to impose those works as articles of communion, was to make them necessary to salvation, and thereby to make void the faith in Jesus Christ. And there is the same reason against imposing any other article of communion which was not imposed from the beginning. All such impositions are teaching another gospel. . . .

"After baptism we are to live according to the laws of God and the king, and to grow in grace and in the knowledge of our Lord Jesus Christ, by practising what we promised before baptism, and studying the Scriptures, and teaching one another in meekness and charity, without imposing their private opinions, or falling out about them."

Parented in part by this traditional religious indoctrination and experience, in part thrust upon him, as it seemed, by indubitable evidences of intelligent purpose in the cosmic order, the now familiar arguments for the divine origin of the world are spread forth upon the pages of his classic works.

The main business of natural philosophy is to argue from phenomena without feigning hypotheses, and to deduce causes from effects, till we come to the very first cause, which certainly is not mechanical; and not only to unfold the mechanism of the world, but chiefly to resolve these and such like questions. What is there in places almost empty of matter, and whence is it that the sun and planets gravitate towards one another, without dense matter between them? Whence is it that nature doth nothing in vain; and whence arises all that order and beauty which we see in the world? To what end are comets, and whence is it that planets move all one and the same way in orbs concentric, while comets move all manner of ways in orbs very eccentric, and what hinders the fixed stars from falling upon one another? How came the bodies of animals to be contrived with so much art, and for what ends were their several parts? [88] Was the eye contrived without skill in optics, or the ear without knowledge of sounds? How do the motions of the body follow from the will, and whence is the instinct in animals? Is not the sensory of animals that place to which the sensitive substance is present, and into which the sensible species of things are carried through the nerves and brain, that there they may be perceived by their immediate presence to that substance? And these things being rightly dispatched, does it not appear from phenomena that there is a being incorporeal, living, intelligent, omnipresent, who, in infinite space, as it were in his sensory, sees the things themselves intimately, and thoroughly perceives them; and comprehends them wholly by their immediate presence to himself? [89]

[88] Cf. also *Principles,* II, 313; *Opticks,* p. 378, ff.

[89] *Opticks,* p. 344, ff.

Here facts whose ultimate causality Newton usually ascribed to the ether seem to be regarded as the direct operation of God, such as gravity and the production of bodily
motion by the will. Likewise the theological grounding of the
postulate of the simplicity of nature is notable, aligning Newton in this respect with his great scientific forbears. Of these
teleological arguments the most cogent to Newton's own mind,
and one which he never tired of stressing, reflects his thorough
acquaintance with the phenomena of the celestial system—
that is, the fact that "planets move all one and the same way
in orbs concentric, while comets move all manner of ways in
orbs very eccentric." [90] In his first letter to Dr. Bentley, on the
occasion of the latter's tenure of the Boyle lectureship in 1692,
this argument is developed in some detail. Bentley had written
to Newton, outlining a vast cosmic hypothesis of the creation
of the universe from matter evenly dispersed throughout all
space, on certain points of which he requested Newton's
advice because he had deduced it, as he believed, from Newtonian principles. The latter's reply approved the main features of the scheme, but devoted itself especially to the above
argument.

> Sir; When I wrote my treatise about our system, I had an
> eye upon such principles as might work with considering
> men, for the belief of a Deity; and nothing can rejoice me
> more than to find it useful for that purpose. But if I have
> done the public any service this way, it is due to nothing
> but industry and patient thought. . . .
>
> The same power, whether natural or supernatural, which
> placed the sun in the centre of the six primary planets,
> placed *Saturn* in the centre of the orbs of his five secondary
> planets; and *Jupiter* in the centre of his four secondary
> planets; and the earth in the centre of the moon's orb; and
> therefore, had this cause been a blind one without con-
> trivance or design, the sun would have been a body of the
> same kind with *Saturn, Jupiter,* and the earth; that is with-
> out light or heat. Why there is one body in our system
> qualified to give light and heat to all the rest, I know no

[90] Cf. *Opticks*, p. 378; *Principles*, II, 310.

reason, but because the author of the system thought it convenient: and why there is but one body of this kind, I know no reason, but because one was sufficient to warm and enlighten all the rest. For the Cartesian hypothesis of suns losing their light, and their turning into comets, and comets into planets, can have no place in my system, and is plainly erroneous: because it is certain, that as often as they appear to us, they descended into the system of our planets, lower than the orb of *Jupiter,* and sometimes lower than the orbs of *Venus* and *Mercury*; and yet never stay here, but always return from the sun with the same degrees of motion by which they approached him.

To your second query I answer, that the motions, which the planets now have, could not spring from any natural cause alone, but were impressed by an intelligent agent. For since comets descend into the region of our planets, and here move all manner of ways, going sometimes the same way with the planets, sometimes the contrary way, and sometimes in crossways, their planes inclined to the plane of the ecliptic, and at all kinds of angles, it is plain that there is no natural cause which could determine all the planets, both primary and secondary, to move the same way and in the same plane, without any considerable variation: this must have been the effect of counsel. Nor is there any natural cause which could give the planets those just degrees of velocity, in proportion to their distances from the sun, and other central bodies, which were requisite to make them move in such concentric orbs about those bodies. Had the planets been as swift as comets . . . or had the distances from the centres, about which they move, been greater or less. . . . or had the quantity of matter in the sun, or in *Saturn, Jupiter,* and the earth, and by consequence their gravitating power, been greater or less than it is; the primary planets could not have revolved about the sun, nor the secondary ones about *Saturn, Jupiter,* and the earth, in concentric circles as they do, but would have moved in hyperbolas or parabolas, or in ellipses very eccentric. To make this system, therefore, with all its motions, required a cause which understood, and compared together the quantities of matter in the several bodies of the sun and planets, and the gravitating powers resulting from thence; the several distances of the primary planets from the sun, and of the secondary ones from *Saturn, Jupiter,* and the earth; and the velocities, with which these planets could revolve about those quantities of matter in the central bodies; and to compare and adjust all these things together in so great a variety of bodies, argues that cause to be not blind or fortuitous, but very well skilled in mechanics and geometry.[91]

That Newton does not allow his teleology to run riot is evidenced by the concluding paragraphs of this interesting argument for the creation of the solar system by an expert mathematician. Dr. Bentley, in his zealous quest for theistic evidences, had suggested the inclination of the earth's axis as an additional proof. Newton thought that this was overdoing the matter, unless the reasoning be cautiously guarded.

Lastly, I see nothing extraordinary in the inclination of the earth's axis for proving a Deity; unless you will urge it as a contrivance for winter and summer, and for making the earth habitable towards the poles; and that the diurnal rotations of the sun and planets, as they could hardly arise from any cause purely mechanical, so by being determined all the same way with the annual and menstrual motions, they seem to make up that harmony in the system, which, as I explained above, was the effect of choice, rather than chance.

There is yet another argument for a Deity, which I take to be a very strong one; but till the principles on which it is grounded are better received, I think it more advisable to let it sleep.

There is nothing in Newton's later writings to indicate whether any of the arguments there advanced is the one here withheld from Dr. Bentley's apologetic zest.

Several times in his Bentley letters Newton took occasion to object to the doctor's assumption that gravity is an essential quality of bodies. This his own experimental principles had

[91]*Opera,* IV, 429, ff.

led him to refuse to do, as we noted in Section 4.[92] At the same time the prestige of his law of gravitation, and its apparent universality in the world of matter, had encouraged a general impression that gravity was innate in matter according to Newtonian principles, an impression that was further advanced by Cotes' explicit championship of the doctrine in his preface to the second edition of the *Principia*. "You sometimes speak of gravity as essential and inherent to matter. Pray do not ascribe that notion to me; for the cause of gravity is what I do not pretend to know, and therefore would take more time to consider it." [93] Nevertheless, Newton held the phenomena to be such, that even with innate gravity the matter of the solar system could not have taken its present form alone; "gravity may put the planets into motion, but without the divine power it could never put them into such a circulating motion, as they have about the sun" [94]; furthermore, if there be innate gravity, it is impossible now for the matter of the earth and all the planets and stars to fly up from them, and become evenly spread throughout all the heavens, without a supernatural power, and certainly that which can never be hereafter without a supernatural power, could never be heretofore without the same power." [95] Hence, whether with gravity essential to bodies or without, a divine creation is implied.

B. God's Present Duties in the Cosmic Economy

Newton thus, because of his powerful religious heritage and with a keen sense for all the facts of order and adaptation in the world, supports with all the vigour of his authoritative pen the view currently accepted by all parties of the ultimately

[92] Cf. *Principles*, II, 161, ff.; 313.

[93] *Opera*, IV, 437.

[94] *Opera*, IV, 436, ff.; 439.

[95] *Opera*, IV, 441.

religious genesis of the universe. God originally created masses and set them in motion; likewise the space and time in which they move, as we saw, he constitutes by his presence and continued existence. He is responsible for that intelligent order and regular harmony in the structure of things that makes them the object of exact knowledge and of reverent contemplation. It is when we inquire into the subsequent relations of the Deity to his handiwork that we fall upon those elements in Newton's theology that became of the most profound historical significance. It will be remembered that none of his predecessors among the mechanical interpreters of nature had ventured to be fully consistent in the conception of the world as a mathematical machine. It seemed either impious or dangerous to detach God from continued connexion with the object of his past creative activity. Thus Descartes, for all his mechanical enthusiasm, spoke of God as maintaining the vast machine by his "general concourse", and even of recreating it constantly because of the supposed discreteness of temporal moments. By More the term "mechanical" was practically confined to the principle of inertia, God being either directly or indirectly responsible for those further principles in virtue of which things were actively held together in a circulating system. Boyle, in spite of his frequent comparison of the world to the Strassburg clock, piously reiterated the "general concourse" of Descartes, though without indicating what meaning might be contained in the phrase, and attempted an analysis of the various ways in which God might be said to exert a present providence over the fruit of his labours. It is in Huyghens and Leibniz that we first meet spirits adventurous enough openly to confine the divine activity to the first creation alone, and the latter contemptuously criticized his English contemporaries for insulting the Deity by the insinuation that he had been unable to make a perfect machine at the beginning, but was under the necessity of tinkering with it from time to time in order to keep it in running condition. "According to their doctrine, God Almighty wants to wind up his watch from time to time, otherwise it would cease to move. He had not, it seems, sufficient foresight to make it a perpetual motion. Nay, the machine of God's making is so imperfect according to these gentlemen, that he is obliged to clean it now and then by an extraordinary concourse, and even to mend it as a clockmaker mends his work; who must consequently be so much the more unskilful a workman, as he is oftener obliged to mend his work and set it right. According to my opinion, the same force and vigour remains always in the world, and only passes from one part of matter to another, agreeably to the laws of nature and the beautiful pre-established order. And I hold that when God works miracles, he does not do it in order to supply the wants of nature, but those of grace. Whoever thinks otherwise, must needs have a very mean notion of the wisdom and power of God." [96]

Now from Newton's writings, as from Boyle's, it is possible to pick passage after passage in which it seems to be assumed that after its first construction the world of nature has been quite independent of God for its continued existence and motion. The world could not have arisen out of a chaos by the mere laws of nature, "though being once formed, it may continue by those laws for many ages" [97]; the frame of nature may be a condensation of various ethereal spirits, "and after condensation wrought into various forms, at first by the immediate hand of the Creator, and ever since by the power of nature, which, by virtue of the command, increase and multiply, became a complete imitator of the copy set her by the Protoplast" [98]; "in him are all things contained and moved, yet neither affects the other—God suffers nothing from the motion of bodies, bodies find no resistance from the omnipresence of God." [99] But when we investigate more thoroughly we find that he, no more than Boyle, had any intention of really divorcing God from present control of, and occasional interference with, his vast engine. It is not enough to have the miracles of scripture and the achievements of spiritual grace to appeal to as evidences of continued divine

[96] Brewster, II, 285.

[97] *Opticks*, p. 378.

[98] Brewster, I, 392.

[99] *Principles*, II, 311.

contact with the realm of human affairs. God must also be given a present function in the cosmos at large; we must not allow him to abandon his toils after six days of constructive labour and leave the world of matter to its own devices. Newton's religious prejudices and his æsthetico-scientific assumptions alike arose in rebellion against such an indeterminate vacation for the Deity.

It is noticeable that Newton, in common with the whole voluntaristic British tradition in medieval and modern philosophy, tended to subordinate in God the intellect to the will; above the Creator's wisdom and knowledge is to be stressed his power and dominion. In some passages this emphasis is not present, but usually the proportions are unmistakable. The famous paragraph on the nature of the Deity in the second edition of the *Principia* is the most striking example:

> This Being governs all things, not as the soul of the world, but as Lord over all; and on account of his dominion he is wont to be called Lord God $\pi\alpha\nu\tau\text{о}\kappa\rho\acute{\alpha}\tau\omega\rho$, or *Universal Ruler* . . . The Supreme God is a Being eternal, infinite, absolutely perfect; but a being, however perfect, without dominion, cannot be said to be Lord God. . . . It is the dominion of a spiritual being which constitutes a God: a true, supreme, or imaginary dominion makes a true, supreme, or imaginary God. And from his true dominion it follows that the true God is a living, intelligent, and powerful Being; and from his other perfections, that he is supreme, or most perfect . . . We know him only by his most wise and excellent contrivances of things, and final causes; we admire him for his perfections; but we reverence and adore him on account of his dominion; for we adore him as his servants; and a god without dominion, providence, and final causes, is nothing else but Fate and Nature. . . . And thus much concerning God; to discourse of whom from the appearances of things does certainly belong to natural philosophy.[100]

Absurd indeed it would be to deprive a being so portrayed of present control of his creation; accordingly we find Newton

[100] *Principles*, II, 311 ff. Cf. also *Opticks*, p. 381.

assigning to God two very important and specific duties in the daily cosmic economy. For one thing, he actively prevents the fixed stars from collapsing together in the middle of space. This is not taught in the *Principia;* Newton there had confined himself to observing that in order to prevent such a collapse God had set these stars at immense distances from one another.[101] Of course, this expedient would hardly suffice through all the ages of time, hence the reader of Newton is surprised that his author nowhere cites this difficulty as a reason for not imputing gravity to matter beyond the reach of our experimental observations: if the fixed stars do not gravitate, obviously there is no problem. We discover, however, that Newton implicitly thinks of them as possessing gravity, for in the *Opticks* and the third letter to Bentley he assigns it as one of the divine functions constantly to maintain them at their proper intervals.[102] In the former note the question: "what hinders the fixed stars from falling upon one another?" In the latter, after approving, in the main, Bentley's creation hypothesis, he adds: "And though the matter were divided at first into several systems, and every system by a divine power constituted like ours; yet would the outside systems descend towards the middlemost; so that this frame of things could not always subsist without a divine power to conserve it. . . ."

In the final query of the *Opticks,* however, we find God made responsible for a much more intricate task in applied mechanics; he is allotted the duty of providentially reforming the system of the world when the mechanism has so far run out of gear as to demand such a reformation. The active principles of the ether provide for the conservation of motion, but they do not provide sufficiently for overcoming the noted irregularities in the motion of the planets and comets, especially the latter. Due to the gradual disintegration of the comets under the influence of solar heat,[103] and the retardation

[101] *Principles,* II, 310 ff.

[102] *Opticks,* p. 344; *Opera,* IV, 439, ff.

[103] *Principles,* II, 293–8.

in their aphelia because of mutual attractions among themselves and between them and the planets; likewise due to the gradual increase in bulk of the planets, owing chiefly to the same causes, the irregularities in nature are on the increase, and the time will come when things must be set right again.

"For while comets move in very eccentric orbs in all manner of positions, blind fate could never make all the planets move in one and the same way in orbs concentric, some inconsiderable irregularities excepted, which may have risen from the mutual actions of comets and planets upon one another, and which will be apt to increase till this system wants a reformation." [104] God is scientifically required, Newton holds, to fulfil this need, since he is a "powerful ever-living Agent, who being in all places is more able by his will to move the bodies within his boundless uniform sensorium, and thereby to form and reform the parts of the universe, than we are by our will to move the parts of our own bodies. And yet we are not to consider the world as the body of God, or the several parts thereof, as the parts of God. He is a uniform being, void of organs, members or parts, and they are his creatures subordinate to him, and subservient to his will. . . . And since space is divisible *in infinitum,* and matter is not necessarily in all places, it may be also allowed that God is able to create particles of matter of several sizes and figures, and in several proportions to space, and perhaps of different densities and forces, and thereby to vary the laws of nature, and make worlds of several sorts in several parts of the universe. At least, I see nothing of contradiction in all this." [105]

Newton thus apparently takes for granted a postulate of extreme importance; he assumes, with so many others who bring an æsthetic interest into science, that the incomparable order, beauty, and harmony which characterizes the celestial realm in the large, is to be eternally preserved. It will not be preserved by space, time, mass, and ether alone; its preservation requires the continued exertion of that divine will which freely chose this order and harmony as the ends of his

[104] *Opticks,* p. 378, ff.

[105] *Opticks,* p. 379.

first creative toil. From the Protoplast of the whole, God has now descended to become a category among other categories; the facts of continued order, system, and uniformity as observed in the world, are inexplicable apart from him.

c. The Historical Relations of Newton's Theism

Contrast this Newtonian teleology with that of the scholastic system. For the latter, God was the final cause of all things just as truly and more significantly than their original former. Ends in nature did not head up in the astronomical harmony; that harmony was itself a means to further ends, such as knowledge, enjoyment, and use on the part of living beings of a higher order, who in turn were made for a still nobler end which completed the divine circuit, to know God and enjoy him forever. God had no purpose; he was the ultimate object of purpose. In the Newtonian world, following Galileo's earlier suggestion, all this further teleology is unceremoniously dropped. The cosmic order of masses in motion according to law, is itself the final good. Man exists to know and applaud it; God exists to tend and preserve it. All the manifold divergent zeals and hopes of men are implicitly denied scope and fulfilment; if they cannot be subjected to the aim of theoretical mechanics, their possessors are left no proper God, for them there is no entrance into the kingdom of heaven. We are to become devotees of mathematical science; God, now the chief mechanic of the universe, has become the cosmic conservative. His aim is to maintain the *status quo*. The day of novelty is all in the past; there is no further advance in time. Periodic reformation when necessary, by the addition of the indicated masses at the points of space required, but no new creative activity—to this routine of temporal housekeeping is the Deity at present confined.

Historically, the Newtonian attempt thus to keep God on duty was of the very deepest import. It proved a veritable boomerang to his cherished philosophy of religion, that as the result of all his pious ransackings the main providential function he could attribute to the Deity was this cosmic plumbery, this meticulous defence of his arbitrarily imposed mechanical laws against the threatening encroachments of irregularity. Really, the notion of the divine eye as constantly roaming the universe on the search for leaks to mend, or gears to replace in the mighty machinery would have been quite laughable, did not its pitifulness become earlier evident. For to stake the present existence and activity of God on imperfections in the cosmic engine was to court rapid disaster for theology. Not immediately, of course, indeed for many contemporary minds the purging of the world from all secondary qualities and the stress laid on the marvellous regularity of its whirrings only brought into fuller rational relief its divine Creator and governing Will.

> What though in solemn *silence* all
> Move round the *dark* terrestrial ball?
> What though no *real* voice nor sound
> Within their radiant orbs be found?
> In reason's ear they all rejoice,
> And utter forth a glorious voice,
> Forever singing as they shine,
> "The hand that made us is divine." [106]

But science moved on, and under the guidance of the less pious but more fruitful hypothesis that it would be possible to extend the mechanical idea over an ever wider realm, Newton's successors accounted one by one for the irregularities that to his mind had appeared essential and increasing if the machine were left to itself. This process of eliminating the providential elements in the world-order reached its climax in the work of the great Laplace, who believed himself to have demonstrated the inherent stability of the universe by showing that all its irregularities are periodical, and subject to an eternal law which prevents them from ever exceeding a stated amount.

While God was thus being deprived of his duties by the further advancement of mechanical science, and men were be-

[106] *The Spacious Firmament on High*, hymn written by Joseph Addison to the chorus of Haydn's *Creation*, 3rd stanza.

ginning to wonder whether the self-perpetuating machine thus left stood really in need of any supernatural beginning, Hume's crushing disposal of the ideas of power and causality along another tack were already disturbing the learned world with the suspicion that a First Cause was not as necessary an idea of reason as it had appeared, and Kant was preparing the penetrating analysis which frankly purported to remove God from the realm of knowledge altogether. In short, Newton's cherished theology was rapidly peeled off by all the competent hands that could get at him, and the rest of his metaphysical entities and assumptions, shorn of their religious setting, were left to wander naked and unabashed through the premises of subsequent thought, unchallenged by thorough criticism because supposed as eternally based as the positive scientific conquests of the man who first annexed the boundless firmament to the domain of mathematical mechanics. Space, time, and mass became regarded as permanent and indestructible constituents of the infinite world-order, while the notion of the ether continued to assume unpredictable shapes and remains in the scientific thought of to-day a relic of ancient animism still playing havoc with poor man's attempts to think straight about his world. The only place left for God was in the bare irreducible fact of intelligible order in things, which as regards the cosmos as a whole could not be quite escaped by Hume the sceptic, and as regards the realm of moral relations was all but hypostasized by that ruthless destroyer of age-long theistic proofs, Immanuel Kant. Newton's doctrine is a most interesting and historically important transitional stage between the miraculous providentialism of earlier religious philosophy and the later tendency to identify the Deity with the sheer fact of rational order and harmony. God is still providence, but the main exercise of his miraculous power is just to maintain the exact mathematical regularity in the system of the world without which its intelligibility and beauty would disappear. Furthermore, the subsequent attempt to merge him into that beauty and harmony had itself to battle for a most discouraging and precarious existence. The bulk of thinking men, ever and inevitably anthropomorphic in their theology, could hardly sense religious validity in such theistic substitutes. For them, so far as they were considerably penetrated with science or philosophy, God had been quite eliminated from the scene, and the only thing left to achieve was a single and final step in the mechanization of existence. Here were these residual souls of men, irregularly scattered among the atoms of mass that swam mechanically among the ethereal vapours in time and space, and still retaining vestiges of the Cartesian *res cogitans*. They too must be reduced to mechanical products and parts of the self-regulating cosmic clock. For this the raw materials had already been supplied by Newton's older English contemporaries, Hobbes and Locke, who had applied in this field the method of explanation in terms of simplest parts, merely dropping the mathematical requirement; they likewise simply needed to be purged of a rather alien theological setting to fit appropriately into an ultimate mechanomorphic hypothesis of the whole universe. Such a universalizing of this clockwork naturalism reached its summation in some of the brilliant French minds of the late Enlightenment, notably La Mettrie and the Baron d'Holbach, and in a somewhat different form in nineteenth-century evolutionism.

To follow such developments is obviously quite beyond the scope of an analysis of the metaphysic of early modern science. The rapid elimination of God, however, from the categories, rendered irreversible the projection upon modern philosophy of the notable problem referred to in the introduction and yet racking the brains of thinkers, whose essential relation to the Newtonian metaphysical scheme can hardly therefore be passed over. I refer to the problem of knowledge. As long as the existence of a God to whom the whole realm of matter was intimately present and known, succeeded in maintaining itself as an unquestioned conviction, the problem of how man's soul, shut within the dark room of a ventricle of the brain, could possibly gain trustworthy knowledge of external masses blindly wandering in time and space, naturally became no terrifying puzzle—a spiritual continuity connecting all links in the infinite scene was supplied in God. This is why Boyle's epistemological comments were so weak. But with the farewell of the Deity, the epistemological difficulties of the situation could hardly fail to offer an overwhelming challenge. How could intelligence grasp an inaccessible world in which there was no answering or controlling intelligence? It was by no means an accident that Hume and Kant, the first pair who really banished God from metaphysical philosophy, likewise destroyed by a sceptical critique the current overweening faith in the metaphysical competence of reason. They perceived that the Newtonian world without God must be a world in which the reach and certainty of knowledge is decidedly and closely limited, if indeed the very existence of knowledge at all is possible. This conclusion had already been foreshadowed in the fourth book of Locke's *Essay*, where a pious theism alone saved the inconsistent author from tumbling into the Avernus of scepticism. None of these keen and critical minds, however —and this is the major instructive lesson for students of philosophy in the twentieth century—directed their critical guns on the work of the man who stood in the centre of the whole significant transformation. No one in the learned world could be found to save the brilliant mathematical victories over the realm of physical motion, and at the same time lay bare the big problems involved in the new doctrine of causality, and the inherent ambiguities in the tentative, compromising, and rationally inconstruable form of the Cartesian dualism that had been dragged along like a tribal deity in the course of the campaign. For the claim of absolute and irrefutable demonstration in Newton's name had swept over Europe, and almost everybody had succumbed to its authoritative sway. Wherever was taught as truth the universal formula of gravitation, there was also insinuated as a nimbus of surrounding belief that man is but the puny and local spectator, nay irrelevant product of an infinite self-moving engine, which existed eternally before him and will be eternally after him, enshrining the rigour of mathematical relationships while banishing into impotence all ideal imaginations; an engine which consists of raw masses wandering to no purpose in an undiscoverable time and space, and is in general wholly devoid of any qualities that might spell satisfaction for the major interests of human nature, save solely the central aim of the mathematical physicist. Indeed, that this aim itself should be rewarded appeared inconsistent and impossible when subjected to the light of clear epistemological analysis.

But if they had directed intelligent criticism in his direction, what radical conclusions would they have been likely to reach?

We have observed that the heart of the new scientific metaphysics is to be found in the ascription of ultimate reality and causal efficacy to the world of mathematics, which world is identified with the realm of material bodies moving in space and time. Expressed somewhat more fully, three essential points are to be distinguished in the transformation which issued in the victory of this metaphysical view; there is a change in the prevailing conception (1) of reality, (2) of causality, and (3) of the human mind. First, the real world in which man lives is no longer regarded as a world of substances possessed of as many ultimate qualities as can be experienced in them, but has become a world of atoms (now electrons), equipped with none but mathematical characteristics and moving according to laws fully statable in mathematical form. Second, explanations in terms of forms and final causes of events, both in this world and in the less independent realm of mind, have been definitely set aside in favour of explanations in terms of their simplest elements, the latter related temporally as efficient causes, and being mechanically treatable motions of bodies wherever it is possible so to regard them. In connexion with this aspect of the change, God ceased to be regarded as a Supreme Final Cause, and, where still believed in, became the First Efficient Cause of the world. Man likewise lost the high place over against nature which had been his as a part of the earlier teleological hierarchy, and his mind came to be described as a combination of sensations (now reactions) instead of in terms of the scholastic faculties. Third, the attempt by philosophers of science in the light of these two changes to re-describe the relation of the human mind to nature, expressed itself in the popular form of the Cartesian dualism, with its doctrine of primary and secondary qualities, its location of the mind in a corner of the brain, and its account of the mechanical genesis of sensation and idea.

These changes have conditioned practically the whole of modern exact thinking. Today new theories on each of these matters are in the making, theories which are more promising than earlier modern attempts to refute the metaphysic of science because they are born of an age in which physical science itself has been forced to break away from its Newtonian moorings and to consider its foundations afresh. In time, out of the clash of these theories will be created a new scientific conception of the world which may last as long and dominate human thinking as profoundly as the great conception of the medieval period. In view of present rapid transformations in the fundamental ideas of the sciences the formation of this new picture in detail cannot be wisely anticipated—it must take its own time to arrive. Yet it ought to be the prime lesson of the present historical study that attempts to formulate this new viewpoint by the mere synthesis of scientific data or the logical criticism of its assumptions are bound to be inadequate in any case. It is of the first importance that they be supplemented by a sound insight into the major factors which have conditioned the rise both of the medieval metaphysic and of its mathematico-mechanical successor which is now seen by all thinkers to demand thorough critical overhauling. Without such insight the new metaphysic, when it arrives, will be but the objectification of the mood of an age, perhaps fitful and temporary, rather than the reasoned expression of the intellectual insight of all ages. Unless we can approximate more closely than has yet been done this generalized interpretation, the new cosmology will hardly be worth the effort required for its construction. But nothing can provide the panorama needed for this effort except extensive historical analysis of the sort that might include the present study as a humble contribution.

It is beyond the scope of a concluding chapter to develop this moralising at any length, but it may be worth while to consider briefly the three fundamental phases just mentioned of the transformation to the mechanical world-view and see what the historical approach might hope to contribute to the clarification of the issues involved.

So far as concerns the problem of the essential nature of reality, it ought to be fairly obvious after the feats of modern physics that the world around us is, among other things, a world of masses moving according to mathematically statable laws in time and space. To bring complaint against so much would be to deny the actual usable results of modern scientific inquiry into the nature of our physical environment. But when, in the interest of clearing the field for exact mathematical analysis, men sweep out of the temporal and spatial realm all non-mathematical characteristics, concentrate them in a lobe of the brain, and pronounce them the semi-real effects of atomic motions outside, they have performed a rather radical piece of cosmic surgery which deserves to be carefully examined. If we are right in judging that wishful thinking in the interest of religious salvation played a strong part in the construction of the medieval hierarchy of reality, is it not an equally plausible hypothesis to suppose that wishful thinking of another sort underlay this extreme doctrine of early modern physics—that because it was easier to get ahead in the reduction of nature to a system of mathematical equations by supposing that nothing existed outside of the human mind that was not so reducible, naturalists proceeded at once to make the convenient assumption? And there is a certain peremptory logic in this. How could the world of physical matter be reduced to exact mathematical formulæ by anybody as long as his geometrical concentration was distracted by the supposition that physical nature is full of colours and sounds and feelings and final causes as well as mathematical units and relations? It would be easy to let our judgment of these giants in the history of thought be over-harsh. We should remember that men cannot do arduous and profound intellectual labour in the face of constant and seductive distractions. The sources of distraction simply had to be denied or removed. To get ahead confidently with their revolutionary achievements, they had to attribute absolute reality and independence to those entities in terms of which they were attempting to reduce the world. This once done, all the other features of their cosmology followed as naturally as you please. It has, no doubt, been worth the metaphysical barbarism of a few centuries to possess modern science. Why did none of them see the tremendous difficulties involved? Here, too, in the light of our study, can there be any doubt of the central reason? These founders of the philosophy of science were absorbed in the mathematical study of nature. *Metaphysics they tended more and more to avoid, so far as they could avoid it; so far as not, it became an instrument for their further mathematical conquest of the world.* Any solution of the ultimate questions which continued to pop up, however superficial and inconsistent, that served to quiet the situation, to give a tolerably plausible response to their questionings in the categories they were now familiar with, and above all to open before them a free field for their fuller mathematical exploitation of nature, tended to be readily accepted and tucked away in their minds with uncritical confidence. This was not quite true of those like Hobbes and More, who were philosophers rather than mathematical physicists, and Descartes is perhaps an exception, though one can hardly feel sure how much his desperate cry for a pure mathematical science of nature conditioned his first philosophy.

Now the growth to a commanding position in modern thought of the chemical, biological, and social sciences has imposed difficulties on this simple scheme which even these redoubtable mechanists would have had to face seriously had mechanical physics not anticipated the exact development of these sciences to the extent that it did. From the standpoint of non-mechanical sciences entities have to be regarded as belonging to the real world beyond the mind for which there is no place in the easy Newtonian metaphysic. At least the secondary qualities and the tertiary ones embodied in human institutions have to be accorded a quite different status than the one congenial to the early mechanical philosophy. These developments strongly suggest that reality can only be consistently regarded as a more complex affair, that the primary qualities simply characterize nature so far as she is subject to mathematical handling, while she just as really harbors the secondary and tertiary ones so far as she is a medley of orderly but irreducible qualities. How to construe a rational structure out of these various aspects of nature is the great difficulty of contemporary cosmology; that we have not yet satisfactorily solved it is evident if one considers the logical inadequacies in the theory of emergent evolution, which appears at present the most popular scheme for dealing with this problem. In this theory we either have to suppose fundamental discontinuities in nature such as permit no inference from qualities earlier existing to those later appearing, or else we have to regard the more complex qualities as somehow existing even before they would have been empirically observable, and co-operating in bringing about their material embodiment. The second of these alternatives carries us back to pre-scientific logic, while the first admits too many irrationalities in the order of nature. It in effect gives up the task of construing a coherent order in the phases of reality. These difficulties suggest that perhaps we need to be much more radical in the explanatory hypotheses considered than we have allowed ourselves to be heretofore. Possibly the world of external facts is much more fertile and plastic than we have ventured to suppose; it may be that all these cosmologies and many more analyses and classifications are genuine ways of arranging what nature offers to our understanding, and that the main condition determining our selection between them is something in us rather than something in the external world. This possibility might be enormously clarified by historical studies aiming to ferret out the fundamental motives and other human factors involved in each of these characteristic analyses as it appeared and to make what headway seemed feasible at evaluating them, discovering which are of more enduring significance and why.

This becomes more evident still when we face the second phase of the Newtonian transformation, the problem of causality. Different thinkers and ages have made widely different assumptions as to what constitutes a sound causal explanation of any event—only historical study can reveal the factors conditioning the appearance of each type and afford us some basis for deciding which of them is the more plausible, or at least which points in the direction of fullest satisfaction of what we want an explanation to do.

Viewed in their historical appearance in western scientific

philosophy, there would seem to have been to date three basically distinct convictions on this matter. One is the teleological position of Platonic and Aristotelian philosophy and expressed with meticulous precision in the scholastic dictum that the cause must be adequate to the effect "either formally or eminently." In simple language we may put it thus: the cause must be at least as perfect as the effect. When worked out in detail this means an essentially religious picture of the world, and a being not dissimilar to the scholastic deity (an *ens realissimum et perfectissimum*) must be postulated as the ultimate and all-embracing cause of events. The second is the mechanical position whose rise to importance we have studied in the preceding pages. Its fundamental assumptions are that all causes and effects are reducible to motions of bodies in time and space and are mathematically equivalent in terms of the forces expressed. From this standpoint the notion of perfection drops out of sight entirely; the task of explanation becomes that of analyzing events into the motions of the elementary mass-units of which they are composed and stating the behaviour of any correlated group of events in the form of an equation. Here there is no such thing as an ultimate explanation except in the form of a most general law exemplified in the specific explanations. Outside of the effort to unify scientific knowledge as far as possible by the discovery of such general laws, an explanation of anything is felt to be entirely adequate if it discovers some other mathematically equivalent event such as will enable the exact prediction of the former or the occurrence of the latter. The Newtonian worldview is a measureably logical metaphysical corollary of this assumption with respect to the nature of explanation, carried through without the admission of any qualification except that provided by the anomalous realm of mind. The third position is the evolutionary one, forced in more recent times by the increasing feeling that the phenomena of growth, both organic and inorganic, require a type of causal explanation essentially different from either of the foregoing. The central assumption of this position is that the cause may be simpler than the effect, while genetically responsible for it. Common to the last two of these causal assumptions is the method of analysing an event to be explained into its simpler (and often pre-existent) components, and likewise the predictability and control of the effect by means of the cause, both of which features are unnecessary and usually absent in explanations from the teleological standpoint. The second attempts to add the element of mathematical exactitude to the relation.

Now it is a possible hypothesis at least that so far as the data of science are concerned we are left undetermined as between these assumptions of what constitutes an adequate causal explanation, and that the factors conditioning a selection between them are to be found primarily in us who think about the world rather than the world we are thinking about. Perhaps it is the rise to a dominating ambition of the human need to control nature's processes, and to do so as exactly as possible, that accounts for our modern preferences in this matter. In this case a historical analysis of the growth of this need, an investigation of the corresponding motives which underlay the assumptions of earlier thought, and a systematic enquiry into the factors which have conditioned the rise and fall of these interests, would certainly be needed if we are to hope for any mature insight into their respective promise of permanence, the possibility of their reconciliation, and the relative plausibility of cosmological constructions which emphasise one or the other of these approaches.

The prejudices of intellectuals have been setting with increasing vigor throughout the modern period against the teleological type of explanation. Some at least of the whys and wherefores of this feeling are evident from the preceding chapters. To-day, however, there are indications of a sense that this prejudice may have been overdone. If one admits that there is such a thing as value in the universe at all, he finds it very difficult to construe it without giving a place to teleology. To analyse a value and reveal its elements, or to study its history and mode of appearance, will answer some questions about a value, but will not account for its nature as value. Certainly this is so if we are to maintain, as sophisticated moderns do, that an ideal may be worth living for, *i.e.,* justify itself as ideal, even though its origin be humble and its empirical destiny very uncertain. This implies that questions of analysis and genesis are irrelevant to the status of value as such, and have we found any way of rationally construing values save that of organising them into a system in which that value which under the circumstances is taken as supreme determines the worth of all the rest? Now it may well be that science, despite its rejection of final causes, reveals the presence and functioning of values in the fundamental categories it selects and the way it applies them. If so, then an adequate scientific metaphysic will not be able to manage without teleology in some form, and it becomes a question of first-rate importance what that form is to be.[1] Surely a comparative study of different stages in the growth of scientific thinking will throw light on this question and suggest hypotheses that could be entertained with more confidence than any reached by a structural study of contemporary scientific procedure alone.

It may be worth while to examine at somewhat greater length the third phase of the Newtonian metaphysic; namely, its doctrine of mind, for it is at this point that philosophical criticism has already shown itself to best advantage in dealing with the metaphysical problems arising from modern science, and it may well be that its distinctive contribution in the future is along this line also. English idealists and realists from Berkeley down have been largely occupied in pointing out that the popular form of the Cartesian dualism, with its conception of mind as substantially different from physical matter and yet to be located in the physical brain, is suicidal to science herself —it makes all knowledge of the world of science impossible and inconsistent—while the German idealists and their followers have largely attempted to show that the very existence of science, as well as of art, philosophy, and human civilisation generally, imply the ascription of a reality and nature to mind widely different from that admitted in the traditional dualism.

Let us critically summarize the situation with reference to each of these points, commencing with the former. An appropriate text for this particular question will be found in

[1] I have dealt in an elementary way with one phase of this question in a little book entitled *Religion in an Age of Science*.

that highly interesting statement of Descartes which has already been twice quoted: "When any one tells us that he sees colour in a body or feels pain in one of his limbs, this is exactly the same as if he said that he there saw or felt something, of the nature of which he was entirely ignorant, or that he did not know what he saw or felt." We have discovered in the course of our historical analysis sufficient reason to believe that in its first inception by Galileo and Descartes this position was buttressed by nothing more than a mathematical apriorism, but, of course, it has rarely, if ever, been avowedly based thereon. As developments continued in the sciences of physiology and of optics, thinkers who had already taken the dualism over from the giants of science supposed themselves to have gathered sufficient empirical arguments to maintain the position. Professor Huxley, in his *Helps to the Study of Berkeley*,[2] offers a typical recent defence of the situation as accepted by the bulk of modern scientists.

Suppose that I accidentally prick my finger with a pin. I immediately become aware of a condition of my consciousness—a feeling which I term pain. I have no doubt whatever that the feeling is in myself alone; and if anyone were to say that the pain I feel is something which inheres in the needle, as one of the qualities of the substance of the needle, we should all laugh at the absurdity of the phraseology. In fact, it is utterly impossible to conceive pain except as a state of consciousness.

Hence, so far as pain is concerned, it is sufficiently obvious that Berkeley's phraseology is strictly applicable to our power of conceiving its existence—its being is to be perceived or known, and, so long as it is not actually perceived by me, or does not exist in my mind, or that of any other created spirit, it must either have no existence at all, or else subsist in the mind of some eternal spirit.

So much for pain. Now let us consider an ordinary sensation. Let the point of the pin be gently rested upon the skin, and I become aware of a feeling, or condition of consciousness, quite different from the former—the sensation

[2] In his *Hume,* New York, 1896, p. 251, ff.

of what I call "touch." Nevertheless this touch is plainly just as much in myself as the pain was. I cannot for a moment conceive this something which I call touch as existing apart from myself, or a being capable of the same feelings as myself. And the same reasoning applies to all the other simple sensations. A moment's reflection is sufficient to convince one that the smell, and the taste, and the yellowness, of which we become aware when an orange is smelt, tasted, and seen, are as completely states of our consciousness as is the pain which arises if the orange happens to be too sour. Nor is it less clear that every sound is a state of the consciousness of him who hears it. If the universe contained only blind and deaf beings, it is impossible for us to imagine but that darkness and silence would reign everywhere.

It is undoubtedly true, then, of all the simple sensations, that as Berkeley says, their *"esse"* is *"percipi"*—their being is to be perceived or known. But that which perceives, or knows, is termed mind or spirit; and therefore the knowledge which the senses give is, after all, a knowledge of spiritual phenomena.

All this was explicitly or implicitly admitted, and indeed insisted upon, by Berkeley's contemporaries . . . . with respect to these secondary qualities.

Huxley proceeds to discuss the idea of primary qualities as held at Berkeley's time, and then returns to his experiment of the pin.

It has been seen that when the finger is pricked with a pin, a state of consciousness arises which we call pain; and it is admitted that this pain is not a something which inheres in the pin, but a something which exists only in the mind, and has no similitude elsewhere.

But a little attention will show that this state of consciousness is accompanied by another, which can by no effort be got rid of. I not only have the feeling, but the feeling is localized. I am just as certain that the pain is in my finger, as I am that I have it at all. Nor will any effort of the imagination enable me to believe that the pain is not in my finger.

And yet nothing is more certain than that it is not, and cannot be, in the spot in which I feel it, nor within a couple of feet of that spot. For the skin of the finger is connected by a bundle of fine nervous fibres, which run up the whole length of the arm, to the spinal marrow, which sets them in communication with the brain, and we know that the feeling of pain caused by the prick of the pin is dependent on the integrity of those fibres. After they have been cut through close to the spinal cord, no pain will be felt, whatever injury is done to the finger; and if the ends which remain in connexion with the spinal cord be pricked, the pain which arises will appear to have its seat in the finger just as distinctly as before. Nay, if the whole arm be cut off, the pain which arises from pricking the nerve stump will appear to be seated in the fingers, just as if they were still connected with the body.

It is perfectly obvious, therefore, that the localization of the pain at the surface of the body is an act of the mind. It is an *extradition* of that consciousness, which has its seat in the brain, to a definite point of the body—which takes place without our volition, and may give rise to ideas which are contrary to fact. . . . Locality is no more in the pin than pain is; of the former, as of the latter, it is true that "its being is to be perceived," and that its existence apart from a thinking mind is not conceivable.

The foregoing reasoning will be in no way affected, if instead of pricking the finger, the point of the pin rests gently against it so as to give rise merely to a tactile sensation. The tactile sensation is referred outwards to the point touched, and seems to exist there. But it is certain that it is not and cannot be there really, because the brain is the sole seat of consciousness; and, further, because evidence, as strong as that in favour of the sensation being in the finger, can be brought forward in support of propositions which are manifestly absurd. For example, the hairs and nails are utterly devoid of sensibility, as every one knows. Nevertheless if the ends of the nails or hairs are touched, ever so lightly, we feel that they are touched, and the sensation seems to be situated in the nails or hairs. Nay more, if a walking-stick, a yard long, is held firmly by the handle and the other end is touched, the tactile sensation, which is a state of our own consciousness, is unhesitatingly referred to the end of the stick, and yet no one will say that it is there.

Further in the essay we need not quote. Professor Huxley is swept along so vigorously by the Berkeleyan argument, that in the end he admits with the good bishop that the primary qualities, just as much as the secondary, must be regarded as states of consciousness and hence, ultimately, if he had to choose between absolute materialism and absolute idealism, he would unhesitatingly adopt the latter. The corollary seems to be that he prefers to remain in the Newtonian dualism.

But now Huxley has offered us here the most plausible scientific argument that has to date been advanced in favour of that dualism, as regards the place it assigns to the mind. Descartes had insisted that secondary qualities must be stripped from extended matter, even pains must be taken out of our limbs, and all but the mathematical qualities bestowed on the soul, which operates from its seat in the pineal gland of the brain. Let us see what we can make of Huxley's defence of this position.

A pin pricks my finger, and I feel, as I say, pain in it. But Professor Huxley assures me that the pain cannot possibly be in the finger, and why? Because if the nerve fibres leading from the finger to the spinal cord are severed, I no longer feel the pinprick; therefore the sensation of pain must really be at the other end of those fibres, namely in the brain. This strikes one at first sight as a curious argument; it is as if one were to say that since the cutting of the Croton aqueduct will cause the passage of water through New York City to cease, therefore the reservoir which we had supposed to exist in the lower Catskills must be really in the city. Furthermore, it can hardly be maintained that the nerve fibres do end in the brain. Normally, in such a situation, there is a continued nerve passage out from the cord or the brain and down through the arm to a muscle which pulls the finger away from the pin.

Therefore, according to this way of arguing, the sensation of pain must be in that muscle. But no one as yet has been willing to maintain this. Do these considerations not suggest that if thinkers were not already convinced that feelings must occur in the brain, they would never have supposed that the notion was supported by such arguments?

But Professor Huxley calls our attention to some further facts. Sever the arm entirely, and prick the attenuated end of that same nerve fibre. Again the pain is felt in the same place, *i.e.*, where the finger would have been. But nothing is there now but empty space, hence, triumphantly exclaims Professor Huxley, the pain certainly must be in the brain. But how in the world does this conclusion follow? Not to repeat the above remark, which would apply here also and require that the argument consistently applied would result in assigning the pain to some muscle of the arm, the facts are certainly widely sundered from the conclusion. It is obvious enough in this situation that the pain I feel and the pricking of the pin do not occur at the same place. But what has led us to fancy that we are resolving this problem by assigning the pain to some third place, namely the brain? I certainly do not feel it there. Other things happen there, as physiologists discover, but not the feeling. If we are to admit what is forced upon us by the simple facts, that the pain and the pricking are in different places, is it not by far the simplest and most consistent way out of the difficulty to hold that the pain is exactly where I feel it, even though to the eye nothing be there but emptiness? Surely no eye would have located it in the brain if he had not been antecedently convinced by some metaphysical prejudice that it must be there.

But the worst is yet to come. Let us adopt and make thoroughgoing Huxley's evident premise. Our sensations are all to be located where the nerve fibres leading from the various parts of the body affected terminate in the brain. Huxley observes, and correctly, that inasmuch as the nerve structure and the immediate perceptions are analogous in the case of all the senses, they are all subject to analogous reasoning at this point; hence, just as the pain felt must be in the brain, so the sound heard must be also in the brain. A step further we ourselves shall add, namely that the coloured and extended thing seen must be in the brain likewise. This is surely nothing but a consistent development of Professor Huxley's admissions and methods. The objects or contents of all the senses are alike concentrated at their proper nerve endings in the brain. But now, having pursued our premises to this result, what has become of the universe we perceive and suppose ourselves to live in? It is all contracted into a series of minute, if not mathematical, points in the brain. But more still—in such an event what in the world can we mean by the brain? Where does it and the nerve fibres that lead into it exist? They too are known only by our various senses; they too must be nothing but minute points—in the same brain? No, that would be unintelligible nonsense—where? Well, stay a moment. After all, I never do perceive my own brain. So far as it is known directly and not merely inferred, it is something perceived by other people who may happen to be interested in investigating it. Therefore the whole of my perceived universe plus the brain in which it exists must be located in someone else's brain. And where does that brain exist? In some third brain, of course. Where now exist those last brains of people who perceive other brains but who are unfortunate enough to have no perceiver for theirs?

Surely we have somewhere run off the track of sane thinking. Is it because we have failed to distinguish between sensed qualities and characters of real objects to which they correspond, the former existing in the brain of the perceiver and the latter in the external world? But what can be meant by characters of real objects if they be something existentially quite different from sensed qualities? What can be meant by correspondence between the two? How can that correspondence be verified if only one term of the relation ever comes within the realm of perception? In practice we correct dubious perceptions by appealing to further perceptions; we never correct them by comparison with something unperceived. And, more challenging still, what can be the relation between the space of real objects and the space of perception? Both seem to be infinite and to contain all the room there is; even the space of perception seems to contain my body as a very small object within it. But on this theory the whole of it must be enclosed within my real brain. How vast a thing the latter must be! The greatest distance that I can measure by any sensible materials or tools must span only a small fraction of my own brain, for all such measurements are within the spatial world of my perception. Stranger still, the brains of other people seem to be very minute as compared with my own; they are but tiny portions of the perceived space all of which exists within my own brain. And on the same assumptions they make equally polite comparisons of my brain with theirs. Something must be off the track again. Or is the brain that I perceive in another man's head but an insignificant point within his own real brain? It is such a point within mine, and mine is the same within his. What then is the spatial relation between his real brain and mine? Which includes the other, and why?

Those who combine realism with the Newtonian dualism have trouble enough on their hands working out consistent answers to the above questions. Sooner or later they are practically compelled to abandon the assumptions involved; the space of perception is too much like the space of real objects to reveal any essential difference from it. All it needs is to be freed from illusions, private images, and other experiences lacking social objectivity, to function quite acceptably as real space. And once this point has been reached there seems no longer any excuse for maintaining the distinction between sensed qualities and the real characters to which they correspond. In veridical perception they are located in the same area of space, and we never in fact attempt to find out what further imperceived things the ones we perceive correspond to. But this is the surrender of the dualism in anything like its Newtonian form. A radically different theory of mind is required to construe the situation in this fashion and to make the fundamental structure of scientific knowledge more than unintelligible nonsense.

The fact is, we can mean by real objects only two things. They are either an entirely transcendent and unknowable X, about which nothing more can be said beyond the bare mention of them; or else they are constancies of relation between groups of sensed qualities. In the latter case they are objects of experience, and the space in which they exist is essentially identical with the space of perception. In common life we all assume this, and take for granted the general validity of judgments of location based on our own spatial perception.

There is simply no science possible of the realm of sensible phenomena unless the trustworthiness of our immediate perception of spatial directions and relations be taken for granted. You think yourself justified in assigning my pain to the brain because you see what happens when the nerve fibres are cut, and you rightly assume that your vision is giving you a correct picture of what is going on in that portion of space occupied by those fibres. You are more than ever confident of it when other observers confirm you. This implies that the spatial world seen is the real spatial world, not something else. But why then should you turn around and accuse me of error when I say that the pain is in my finger? There is surely no logical impossibility in its being there, even in its being in otherwise empty space after my arm has been lopped off. The only people to whom it is an impossibility are those who already assume that the feeling must be in the brain, and if they were consistent they would acknowledge the seeing to be in the brain likewise—and where such reasoning ends we have just observed. Hence why, pray, is my feeling to be presumed a liar, and your vision always veracious? Why not admit that the feeling is where I feel it, inasmuch as you cannot avoid assuming that the seeing is where you see it? As long as I adhere to an empirical standard of truth, in fact, you shall be unable to convince me that something which I immediately feel is located in a different place from where I feel it. Empirically, there is no difference whatever between the senses in this respect. Through all of them we immediately experience things in various spatial relations, locations, or directions. There are doubtless important and interesting problems thrust upon us in the experiences Huxley cites, such as the matter of the nerve stump, of feeling with a cane, and the like, just as there are problems about visual illusions, but such problems can hardly be solved in either case by a total denial of the trustworthiness of the senses, but only by a more careful analysis of the judgments which we pass on the basis of our sensible experiences. When I feel pain in a certain spatial locus, granted that the testimony of feeling is clear on the point, how can I empirically deny that I feel it there, even though to the eye that locus be some distance from the body? In that case I must simply affirm that the ordinary spatial correlation of the various senses does not obtain. Analogously, if I see a ghostly form where other people tell me there is nothing, or if I call objects green which they call red, still I can hardly deny that I see what I see, and in certain definite spatial relations with the other objects of my vision.[3] In so far as I am a social being, however, I need also to get at a common spatial world which is verifiably there for all people; likewise, in order to live successfully I must get at an orderly, dependable world, and learn to distinguish clearly my purely individual and untrustworthy spatial experiences from those which make up that common dependable world. But to substitute for this thoroughly empirical process of the improvement and social correction of the senses a speculative apriorism that flatly contradicts the immediate testimony of sense and places its objects in spatial relations wholly different from those in which they are sensed, can only lead, if carried out to its logical conclusion, to the complete confusion and mystification of science.

Philosophers since the days of Newton have gradually become cognizant of these considerations. But when it comes to the question of replacing this impossible doctrine by a positive theory of mind, there has been a radical diversity of opinion and a philosophy which will be fair to all the data and meet all the basic needs clamoring to guide their interpretation is yet to be invented. In general, it may be said that two main directions have been pursued. On the one hand there have been those eager to make mind itself, the knower of physical nature, an object of scientific study. To do this with exactitude and objectivity has meant breaking down the dualism by in-

[3] The immediate testimony of sight, of course, covers only the direction and spatial relations of the things seen, not their distance from the seer, nor their relative magnitudes as seen from the same distance. Each of the other senses has its limitations likewise.

corporating mind somehow into the world of bodily motions. On the other hand there have been those anxious to substantiate on a basis more acceptable in modern times the medieval accordance to mind of a high place and destiny in cosmic affairs. In general these two trends have been in violent conflict with each other.

To put ourselves briefly at the point of view of the former group, it does seem like strange perversity in these Newtonian scientists to further their own conquests of external nature by loading on mind everything refractory to exact mathematical handling and thus rendering the latter still more difficult to study scientifically than it had been before. Did it never cross their minds that sooner or later people would appear who craved verifiable knowledge about mind in the same way they craved it about physical events, and who might reasonably curse their elder scientific brethren for buying easier success in their own enterprise by throwing extra handicaps in the way of their successors in social science? Apparently not; mind was to them a convenient receptacle for the refuse, the chips and whittlings of science, rather than a possible object of scientific knowledge.

To be sure, some thinkers in those days were willing to make ventures that might, if wisely and prophetically developed, have led in the direction of an objective science of mind. Outside of Hobbes' crude anticipations of behaviorism, Henry More's doctrine of the spatial extension of mind is interesting to explore from this standpoint. More was willing to grant the materialists that everything really existing occupies space. Mind, too, then, is an occupant of space and has its own geometry, to be studied by comparable techniques to those by which the geometry of bodily motion is determined. Thus, seemingly, a verifiable science of mind might be worked out. Let us allow our fancy to wander along the route that this speculation might indicate. "When I feel pain in my hand," a champion of this view would say, "resistance of the earth against my feet, and gaze at a glorious sunset beyond the hills —all at the same time—am I not extended in space? And if to these experiences be added a memory of some previous and more glorious sunset, together with an anticipation of the twilight soon to descend, am I not extended in time also? To be sure, there are important differences between my spatio-temporal extension and that of material bodies. The latter are regular, dependable, divisible into parts, and orderly, at least as regards their mathematical qualities and behaviour; the space and time which I occupy is a monstrous, irreducible unit, fluctuating rapidly and violently in size, shape, and centre of attention. But certainly my immediate experience through all the senses negates the notion that the difference between them and me lies in the fact that they are extended while I am not. Science depends entirely on the validity of my spatial perceptions of direction and relation—how in the world can they be either spatial or valid unless I am already an occupant of space? Indeed, can the bulk of modern thought be blamed for turning away from the more logically consistent form of Descartes' dualism, which reached its grandest expression in Spinoza, to a view which at least left some spatial locus for the soul, and offered a practical, though absurdly inconsistent, way of interpreting its relations with extended matter? For the relations exist. We know our spatial world, we live in it, enjoy it, use it. How could this be possible if we were absolutely unspatial ourselves? Can we clearly conceive anything as existing without occupying space and time, except a mathematical point?

"Now if the extension of the mind be thus demanded," he would continue, "where shall we limit that extension? We feel in every part of the body, nay, perhaps beyond the body under certain conditions which ought to be analysed and determined. But can we confine ourselves to More's doctrine of the extension of spirit, which limits that extension to a thin effluvium surrounding the body? Are the things heard in the body, or the things seen, no farther than the boundary of such a ghostly fringe? And how about memory and purpose? Is there any cogent reason to suppose that ideals and memory-images are in the present body at all? Have not the psychological and physiological difficulties about them arisen largely because we are determined to push them somehow into the brain? There is no help for it, we must declare unreservedly that a consistent empiricism cannot stop short of maintaining that the mind is extended in time and space throughout the whole realm that is spanned by its knowledge and contemplation. How else can the facts be expressed?"

But this outcome, of course, reveals how impossible it will be to make an exact science of mind by the aid of these conceptions. The mind thus studied is still an object of introspection, not of co-operative analysis; the space it occupies is a widely fluctuating unit, not determinable by any of the techniques of exact measurement which we apply to the objects of other sciences. No, this motive will lead clearly in the direction of identifying mind with activities of the organic body, which supply something objectively manipulable by accredited scientific methods and which are sufficiently correlated with mental events in the traditional sense so that the extent of the transformation is somewhat masked and the radical novelty of the doctrine minimized. When this is done with no qualification or reservation, psychology retaining no uniqueness but becoming a sheer branch of objective physiology, the outcome is behaviorism; when the same motives are dominant but qualitative uniquenesses of terms and relations are permitted to each science, a less extreme functional conception of mind results. Thus mind becomes an empirical object of co-operatively verifiable procedures, and the problem of the subjective as such, forfeited by a psychology which has thus crossed the Rubicon, is handed over to philosophy.

Granted, however, the legitimacy of the motives which wish to render mind material for exact prediction and control after the fashion of objects of the other sciences—were the ancients and medievalists entirely astray in their doctrine that mind is in some sense a privileged and superior entity in face of the vastness of physical nature? Is there anything in the scientific situation itself which implies such a status for that which knows the world of science? Many philosophers have reacted to Newtonianism by elaborating affirmative answers to these questions. We may open consideration of their reflections by reminding ourselves of the rather suggestive fact that all schools of Greek thought, even the atomists, were agreed in assigning unique prerogatives and powers to mind; it may be that our modern hesitation to do so is due mainly to the abuse of such speculations by religionists eager to prove the immateriality and immortality of the soul. To be sure, since when we think and speak we are functioning as minds, it is well to be modest about our cosmic status, and if stressing certain truths about the wonder of mind is apt to encourage tender souls to bask in sweet dreams about their importance in the universe, perhaps these truths should not be stressed. None the less, there is a definite sense in which mind is the living perspective of the totality of human experience, the active and focal organization of the entire current of events and their meanings of which we humans become cognizant.

The whole vast realm which science reveals finds its rational order and meaning in the knowing activity of mind. So far from being a curious sensitive substance present in a small corner of the brain, or even an activity of the nervous system, mind seems to be a unique something to which the spatio-temporal realm, including the brain and the body, is or can be present. Or if objecting realists plead that the structure of meaning is as external to mind as physical nature, at least it must be admitted that mind is that something in the existential world most capable of actively participating in this realm of meaning. To note this circumstance and what it involves is not mere matter of silly self-congratulation. The so-called higher mental powers of human persons seem to be the completest perspectives of reality so far as revealed in our experience; as Aristotle insisted, they include all that other orders of being do and more besides. In their larger attainments reason, feeling, and purpose compose a marvellous unity of functions. When we see them at work in the smile and genial conversation of a friend we give free rein to our admiration and delight, whatever conscientious scruples seem to require when we come to philosophize. I had almost introduced the word "spirit" here, forgetting for a moment that at the sight of such a word sophisticated moderns would brand me at once a hopeless anachronism. Perhaps it might be well to surrender the old term mind to the mercies of behaviorists if we might recover in its place the term spirit from the fog of obscurantist mythology, and express by its aid such facts as these. Let the order of nature be ever so vast and all-absorbing—it is still but the object of rationally conceiving mind. And as for purpose, do we not empirically note that every object of mind is likewise a *means* for the realization of further *ends?* Among the irreducible relations of a thing known, is there not its relation to a more valuable end which it may be made to serve? If this be the case, then purpose is an even more ultimate function than knowledge and feeling, and mind, embracing by this term such knowing, appreciating, and purposive activity, must find its total explanation beyond the material world. Mind appears to be an irreducible something that can know the world of extended matter, love ardently its order and beauty, and transform it continually in the light of a still more attractive and commanding good. Mind has the power to feel, to idealize, to recreate its world into something significantly better, as well as to know it.

Strange dualism between the theory and practice of us moderns—electrons are the only real things, but yet by applied science the world of electrons has been reduced as never before to a means for the achievement of ideal ends! The natural world after all is more the home and theatre of mind than its unseen tyrant, and man as expressing the functions of reason and spirit gathers to a focus far more of the flavour and creative fertility of the universe than the whole spatio-temporal object of his eager contemplation.

Mayhap we must wait for the complete extinction of theological superstition before these things can be said without misunderstanding. Such is the misfortune of modern thought as compared with that of Greece. But in these two-sided considerations is bared the terrific difficulty of the modern problem of metaphysics. An adequate cosmology will only begin to be written when an adequate philosophy of mind has appeared, and such a philosophy of mind must provide full satisfaction both for the motives of the behaviorists who wish to make mind material for experimental manipulation and exact measurement, and for the motives of idealists who wish to see the startling difference between a universe without mind and a universe organized into a living and sensitive unity through mind properly accounted for. I hope some readers of these pages will catch glimmerings how this seemingly impossible reconciliation is to be brought about. For myself I must admit that, as yet, it is beyond me, and only insist that whatever may turn out to be the solution, an indispensable part of its foundation will be clear historical insight into the antecedents of our present thought-world. If the volume in hand has aided somewhat in the clarification of these it has fulfilled its modest pretensions.

BIBLIOGRAPHY

The secondary literature on the men treated in the foregoing chapters is so extensive that this bibliography makes no claim to completeness. Its purpose is merely to include those works which have been found helpful in pursuing this study, thus furnishing a guide to supplementary literature for those interested in the metaphysical aspect of their work.

I. *Works dealing with the whole,*
or a considerable part of the field

E. F. APELT, Die Epochen der Geschichte der Menscheit, 2 vols., Jena, 1845.

Theorie der Induktion, Leipzig, 1854.

J. J. BAUMANN, Die Lehren von Raum, Zeit, und Mathematik in der neuren Philosophie, Berlin, 1868.

ARTHUR BERRY, A Short History of Astronomy, London, 1910.

THOMAS BIRCH, History of the Royal Society of London, 4 vols., London, 1756.

M. CANTOR, Vorlesungen über Geschichte der Mathematik, 4 vols., Leipzig, 1900–8.

E. CASSIRER, Das Erkenntniss-problem in der Philosophie und Wissenschaft der neueren Zeit, 3 vols., Berlin, 1906–20.

J. P. DAMIRON, Mémoires pour servir à l'histoire de philosophie au dix-huitième siècle, Paris, 1858, ff. Essai sur l'histoire de la philosophie en France au dix-septième siècle, Bruxelles, 1832.

P. DUHEM, L'évolution des théories physiques, Louvain, 1896.

E. DÜHRING, Kritische Geschichte der allgemeinen Prinzipien der Mechanik, Leipzig, 1887.

JOS. EPSTEIN, Die logischen Prinzipien der Zeitmessung, Berlin, 1887.

L. FEUERBACH, Geschichte der neueren Philosophie von Bacon von Verulam bis Benedikt Spinoza (in his Werke, Stuttgart, 1903–11).

E. GRIMM, Zur Geschichte des Erkenntniss-problems von Bacon zu Hume, Leipzig, 1890.

J. HEINRICI, Die Erforschung der Schwere durch Galilei, Huyghens, Newton, als rationelle Kinematik und Dynamik historisch-didaktisch dargestellt, Heidelberg, 1885.

H. HÖFFDING, A History of Modern Philosophy (Meyer translation), London and New York, 1900.

F. LANGE, Geschichte des Materialismus und Kritik seiner Bedeutung in der Gegenwart, Iserlohn, 1887. English translation by Thomas, 3 vols., London, 1890–2.

L. LANGE, Die Geschichtliche Entwickelung des Bewegungs-begriffes und ihr voraussichtliches Endergebniss, Leipzig, 1886.

K. LASSWITZ, Geschichte der Atomistik vom Mittelalter bis Newton, Hamburg, 1890.

OLIVER LODGE, Pioneers of Science, London, 1913.

L. MABILLEAU, Histoire de la philosophie atomistique, Paris, 1895.

E. MACH, The Science of Mechanics (McCormack translation of his Die Mechanik in ihrer Entwickelung historisch-kritisch dargestellt) 4th ed., Chicago and London, 1919.

F. A. MÜLLER, Das Problem der Continuität in der Mathematik und Mechanik, Marburg, 1886.

P. NATORP, Die logischen Grundlagen der exakten Wissen-schaften, Leipzig, 1910.

CARL NEUMANN, Uber die Prinzipien der Galilei-Newton'-schen Theorie, Halle, 1870.

F. PAPILLON, Histoire de la philosophie moderne dans ses rapports avec le développement des sciences de la nature, 2 vols., Paris, 1876.

J. C. POGGENDORFF, Geschichte der Physik, Leipzig, 1879.

S. J. RIGAUD, Correspondence of Eminent Scientific Men of the Seventeenth Century, Oxford, 1841.

P. VOLKMANN, Einführung in das Studium der theoretischen Physik, Leipzig, 1900.

Erkenntnisstheoretische Grundzüge der Naturwissenschaften, Leipzig, 1896.

H. WEISSENBORN, Die Prinzipien der höheren Analysis, als historisch-kritischer Beitrag zur Geschichte der Mathematik, Halle, 1856.

W. WHEWELL, History of the Inductive Sciences from the Earliest to the Present Time, new and revised edition, 3 vols., London, 1847.

The Philosophy of the Inductive Sciences, London, 1840.

W. WINDELBAND, History of Philosophy (Tufts translation), New York, 1907.

II. *Works dealing primarily with
the material of the separate chapters*

CHAPTER II. SOURCES

NICHOLAUS COPERNICUS, De Revolutionibus Orbium Coelestium, Nüremberg, 1543; German translation, Thorn, 1879.

NICOLAI COPERNICI, De hypothesibus motuum coelestium a se constitutis Commentariolus, ed. A. Lindhagen, Stockholm, 1881.

Joannis Kepleri Astronomi Opera Omnia, ed. Ch. Frisch, 8 vols., Frankfurt and Erlangen, 1858, ff.

SECONDARY

W. W. R. BALL, A Short Account of the History of Mathematics, 4th ed., London, 1912.

M. CARRIÈRE, Die philosophische Weltanschauung der Reformationszeit in ihrer Beziehung zur Gegenwart, Leipzig, 1887.

M. CURTZE, Uber eine neue Copernicus-handschrift, Königsberg, 1873.

J. L. E. DREYER, Planetary Systems from Thales to Kepler, Cambridge, 1919.

Tycho Brahe, a Picture of Scientific Life and Work in the Sixteenth Century, Edinburgh, 1890.

P. DUHEM, Essai sur la notion de théorie physique de Platon à Galilée, Paris, 1908.

Etudes sur Leonard de Vinci, Paris, 1906–13.

Le système du monde: histoire des doctrines cosmologiques de Platon à Copernic, 5 vols., Paris, 1913, ff.

R. EUCKEN, Johann Kepler (Philosophische Monatshefte), 1878.

Nicholas von Kuss (Philosophische Monatshefte, 1878.)

C. FLAMMARION, Vie de Copernic et histoire de la decouverte du système du monde, Paris, 1872.

CH. FRISCH, Vita Joannis Kepleri (in his edition of the latter's Opera Omnia, Vol. VIII, pp. 668–1028).

E. GOLDBECK, Keplers Lehre von der Gravitation, Halle, 1896.

J. HASNER, Tycho Brahe und J. Kepler in Prag; eine Studie, Prag, 1872.

C. LIBRI, Histoire des sciences mathématiques en Italie depuis la renaissance des lettres, 2nd ed., Halle, 1865, 4 vols.

K. PRANTL, Galilei und Kepler als Logiker (Sitzungsbericht der Müncher Akademie, 1875).

Leonardo da Vinci als Philosoph (same, 1885).

L. PROWE, Nicholaus Copernicus, 3 vols., Berlin, 1883, ff.

H. RASHDALL, Universities of Europe in the Middle Ages, 2 vols., Oxford, 1895.

T. A. RIXNER and T. SIBER, Leben und Lehrmeinungen berühmter Physiker am Ende des sechszehnten und am Anfange des siebzehnten Jahrhunderts, 3 vols., Sulzbach, 1820–9.

J. SCHMIDT, Keplers Erkenntniss-und Methodenlehre, Jena, 1903.

F. SIGWART, Kleine Schriften, 2 vols., Freiburg, 1889. (Vol. I contains anniversary address on Kepler.)

CHAS. SINGER, Studies in the History and Method of Science, Vol. II, Oxford, 1921. Includes:

ROBERT STEELE, Roger Bacon and the State of Science in the Thirteenth Century, p. 121, ff.;

H. HOPSTOCK, Leonardo as Anatomist, p. 151, ff.;

J. J. FAHIE, The Scientific Works of Galileo, p. 206, ff.;

J. L. E. DREYER, Mediæval Astronomy, p. 102, ff.

K. F. STAUDLIN, Uber Johann Keplers Theologie und Religion (Beiträge zur Philosophie der Religion, 1797–9, vol. I, pp. 172–241).

DOROTHY STIMSON, The Gradual Acceptance of the Copernican Theory of the Universe, New York, 1917.

H. O. TAYLOR, The Mediæval Mind, 2nd ed., 2 vols. London, 1914.
Thought and Expression in the Sixteenth Century, 2 vols., London, 1920.

CHAPTER III. SOURCES

GALILEO GALILEI, Dialogues Concerning the Two Great Systems of the World. Translated by Thomas Salusbury, and included in his Mathematical Collections and Translations, Vol. I, London, 1661.

GALILEO GALILEI, Dialogues and Mathematical Demonstrations Concerning Two New Sciences, Crew and de Salvio translation, New York, 1914.

GALILEO GALILEI, Opere Complete di G. G., 15 vols., Firenze, 1842, ff.

GALILEO GALILEI, Letter to the Grand Duchess Cristina, 1615. (In Salusbury, Vol. I.)

GALILEO GALILEI, Le Opere: Edit. nazionale, vols. I–XX, Firenze, 1890–1909. (This is the best and most complete edition. That referred to in the text is the usually more accessible edition of 1842, ff.)

SECONDARY

COUNT VON BROCKDORFF, Galileis philosophische Mission. (Vierteljährig-Schr. für wiss. Philos., 1902.)

S. F. DE DOMINICIO, Galilei e Kant; o, l'esperienza e la critica nella filosophia moderna, Bologna, 1874.

E. GOLDBECK, Die Gravitation bei Galileo und Borelli, Berlin, 1897.

W. JACK, Galileo and the Application of Mathematics to Physics, Glasgow, 1879.

334

K. LASSWITZ, Galileis Theorie der Materie (Vierteljährig-Schr. für wiss. Philos., 1888).

L. LÖWENHEIM, Der Einfluss Demokrits auf Galilei (Archiv f. Gesch. d. Philos., 1894).

H. MARTIN, Galilée, les droits de la science et la méthode des sciences physiques, Paris, 1868.

L. MÜLLNER, Die Bedeutung Galileis für die Philosophie, Wien, 1895.

P. NATORP, Galilei als Philosoph (Philosophische Monatshefte, 1882).
Nombre, temps, et espace dans leurs rapports avec les fonctions primitives de la pensée. (Philosophie générale et métaphysique, 1900, pp. 343–89.)

E. DE PORTU, Galileis Begriff der Wissenschaft, Marburg, 1904.

A. RIEHL, Uber den Begriff der Wissenschaft bei Galilei (Vierteljährig-Schr. für wiss. Philos., 1893).

F. WIESER, Galilei als Philosoph, Basel, 1919.

E. WOHLWILL, Die Entdeckung des Beharringsgesetzes. (Zeitschrift für Völker psychologie, 1884, vols. XIV, XV.)

CHAPTER IV. SOURCES

RENÉ DESCARTES, Oeuvres (Cousin edition), 11 vols., Paris, 1824, ff.
Oeuvres (Adam et Tannery edition), 10 vols., Paris, 1897–1910.
Philosophical Works (Haldane and Ross translation), 2 vols., Cambridge, 1911.

SECONDARY

F. BARK, Descartes' Lehre von den Leidenschaften, Rostock, 1892.

A. BARTHEL, Descartes' Leben und Metaphysik auf Grund der Quellen, Erlangen, 1885.

F. C. BOUILLER, Histoire de la philosophie cartésienne, 3rd ed., 2 vols., Paris, 1868.

B. BOURDON, De qualitatibus sensibilibus apud Cartesium, Paris, 1892.

E. CASSIRER, Descartes' Kritik des mathematischen und naturwissenschaftlichen Erkenntniss, Marburg, 1899.

P. F. EBERHARDT, Die Kosmogonie des Descartes im Zusammenhang der Geschichte der Philosophie, Erlangen, 1908.

C. FELSCH, Der Kausalitätsbegriff bei Descartes, Bern, 1891.

A. FOUILLÉE, Descartes, Paris, 1893.

E. GOLDBECK, Descartes' mathematisches Wissenschaftsideal, Halle, 1892.

B. GUTZEIT, Descartes' angeborene Ideen verglichen mit Kants Anschauungs-und Denkformen a priori, Bromberg, 1883.

E. GRIMM, Descartes' Lehre von den angeborenen Ideen, Jena, 1873.

E. S. HALDANE, Descartes, His Life and Times, London, 1905.

O. HAMELIN, Le système de Descartes, Paris, 1911.

A. HOFFMANN, Die Lehre von der Bildung des Universums bei Descartes in ihrer geschichtlichen Bedeutung, Berlin, 1903.

M. L. HOPPE, Die Abhängigkeit der Wirbeltheorie des Descartes von William Gilberts Lehre vom Magnetismus, Halle, 1914.

R. JÖRGES, Die Lehre von den Empfindungen bei Descartes, Düsseldorf, 1901.

K. JUNGMANN, Die Weltentstehungslehre des Descartes, Bern, 1907.

L. KAHN, Metaphysics of the Supernatural as illustrated by Descartes, New York, 1918.

R. KEUSSEN, Bewusstsein und Erkenntniss bei Descartes, Bonn, 1906.

A. KOCH, Die Psychologie Descartes' systematisch und historisch-kritisch bearbeitet, München, 1881.

L. LIARD, Descartes, Paris, 1911.

J. P. MAHAFFY, Descartes, Edinburgh and London, 1880.

G. MILHAUD, Descartes savant, Paris, 1921.

J. MILLET, Histoire de Descartes avant 1637, Paris, 1867.

P. NATORP, Untersuchungen über die Erkenntnisstheorie Descartes, Marburg, 1882.

G. OPRESCU, Descartes' Erkenntnisslehre, Leipzig, 1889.

R. F. PFAFF, Die Unterschiede zwischen der Naturphilosophie

336

Descartes' und derjenigen Gassendis und der Gegensatz beider Philosophen überhaupt, Leipzig, 1905.

G. RICHARD, De psychologico apud Cartesium mechanismo, Neocastri, 1892.

H. SCHNEIDER, Die Stellung Gassendis zu Descartes, Halle, 1904.

NORMAN SMITH, Studies in the Cartesian Philosophy, London, 1902.

A. TEUCHER, Die geophysikalischen Auschauungen Descartes, Leipzig, 1908.

K. TWARDOWSKI, Idee und Perception: eine erkenntniss-theoretische Untersuchung aus Descartes, Wien, 1892.

CHAPTER V. SOURCES

ISAAC BARROW, Geometrical Lectures (Child translation, with many omissions), Chicago and London, 1916.
Geometrical Lectures (Sir I. Newton's edition), London, 1735.
The Mathematical Works of Isaac Barrow, D.D. ed., W. Whewell, 2 vols. in 1, Cambridge, 1860.

RALPH CUDWORTH, The True Intellectual System of the Universe, 3 vols., London, 1845. (First published 1678.)

THOMAS HOBBES, Works, Molesworth edition, 16 vols., London, 1839, ff.

HENRY MORE, Immortality of the Soul, Antidote against Atheism. (Included in A Collection of Several Philosophical Writings, 4th ed., London, 1712.)
A Platonic Song of the Soul. (First published, Cambridge, 1642; many subsequent editions.)
Divine Dialogues, 2nd ed., London, 1713.
Enchiridion Metaphysicum, London, 1671.
Opera Omnia, 4 Vols. (The English works are here rendered into Latin.) London, 1675–9.

SECONDARY

G. BRANDT, Grundlinien der Philosophie von Thomas Hobbes, insbesondere seine Lehre vom Erkennen, Kiel, 1895.

A. GASPARY, Spinoza und Hobbes, Berlin, 1873.

B. GÜHNE, Uber Hobbes' naturwissenschaftliche Ansichten, und ihrem Zusammenhang mit der Naturphilosophie seiner Zeit, Dresden, 1886.

MAX KÖLHER, Hobbes in seinem Verhältniss zu der mechanischen Naturanschauung, Berlin, 1902.

Also articles on Hobbes in Archiv f. Geschichte der Philosophie, vols. xv, xvi.

L. H. SCHÜTZ, Die Lehre von den Leidenschaften bei Hobbes und Descartes, Hagen, 1901.

H. SCHWARTZ, Die Lehre von den Sinnesqualitäten bei Descartes und Hobbes, Halle, 1894.

SIR LESLIE STEPHEN, Hobbes, New York and London, 1904.

F. TÖNNIES, Hobbes, Leben und Lehre, Stuttgart, 1896.

R. ZIMMERMANN, Henry More und die vierte Dimension des Raumes (Sitzungsbericht d. Königliche Akademie d. Wissenschaft, Lex. 8, p. 48).

CHAPTER VI. SOURCES

FRANCIS BACON, Philosophical Works. Edited by J. M. Robertson, after the text and translation of Ellis and Spedding, London, 1905.

ROBERT BOYLE, The Works of the Honourable Robert Boyle, ed. Thomas Birch, 6 vols., London, 1672.

P. GASSENDI, De Vita et Moribus Epicuri, Lugdovici, 1647.

WILLIAM GILBERT, De mundo nostro sublunari Philosophia Nova, Amsterdam, 1651.

WILLIAM GILBERT OF COLCHESTER, On the Loadstone and Magnetic Bodies (Mottelay translation), New York, 1893.

WILLIAM HARVEY, On the Motion of the Heart and Blood in Animals, London and New York, 1908.

SECONDARY

F. X. KIEFL, P. Gassendis Erkenntnisstheorie und seine Stellung zum Materialismus, Fulda, 1893.

J. MEIER, Robert Boyles Naturphilosophie, etc., München, 1907.

S. MENDELSSOHN, Robert Boyle als Philosoph, Würzburg, 1902.

338

CHAPTERS VII–VIII. SOURCES

Isaaci Newtoni Opera quae exstant Omnia. Commentariis il-
lustrabat Samuel Horsley, LL.D., etc. 5 vols., London,
1779–85.

SIR ISAAC NEWTON, The Mathematical Principles of Natural
Philosophy (Motte translation), to which are added Newton's System of the World, etc., 3 vols., London, 1803.

Optical Lectures Read in the Publick Schools of the University
of Cambridge, Anno Domini, 1669. (English translation),
London, 1727.

Opticks: or, a Treatise of the Reflections, Refractions, Inflec-
tions, and Colours of Light, 3rd ed., corrected, London,
1721.

Universal Arithmetick: or, a Treatise of Arithmetical Composition and Resolution, etc. (Ralphson and Cunn translation),
3rd ed., London, 1769.

A Catalogue of the Portsmouth Collection of Books and
Papers written by or belonging to Sir Isaac Newton, Cambridge, 1888.

C. J. GRAY, Bibliography of the Works of Sir Isaac Newton,
together with a list of Books illustrating his Life and Works,
2nd ed., Cambridge, 1907.

SECONDARY

JOSEPH ADDISON, Oration spoken in the Theatre at Oxford,
July 7, 1693. (In Fontenelle, Plurality of Worlds, Gardiner
translation, 1757.)

R. AVENARIUS, Der menschliche Weltbegriff, Leipzig, 1891.
Philosophie als Denken der Welt, gemäss dem Prinzip des
kleinsten Kraftmasses, Leipzig, 1876.

W. W. R. BALL, A History of the Study of Mathematics at
Cambridge, Cambridge, 1889.

RICHARD BENTLEY, Correspondence, ed. Christopher Words-
worth, 2 vols., London, 1842.
Eight Sermons against Atheism, preached at Boyle's Lecture,
London, 1693.

GEO. BERKELEY, Works, ed. A. C. Fraser, 4 vols., Oxford, 1871.

L. BLOCH, La philosophie de Newton, Paris, 1908.

SIR DAVID BREWSTER, Memoirs of the Life, Writings, and Discoveries of Sir Isaac Newton, 2 vols., Edinburgh, 1885.

JAMES CHALLIS, On Newton's Regula Tertia Philosophandi (Philosophical Magazine, Jan., 1880).

S. CLARKE, A Discourse Concerning the Being and Attributes of God, etc., London, 1706.

WM. DANMAR, Die Schwere: ihr Wesen und Gesetz; Isaac Newton's Irrthum, Zürich, 1897.

J. T. DESAGULIER, The Newtonian System of the World, the best model of government, an allegorical poem, etc., Westminster, 1728.

C. DIETERICH, Kant und Newton, Tübingen, 1876.

JOS. DURDIK, Leibnitz und Newton: ein Versuch über die Ursachen der Welt auf Grundlage der positiven Ergebnisse der Philosophie und Naturforschung, Halle, 1869.

J. EDLESTON, Correspondence of Sir I. Newton and Prof. Cotes, including letters of other eminent men, etc., London, 1850. (Contains appendix with other unpublished letters and papers by Newton.)

P. and J. FRIEDLANDER, Absolute und relative Bewegung, Berlin, 1896.

H. R. FOX BOURNE, The Life of John Locke, 2 Vols., New York, 1876.

P. GERBER, Uber die räumliche und zietliche Ausbreitung der Gravitation (Zeitschrift für Math. und Phys., 1898, vol. II).

GEO. GORDON, Remarks upon the Newtonian Philosophy; wherein it is proved to be false and absurd, London, 1719.

H. GREEN, Sir Isaac Newton's Views on Points of Trinitarian Doctrine, etc., 1856.

H. HERTZ, Die Prinzipien der Mechanik in neuem Zusammenhange dargestellt, Leipzig, 1894.

GEO. HORNE, A Fair, Candid, and Impartial State of the Case between Sir I. Newton and Mr. Hutchinson. In which it is shown how far a system of physics is capable of mathematical demonstration, etc., Oxford, 1753.

CH. HUYGHENS, Opera mechanica, geometrica, astronomica, et

miscellanea, ed. C. J. Gravesande, 4 vols. in I., Ludg. Bat, 1751.

DAVID HUME, Philosophical Works, ed. by T. H. Green and T. H. Grose, London, 1874.

J. HUTCHINSON, Moses' Principia, London, 1724.

J. JURIN (Philalethes Cantabrigiensis), Geometry No Friend to Infidelity; or, a Defence of Sir Isaac Newton, London, 1734.

(Philalethes Cantabrigiensis), The Minute Mathematician. . . . Containing a defence of Sir Isaac Newton, etc., London, 1735.

P. LIND, Uber das Verhältnis Lockes zu Newton, Berlin and Leipzig, 1915.

J. H. MONK, Life of Richard Bentley, 2nd ed., 2 vols., London, 1833.

LORD MONTBODDO, Ancient Metaphysics, containing an Examination of Sir I. Newton's Philosophy, 6 vols. Edinburgh, 1779, ff.

HENRY PEMBERTON, A View of Sir Isaac Newton's Philosophy, London, 1728.

S. P. RIGAUD, Correspondence of Scientific Men of the Seventeenth Century, including letters of Barrow; Flamstead, Wallis, and Newton, etc., 2 vols., Oxford, 1841.

Historical Essay on the First Publication of Sir I. Newton's Principia, London, 1838.

BRYAN ROBINSON, Dissertation on the Ether of Sir I. Newton, Dublin, 1743, 2nd ed., with Appendix, 1747.

JACQUES ROHAULT, System of Natural Philosophy, illustrated with Dr. Samuel Clarke's notes taken mostly from Sir I. Newton (J. Clark translation), London, 1710.

F. ROSENBERGER, Newton und seine physikalischen Prinzipien, Leipzig, 1895.

H. SEELIGER, Uber das Newtonsche Gravitationsgesetz (Sitzungsbericht der Münchner Akademie, 1896).

H. G. STEINMANN, Uber den Einfluss Newtons auf die Erkenntnistheorie seiner Zeit, Bonn, 1913.

H. STREINTZ, Die physikalischen Grundlagen der Mechanik, Leipzig, 1883.

EDMUND TURNER, Collections for the History of the Town

and Soke of Grantham, containing authentic memoirs of Sir I. Newton now first published, London, 1806.

P. VOLKMANN, Uber Newtons Philosophia Naturalis, Königsberg, 1898.

F. M. A. DE VOLTAIRE, Eléments de la philosophie de Newton, Amsterdam, 1738. (Eng. translation by John Hanna, in the same year.)

The Metaphysics of Sir Isaac Newton, Baker translation, London, 1747.

Response à toutes les objections principales qu' on a faites en France contre la philosophie de Newton, Amsterdam, 1739.

E. T. WHITTAKER, History of the Theories of Ether and Electricity from the Age of Descartes to the Close of the Nineteenth Century, London and New York, 1910.

INDEX

Absolute motion, justification of, 254 ff.
Absolute space and time, analysis of, 256 ff.
Actuality, 26, 94 ff.
Alfarabi, 46
Analytical geometry, 106
Archimedes, 193
Arianism, Newton's, 284 f.
Aristarchus, 79
Aristotle, 37, 45, 52 f., 67, 70, 78, 89 ff., 153, 308, 323
Astronomy, pre-Copernican, 19, 44 ff.
Astronomy, Copernican, 49 ff., 73 f., 79, 84, 164
Atomism, 68, 87 f., 168; More's theory of, 135; Newton's, 231 ff., 242

Bacon, Francis, 87, 125 f., 168, 194
Bacon, Roger, 42, 46, 53
Ball, W. W. R., 42 ff.
Barrow, Issac, 58, 150 ff.; brief summary, 205
Beale, John, 193
Bentley, Richard, 194, 258, 266, 282, 288 ff., 295 f.
Bergson, 25, 95
Berkeley, 25, 32, 34, 258, 311 ff.
Bessarion, 54
Bessel, 38
Boehme, Jacob, 60, 202
Boyle, 113, 125 f., 137, 162, 167 ff., 241 f., 259, 265, 275 ff., 292, 300; brief summary, 205 f.; lectures, 193 f.

Broad, 28
Bruno, 53 f., 56

Campanella, 67, 84
Cardanus, 44
Cartesian dualism, 90, 105, 115, 118 ff., 142, 150, 301, 304 ff.;
    Hobbes attack on, 126 ff.
Cassirier, 28 f.
Categories, 55; change in, 306 ff.; of metaphysics, 26 f., 29,
    33, 34; of modern science, 126
Cavalieri, 58, 72
Causality, 26, 30, 32, 134 f.; Galileo's view of, 98 ff.; Hobbe's
    view of, 133 ff.; Keppler's view of, 64 f.; nature of, 307
Chemistry, Boyle's revolution of, 170
Cohesion, 139, 142, 148, 273, 276
Colour harmony, Newton's theory of, 236
Commercial Revolution, 40
Conservation of energy, 101, 267
Contrast between medieval and modern thought, 17 ff., 24,
    89 ff., 94 ff., 123 f., 160 f., 297 ff., 303 f.
Copernicus, 35, 36 ff.; brief summary, 203
Cosmic hypothesis, Newton's suggestion of, 271 ff., 281 f.
Cudworth, Ralph, 148 f.

Dante, 20 ff., 238
Deduction, Newton's use of, 224 f.
Democritus, 68, 87 f.
Desargues, 58
Descartes, 97, 104, 105 ff., 166, 167 ff., 174 f., 190 ff., 264 f.,
    292 f., 306 f.; brief summary, 204 f.
Dimension, nature of, 109
Duhem, P., 45
Dynamics, 73 f., 97 f.

Eddington, 28
Einstein, 27

Empiricism, 38, 52, 61, 71, 116 f., 163, 168, 314 ff.; Galileo's, 76 ff.; Newton's attitude toward, 213 ff., 220 f., 231 ff., 242 ff., 256

Enclyclopaedists, French, 34

Epicurus, 68, 87, 172, 266

Epicycles, 38, 47 f.

Ether, Boyle's conception, 189 ff.; Descartes' view, 111 ff., 271 ff.; functions of, 190 ff., 265 ff.; Gilbert's view of, 165 f.; Newton's use of, 234 f., 242 f., 264 ff.

Euclid, 45

Evolutionary biology, 30

Experimental method, 32; Boyle's, 170 f.; Galileo's, 81

Experimental verification, Newton's use of, 214 f.

Explanation, nature of, 177 ff.

Fichte, 25

Force, 26, 35, 87, 92, 97, 98 ff., 109 f., 152, 161, 241 ff., 250 ff.

Form, Boyle's conception, 176 f.

Four elements, 37

Fourth dimension, 137

Fulbert, 53

Galileo, 37, 44, 70, 72 ff., 126, 311 f.; brief summary, 203 ff.

Gassendi, 87, 167 f., 173 f.

Gauss, 240

Gerbert, Pope, 53

Gilbert of Colchester, 41, 163 f., 205, 282

Glanvill, 169

God, Boyle's conception of, 194 ff.; Descartes' appeal to, 113, 115, 121; Hobbes's view of, 128; Galileo's view of, 98 ff.; More's theory of, 143 ff.; Newton's view of, 282 ff., 293 ff.

God's relation to space and time, 154 ff.; Newton's view, 257 ff.

God's relation to the world, 194 ff., 295 ff.

Gravity, 100, 139 f., 142, 148, 177 f., 192, 226, 241, 243, 266, 273 f., 276 f., 281, 287 f., 291, 295

Halley, 274

Harvey, William, 166, 186, 205

Hegel, 25, 35

Hipparchus, 60

Hobbes, 44, 73, 122, 125 ff., 166, 306, 320; brief summary, 204; Boyle's refutation of, 170

Holbach, 300

Hooke, 169, 192, 217, 266

Horne, 32

Hume, 25, 34, 230, 299, 301

Huxley, 311 ff.

Huyghens, 101, 206, 240, 292

Hypothesis, 33, 155; Boyle on, 186 f.; Copernicus on, 56 f.; Kepler's view of, 65 ff.; Newton's attack on, 215 ff., 222 ff.; Newton's use of, 269 ff.

Induction, Newton's use of, 223 f.

Inertia, 241

James, William, 25

Kant, 25, 34, 230, 299, 301

Kepler, 42, 56 ff., 140 f.; brief summary, 203

La Mettrie, 300

Laplace, 96, 230, 298

Law, Boyle's conception of, 198 ff.

Laws of planetary motion, 61 f.

Leibniz, 34, 58, 101, 113, 206, 267, 292

Leonardo da Vinci, 42 f., 53

Local motion, 72 ff.

Locke, 31, 113, 134, 169, 185, 300 f.

Logic v. mathematics, 75 f.

Lucretius, 172

Mach, 28

Magnenus, 87

Magnetism 139, 142, 162 ff., 273

Malebranche, 147, 206

Man, nature of, 329; Boyle's theory of, 181 ff.; Galileo's picture of, 88 ff.; Newton's view of, 233 ff.

Marcilius, Ficinus, 54

Mass, 26, 33, 97, 109 f., 164, 166, 239 ff.

Mästlin, 57

Materialism, 132, 133, 314

Mathematical interpretation of the world, 74 ff., 78 ff., 106 ff., 110 ff., 115 f., 168, 172 ff.; Newton's conception of, 209 f.

Mathematical method, 32; Barrow's conception of, 220 ff.; of Descartes, 107 f.; Newton's theory of, 209 f.

Mathematics, Aristotelian conception of, 54 f.; Barrow's view of, 151 ff.; Boyle on, 172 f.; certainty of, 118 f.; Descartes' theory of, 107 ff.; pre-Copernican, 41 f.

Mechanical view of the world, 24 f., 101 f. 113, 173 f., 238 f., 244, 267, 301 f.; Boyle's, 201 f. More's criticism, of, 137 f.; Newton's, 293 ff.

Mechanics, Newton's conception of, 214 f.

Medieval physics, 17 ff.

Mersenne, 115, 126

Metaphysical ideas, types of, 229 f.

Metaphysics, nature of, 228 f.

Milton, 238

Mind, nature of, 317 ff.; Hobbes's theory of, 126 ff., 132, 133 ff.

Mind and body, problem of, 121 ff., 138 f.

Mind and Brain, 122, 136 f., 307 ff., 323; Boyle's theory of, 184 ff.; Newton's view of, 237 ff.

Mind and space, 319 ff.

Minkowski, 28

Miracles, Boyle's admission of, 200 ff.; Newton's view of, 299 f.

Montaigne, 67

Morals and metaphysics, relation of, 323

More, Henry, 125, 135 ff., 169, 257 f., 282, 292, 306, 320 f.; brief summary, 205

Naturalism, 26, 330; Hobbes's, 129

Nature, Boyle's conception, 177

Neo-Platonism, 53 f., 58, 70

Newton, Sir Isaac, 29 ff., 58, 92, 104, 125, 150 f., 162 f., 167, 169, 185, 192, 202, 207 ff., 304, 310; genius of, 207 f.; as philosopher, 32 f., 207 f.; his problem, 208 f.

Nicholas of Cusa, 41, 53 f.

Nominalism, 128, 132 f.

Novara, Dominicus Maria de, 54, 55

Oldenburg, 220, 271

Optics, Newton's work in, 211 f., 215 ff., 235 f.

Pacioli, 43

Pardies, 266

Pascal, 206

Patrizzi, 54

Pemberton, 31

Pearson, 28

Philosophy of science, Kepler's, 63 ff.

Pico of Mirandola, John, 54

Plato, 42, 53 f., 68 f., 89 f., 308

Pletho, 54

Pluralism, 228

Poincaré, 28

Point of reference in astronomy, 39 f., 46, 48 f., 52

Pope, 31

Positivism, 34, 45 f., 153, 227 ff.; Boyle's, 186 ff.; Galileo's, 101 ff.; Newton's, 282

Potentiality, 26, 94 ff.

Practical interest, Newton's, 214 f.

Primary and secondary qualities, 33, 306; Boyle's treatment of, 181 ff.; Cudworth on, 149 f.; Descartes' treatment, 116 ff.; Hobbes's view of, 130 ff.; Galileo's view of, 83 ff.; Kepler on, 67 f.; More's view of, 135 f.; Newton on, 235 ff.

Problem of knowledge, 15 f., 123 f., 185 ff., 300 f., 308

Providence, Newton's view of, 291 ff.

Psychology, contemporary, 318 f.

Ptolemy, 36, 38 ff., 45 ff., 52, 62

Pythagorean metaphysics, 42, 45, 52 f., 55, 63 f., 68 ff., 88

Qualitative explanations, Boyle's use of, 177 ff.

Quantity, nature of, 67 f.

Reason and experience, relation of, 170 f.

Relativity, of motion, 44, 47, 113 f., 145 f.; Newton's attack on, 245 f., 249 ff., 255; of space, 113 f.

Religion, 19 f., 40; Boyle's, 193 ff.; Galileo's, 82 f.; Newton's, 258 ff., 261 f., 283 ff.

Renaissance, 40

Res extensa and res cogitans, 115 ff.

Rheticus, 45

Robb, 28

Royal society, 194

Rules of reasoning, Newton's, 218 ff.

Russell, Bertrand, 23

Sanchez, 67

Science, nature of, Newton's conception, 226

Scientific method, analysis of Newton's, 220 ff.

Sensation, nature of, 135, 184, 273, 311 ff.

Senses, nature of, 84, 115 f., 123, 132, 314 ff.

Sensorium, 135, 236 ff.; God's, 259 f.

Simple natures, Descartes' conception, 108 f.

Simplicity, postulate of, 38 f., 50 f., 55 f., 57 f., 74 f., 218, 287 f.

Space, 26, 33 ff., 44 f., 106, 316 f.; Barrow's view of, 161; Galileo's conception of, 92 f.; Hobbes's view of, 133 f.; More's theory of, 144 ff.; Newton's view of, 244 ff.; criticism of, 256 ff.; post-Newtonian view, 262; psychology of, 316 f.

Spinoza, 134, 169, 206, 321

Spirit, Boyle's theory of, 183 f.; Gilbert's theory of, 165 f.; More's theory of, 136 ff.

Spirit of nature, 140 ff., 162 ff., 177

Stevinus, 43, 193

Sun-worship, Kepler's, 58 f.

Sydenham, 169

Tartaglia, 43

Teleology, 18, 98 f., 161, 169, 308 f.; Boyle's attitude toward, 178 f.; Galileo's attitude toward, 91, 93 ff.; Hobbes's significance for, 133 ff.; Newton's, 288 ff.

Theology, Kepler's, 60 f.

Thinking, modes of, 120

Time, 26, 33 f., 305; Barrow's theory of, 155 ff.; Boyle's thought of, 188 f.; Galileo's view of, 92 ff.; Hobbes's view of, 132; Newton's view of, 244 ff.; criticism of, 256 f.; post-Newtonian view, 262; problems of, 93 ff., 262 ff.

Torricelli, 92

Tycho Brahe, 60 f., 64, 71, 96

Uniformity of nature, Newton's view of, 219 f.

Vortex theory, of Descartes, 112 f., 140

Vacuum, 133, 145, 190

Vives, 67, 84

Weyl, 28

Whitehead, 28

William of Conches, 53